SPOKEN ARABIC

SPOKEN ARABIC

Students Book

Cassette to accompany Students Book

Spoken Arabic

David Harvey B.A.

HODDER AND STOUGHTON
LONDON SYDNEY AUCKLAND TORONTO

British Library Cataloguing in Publication Data
Harvey, David
  Spoken Arabic.
  1. Arabic language – Spoken Arabic
  2. Arabic language – Grammar
  I. Title
  492′.7′83421   PJ6307

ISBN 0-340-23681-7
ISBN 0-340-23376-1 Pbk
First published 1979
Second impression 1980

Printed in Great Britain for Hodder and Stoughton Educational,
a division of Hodder and Stoughton Ltd,
Mill Road, Dunton Green, Sevenoaks, Kent
by Richard Clay (The Chaucer Press), Ltd,
Bungay, Suffolk.

FOREWORD

Elements of the Course

1. The Materials: the materials consist of a book and a cassette.

(*a*) The book contains 21 lessons (including two revision lessons), each designed to cover a coherent chunk of the language rather than be absorbable within (say) an hour's study. Indeed it will take several hours for the average student to master each lesson. Nearly every lesson falls into the following divisions:

(1) dialogue and/or narrative (presented with facing translation).

(2) vocabulary – which may include extra notes on certain grammatical features.

(3) questions on the dialogue/narrative with provided answers. The aim being to provide closely guided practice in varying the language presented.

(4) Notes on Grammar and Usage: in this section grammatical points are explained and illustrated.

(5) Exercises: there is usually a translation exercise (with answers provided at the end of the lesson) and various drills, usually of a substitution type. A good deal of the vocabulary suggested for use in these exercises comes from earlier lessons, for the intention is to encourage a constant revision process.

(*b*) The book also contains an Arabic–English Glossary which includes most of the 700 or so words used in the course.

(*c*) A special feature is the English–Arabic Glossary, containing rather more than 3 000 words. The student, having learnt the basic grammar, will have ready access to fresh vocabulary which he will be able to fit into the structures he already knows.

(*d*) There is also an appendix giving a concise account of the main differences between some of the more important dialects.

(*e*) Finally, the cassette, indispensable for acquiring an acceptable pronunciation, carries recordings of the Introduction (The Sounds of Arabic) together with recordings of all the dialogues and narratives.

2. The Language Chosen for the Course: the following points should be noted:

(*a*) Arabic is a language with one written language but many distinct spoken dialects. The "written" language is heard spoken on the radio, in plays and in the language used on rather formal occasions. This formal variety of Arabic is understood by all educated Arabs and the one towards which Arabs may move if they wish to speak with an Arab from another dialect area. The written language is felt, however, to be too formal an instrument for everyday use, so, in what one might call "elevated colloquial", a good deal of the complex grammar of the written language has been simplified or done away with altogether.

(*b*) The aim in this course is to teach an "elevated colloquial" which one might regard either as a relaxed version of the universally understood written language or as a "corrected" colloquial.

(*c*) The regional element in the variety of language chosen is that of the Greater Syrian dialect area (this area includes Syria, Jordan, Lebanon and Palestine). Geographically and linguistically this lies between Egypt, the greatest cultural centre of the Arab World, and the oil rich states to the east. It should be mentioned at this point that the majority of the population in many Gulf states are immigrant Arabs, many of these coming from the more "westernised" but poorer countries of Egypt, Lebanon and Palestine to the west. Pure "Gulf" Arabic is growing more difficult to find as people speaking higher prestige dialects move in.

(*d*) Especially when teaching verbs, care is taken to present not only the more colloquial forms but also the more "classical" versions of the written language. The words that are used in this book will be understood from Egypt to the Gulf and throughout the Arabian Peninsula.

(*e*) Libya, Tunisia, Algeria and Morocco have been excluded from the claims made for the course. This is because these "western" dialects are distinct from the eastern dialects (and grow more distinct as one moves further west – Moroccan Arabic having a strong admixture of Berber). It may happen, however, that with improved education and the ever closer links made possible by modern communications, the generally understood Arabic of the kind used in this book will spread to these areas too.

CONTENTS AND GRAMMATICAL REFERENCE

The themes and grammatical topics handled in each lesson are given below. Most grammar is dealt with in the sections entitled "Notes on Grammar and Usage", occasional matters occurring in Vocabulary sections. Where this happens, the Arabic word in question is preceded by the abbreviation 'Vocab:' . . .

Introduction   The Sounds of Arabic (Consonants – Sun Letters – Vowels – Diphthongs – Stress)

Lesson 1

Theme   Greetings and Farewells
Grammar   1. The definite article.
2. "You" and "your" expressed by -*ak*, -*ik* and -*kum*.
3. Subject pronouns for "you".
4. Feminine ending -*a* for adjectives.
5. The Dual.

Lesson 2

Theme   More Greetings and Farewells, Various Formal Phrases
Grammar   1. Vocab: no translation for "am/are/is/be".
2. Vocab: plural ending -*iin* for adjectives.
3. Plural ending -*aat* for feminine nouns.
4. All subject pronouns.
5. Subject pronoun + active participle = present continuous.
6. All possessive and pronoun suffixes.

Lesson 3

Theme   Introductions – polite enquiries – leave taking
Grammar   1. The triliteral root.
2. The demonstratives *haádha* and *haádhi*.
3. Relative adjectives.

7

4. *bidd* = "want".
5. *mush* and *ma*.
6. The Imperfect Tense (*yáshkur, yaruúH & yíji*).

Lesson 4

Theme   Directions (prepositions, adjectives and adverbs of place)

Grammar 1. Agreement of adjectives with singular nouns.
2. The *b-* prefix to the imperfect.
3. The structure of Arab names.

Lesson 5   (Revision Lesson)

Lesson 6

Theme   Possession

Grammar 1. Translations of "to have".
2. The possessive relationship between nouns ("Construct").
3. "Construct" – the position of adjectives.
4. Some forms of address.

Lesson 7

Theme   Discussing the Past

Grammar 1. The Perfect Tense (of regular verbs).
2. Preliminary sketch of Derived Forms of the Verb.
3. Numbers 1–12.
4. Telling the time (hours only).

Lesson 8

Theme   Further Discussion of the Past

Grammar 1. The perfect and imperfect of hollow verbs.
2. The perfect of defective verbs.
3. The perfect and imperfect of *'aja*.

Lesson 9

Theme   A Story set in the Past

Grammar 1. The perfect of doubled verbs.
2. The perfect of *nisi*.
3. "Sound" and "Broken" plurals.
4. Stress changes caused by affixing pronouns.

Lesson 10

Theme and Grammar Numbers (excluding ordinals and fractions)

Lesson 11 (Revision Lesson)

Themes Noun plurals – Sentence construction – polite formulae

Lesson 12

Theme Daily routine in both past and present
Grammar 1. Ordinals.
2. Fractions
3. Telling the time.
4. Imperfects of defective verbs.
5. Imperfects of verb beginning with 'a-.

Lesson 13

Theme Daily routine in the office (present and past)
Grammar 1. Agreement of adjectives with plural nouns.
2. Agreement of verbs and pronouns with nouns.

Lesson 14

Theme Description and comparison of two houses
Grammar 1. Relative Clauses.
2. Comparison of adjectives.
3. The superlative of adjectives.
4. Colour adjectives.

Lesson 15

Theme 1. In the bank – In the post-office – Handling money
Grammar 1. Vocab: *li'an* = because.
2. Vocab: *hayyaa* = here is.
3. Vocab: *'iyyaa.*
4. Active participle (1st form verb).
5. Passive participle (1st form verb).

Lesson 16

Theme Orders to a servant
Grammar 1. Imperatives (affirmative and negative)
2. Nouns of Place and Instrument.

9

Lesson 17

Theme   Shopping for food – Bargaining
Grammar 1. Collectives.
           2. Arab Currencies.
           3. Weights and Measures.
           4. Days of the Week.

Lesson 18

Theme   On the telephone – arranging meetings
Grammar 1. Vocab: *talfan* – conjugation of quadriliteral verbs.
           2. Vocab: *raqm talfawnak* – possessives and compound nouns.
           3. Conditional Sentences.
           4. *lawla – ya rayt – kullma* etc.
           5. Compound tenses.

Lesson 19

Theme   Conversation at a party – time expressions
Grammar 1. *Saar.*
           2. "To owe."
           3. "As/so long as."
           4. "Still . . . not yet."
           5. "In order to."
           6. "For, for the sake of."

Lesson 20

Theme   Going on leave. Travel
Grammar 1. Derived forms of the verb (Forms 2, 3, 4, 5 & 6).

Lesson 21

Theme   Travel
Grammar 1. Derived forms of the verb (Forms 7, 8, 9 & 10).

Appendix

     A.   Some Differences between the Main Dialects
     B.   Arabic–English Glossary
     C.   Christian and Muslim Months
     D.   Gazetteer
     E.   English–Arabic Glossary

INTRODUCTION

THE SOUNDS OF ARABIC

Consonants similar to English ones

b – as in English.

d – tip of tongue on teeth rather than tooth ridge.

f – as in English.

g – hard as in "gate".

h – as in English.

k – as in English, but no aspiration.

l – like the l in "leaf" (for British English speakers) not as in "feel".

m – as in English.

n – as in English.

p – normally only in foreign words. No aspiration.

r – trilled as in Spanish.

s – a little tenser than in English.

t – tip of tongue on teeth rather than tooth ridge. No aspiration.

v – normally only in foreign words.

w – as in English.

y – as in English.

z – as in English.

The following three consonants present no difficulties as regards pronunciation. They are represented by two letters in the transliteration because of the deficiencies of the English alphabet.

th – as in "*th*in".

sh – as in "*sh*op".

dh – as in "*th*at"

N.B. Where these two letter combinations represent two individual sounds rather than one, a hyphen is inserted: e.g. *mud-hish* (= surprising)

Consonants not found in English

H – this must be distinguished from the sound represented by *h* in the list of consonants given above. The sound is produced by ejecting air sharply from the lungs, more sharply than for *h*, together with a slight "whisper" produced in the pharynx (the area between the root of the tongue and the back of the throat). Blow on imaginary spectacles as if to clean them. This will give the strong ejection of air required. Try a stage whisper. You should feel the re-

11

quired friction at the back of the throat. Listen to the cassette and repeat the examples when you feel ready.

Examples:

Initial H – *Haal*   *Hamd*   *Hisaáb* (= state – praise – account)
Medial H – *ráHma*   *ríHla*   *laHm*   (= mercy – journey – meat)
Final H –   *raaH*   *nábaH*   *shábaH* (= went – bark – ghost)
Compare *H* with *h* – *Harb*   *harb*   (= war – flight)
                        nábaH   *nábah*   (= bark – notice)

Notice how the *h* is pronounced even at the end of a syllable in *nábah*.

x – this represents the scrape heard at the end of the Scottish word "loch". English speakers may tend to confuse it with *H* above. But the sound represented by *x* is produced by friction between the back part of the tongue and the roof of the mouth, not in the throat.

Examples:

Initial x – *xubz*   *xámsa*   *xayr* (= bread – five – good)
Medial x – *'áxad*   *yaáxud*   *'axiir* (= took – take – last)
Final x –   *'ax*   *shayx*   *muxx* (= brother – sheikh – brain)
Compare *x* with *H* –*xaal*   *Haal* (= uncle – state)

9 – various amusing and even embarrassing ways have been suggested for mastering this sound. One expert advises singing to one's lowest note and then trying to sing a note lower. This should produce the authentic snarl. Another recommends tensing the throat muscles as if to retch and then trying to produce an "a" vowel. Yet another counsels starting with the long "aa" a doctor might ask a patient to produce, then moving the root of the tongue further and further back till a satisfactory amount of friction is produced between the root of the tongue and the back of the throat. Here we seem to be back with *H* but there is no strong ejection of air and the vocal cords are vibrating.

This consonant has been heard as an "a" vowel by most Europeans.

Examples:

Initial 9 – *9árab*   *9ámal*   *9ind*   (= Arabs – work – "chez")
Medial 9 – *ná9am*   *ba9d*   *ba9dáyn* (= yes – after – afterwards)
Final 9 –   *rub9*   *rabii9*   *shaári9* (= quarter – Spring – street)

12

' – this symbol represents the "glottal stop", which is produced by penning air back behind the vocal cords and then suddenly releasing it. In English it occurs in the speech of Cockneys where it can replace a "t" – e.g. "li"le" rather than "little". It is often used at the beginning of a word commencing with a vowel – e.g. "'apple".

Examples:

Initial ' –	*'ibn*	*'ax*	*'uxt* (= son – brother – sister
Medial ' –	*sá'al*	*mas'uúl*	*zaá'ir* (= asked – responsible – visitor)
Final ' –	*Hamraá'*	*sawdaá'*	*samraá'* (= red – black – brown)

q – this represents a "k" pronounced very far back, on the uvula in fact. It sounds and feels very "exaggerated".

Examples:

Initial q –	*qalb*	*qadiim*	*'al-qur'aán* (= heart – old – Koran)
Medial q –	*maqbuúl*	*báqar*	*'intáqal* (= acceptable – cattle – transfer)
Final q –	*suuq*	*saaq*	*Tariiq* (= market – drove – road)

Note how the vowels near *q* are further "back" than normal.

q tends to be replaced in most dialects by other consonants, the choice of which one depending on the area. In "urban" dialects (Cairo, Beirut, Damascus – but *not* Baghdad) *q* is usually replaced by the glottal stop '.

Examples:

instead of *qalb* '*alb* (= heart)
instead of *báqar* *bá'ar* (= cattle)
instead of *suuq* *suu'* (= market)

It remains in certain words even so:

e.g. *'al-qur'aán* *'al-qaáhira* (= Koran – Cairo)

In "nomad" dialects *q* is normally replaced by "g" (Arabia, Iraq, Upper Egypt, Sudan).

13

Examples:

instead of *qalb*   *galb*
instead of *báqar*   *bágar*
instead of *suuq*   *suug*

D, S, T, Z – these represent sounds like those designated by the corresponding small letters. The sounds are, however, modified by changes in the shape of the mouth and the positioning of the tongue. More traditional grammars call these sounds "emphatics" while the more modern talk of "velarisation" i.e. modifications produced at the back of the mouth in the soft palate area. It is fortunate that velarisation occurs in English too. Compare the "l" in "leaf" and that in "feel". British English speakers will notice that the "l" at the end of "feel" is "darker" than the one at the beginning of "leaf". Try to pronounce the dark final one at the beginning of a word (how would an American pronounce the word "lovely"?). D, S, T and Z are pronounced in exactly the same place in the mouth as dark "l". To pronounce them the tongue is humped up at the back just as for dark "l".

Examples:

D – *Dúhur*	*faáDi*	*báraD*	(= noon – free – germinate)
S – *SaáHib*	*biSiir*	*baSS*	(= owner – become – bus)
T – *Tiin*	*fuTuúr*	*DaábiT*	(= clay – breakfast – officer)
Z – *Zann*	*maZaáhir*	*HaáfiZ*	(= thought – phenomena – keeper)

As with *q*, the vowels near the "emphatics" tend to be further back than normal, so that *a* will resemble "o" as in "hot".

Compare the pronunciations of the following pairs of words.

Normal	Emphatic	
faádi	*faáDi*	(= redeemer – free)
saáHib	*SaáHib*	(= withdrawer – owner)
tiin	*Tiin*	(= figs – clay)
Haáfiz	*HaáfiZ*	(= incentive – keeper)

gh – this represents a scraping sound produced in the region of the uvula. It is the sound made when gargling and resembles the French "r".

Examples:

Initial gh –	*ghaáli*	*ghábi*	*ghazaál* (= dear – stupid – gazelle)

14

Medial gh – *dúghri* *shughl* *'ishtághal* (= straight – work –
                                                 worked)
Final gh – *bálagh* *máblagh* *faraágh* (= reached – sum –
                                                 leisure)

j – none of the sounds represented by this symbol are difficult for
the English speaker. In Egypt it is pronounced as "g". In Lebanon
and Syria it is pronounced as the "s" in "leisure". The sound of the
English "j" in "judge" is accepted everywhere.

Doubling of Consonants

When written double, consonants must be pronounced as if double.
A double *dd* must be pronounced as in "bad dog", not as in
"redden".

Examples:

Compare *Sádar* with *Sáddar* (= be issued – export)
   „   *kásar*   „   *kássar* (= break – smash)
   „   *mára*   „   *márra* (= woman – occasion)

"Sun" Letters

The definite article ("the") in Arabic is *'al-* (the vowel may change
according to environment so producing such variants as *'el, 'il, 'ul*
etc.). It is felt to be very closely attached to its noun, so in the
transliteration used in this book the definite article is connected by
a hyphen to the following noun e.g. *'al-bayt* (= the house).
    When the following noun begins with *t, d, r, z, s, sh, S, Z, D, T, l*
or *n*, the *l* of the definite article is assimilated into that initial letter
and the letter is pronounced double.

Examples:

'ash-shams (not *'al-shams*. . . . the word *shams* is a good example of
    the consonant doubling feature with the definite article, hence the
    name of "sun" letters for the whole group of consonants which
    so behave, for *shams* = sun)
'ar-rájul (= the man)   *'aD-DaábiT* (= the officer)

The phonetic reason for this is that all these consonants are pronounced on the teeth or tooth ridge. It is a simplification of articu-
lation to omit the l of *'al-* and move directly to a following related
consonant.
    Sometimes *j* is included in the list of "sun" letters.

15

The "glottal stop" of 'al-

The glottal stop of *'al-* is only pronounced at the beginning of a sentence or after a pause. And indeed the vowel of *'al-* takes the sound of any preceding vowel, so that when there is a preceding vowel the *a* of *'al-* is not written in the transliteration used.

Examples:

' pronounced	' unpronounced	vowel omitted
'al-bayt	wayn al-bayt?	'ila l-bayt
(the house)	(where is the house?)	(to the house)
'ar-rájul	wayn ar-rájul?	lir-rájul (to the . . .)

Vowels

There are three vowels in Arabic which occur in both long and short forms. They are *a* and *aa*, *i* and *ii*, *u* and *uu*. Some details on their pronunciation follow:

a – a rather "flat" fronted sound like the "a" in Southern English "man", but as has been already mentioned in the section on consonants, the vowels are very liable to change when near certain consonants.

Examples: (notice the differences between the various manifestations of *a*)

bass (= only)   *sáwda* (= black)   *raH*   *baTT* (= duck)

aa – a similar vowel quality to the short *a*, and subject to the same influences from consonants.

Examples:

maáshi (= walking) *kaan* (= was) *baárid* (= cold) *Zaálim* (unjust)

i – a sound like the "i" in "hit". It may be modified by consonants.

Examples:

'idha (= if)   *Sábi* (= boy)   *niZaám* (= system)

ii – similar to the English vowel of "seen", but tenser and not diphthongised.

Examples:

bariíd (= mail)   *jiib* (= bring!)   *biSiír* (= become)

u – like the "oo" of "foot".

Examples:

lúgha (= language)   *dúwal* (= nations)   *wuSuúl* (= arrival)

uu – rounder and tenser than the vowel in "soon".

Examples:

shuuf (= look!)   *wujuúd* (= existence)   *byuúSal* (= he arrives)

Diphthongs

In addition to the pure vowels, there are two further vowel sounds which are always long. They may be heard as the diphthongs they originally were or (more usually) be pronounced as pure vowels. Hence *ay* may be pronounced as a diphthong (vowel combination) as in "fight" or as a pure vowel rather like the vowel in "fate". Its fellow *aw* may be pronounced as a diphthong as in "cow" or a pure vowel rather like the vowel in "soap". The examples given here are of the pure vowels only and one should note that though the vowels *resemble* those in "fate" and "soap", they are pure and do not have the glide characteristic of the English vowels.

Examples:

ay – *bayt* (= house)   *shayx* (= sheikh)   *SayD* (= hunting)
aw – *lawn* (= colour)   *zawj* (= husband)   *qawl* (= utterance)

In an occasional word, the *y* has been used not as a consonant but as a very short *i*.

Examples:

shaay (= tea)   *'abuuy* (= my father)   *mayy* (= water)

Stress

There are short syllables and there are long syllables. A short syllable is made up of consonant + short vowel + (possibly) one consonant: e.g. *kátab* (= he wrote) – *ka* – *tab* (both short).

A long syllable has a long vowel or is followed by more than one consonant: e.g. *kaátab* (= he corresponded) – *kaa* – *tab* (first long)
katábt (= I wrote) – *ka* – *tabt* (second long)

The general rule is that the last long syllable in a word is stressed. If there are no long syllables, the first syllable is stressed. It is rare to find in Arabic four syllable words without a single long vowel. In such cases, however, the syllable third from the end is stressed: e.g. *muttáhida* (= united)

17

Examples of Stress:

kátab — first syllable stressed because all syllables are short.

kitaáb — last syllable stressed because it has a long vowel.

katábt — last syllable stressed because it ends in two consonants.

makaátib — second syllable stressed because it has a long vowel.

makaatiíb — last syllable stressed because it is the last long syllable.

yusállim — second syllable stressed because it is followed by a double *ll*.

yusallímkum — third syllable is stressed because its vowel is followed by two consonants *mk* and it has become the last long syllable in the word.

xaáTrak — first syllable stressed because it has a long vowel.

xaaTírkum — second syllable stressed because its vowel is followed by two consonants *rk* and it has become the last long syllable in the word.

N.B. There are occasional exceptions to the above rules.

Examples are:

byashtághil (= he works) — stress should fall on the first syllable according to rule.

muxtálif (= different) — same remark.

byankásir (= be broken) — same remark.

These are all parts of 7th and 8th form verbs.

The stress on all words is in fact indicated by an acute accent over the stressed syllable, as in the examples above.

ABBREVIATIONS AND GRAMMATICAL TERMS

1. The following abbreviations have been used:

coll. = collective (See Lesson 17)
f.   = feminine
m.   = masculine
pl. = plural
s.   = singular

2. The *definite article* in English is "the", while the *indefinite article* is "a/an". The definite article in Arabic is *'al-*, but there is no indefinite article – a noun standing alone is as if it has an indefinite article in front:

e.g. 'al-bayt = the house   bayt = a house

3. A *suffix* is an element attached to *the end* of an already existing word so changing the meaning of that word:

e.g. parent + hood (a suffix) = parenthood

A *prefix* is attached to *the beginning* of a word:

e.g. draw + re (a prefix) = redraw

4. An *adverb* adds to the meaning of a verb, an adjective or another adverb:

e.g. He ran quickly (*quickly* is an adverb going with *ran*).
    It is very hot today (*very* is an adverb going with *hot*).
    He drives too fast (*too* is an adverb going with *fast*).

5. A *pronoun* stands instead of a noun:

e.g. John is here. He came by bus. (*He* is a pronoun.)

6. A *preposition* is placed before a noun or pronoun to show the relationship between these and other words in the sentence:

e.g. Go with peace! (*with* is a preposition).
    Go to him! (*to* is a preposition).

7. *A conjunction* is a word used to link words, phrases or sentences together:

e.g. John *and* Mary. . . . *before* you came. . . . *neither* true *nor* kind . . .

FIRST LESSON – *'ad-dars al-'awwal* (= the lesson the first)
GREETINGS AND FAREWELLS

Suggestions for using the dialogues:

1. Listen to the recording of the dialogue on the cassette.
2. Listen to the dialogue sentence by sentence, working out the meaning with the aid of the book.
3. Listen to the dialogue sentence by sentence, pausing the cassette to allow you to repeat each sentence. Repeat each sentence several times if necessary. Keep the meaning of the sentence in mind. It is better if you can do without the book at this stage, but glance at it if necessary.
4. Listen to the dialogue right through for comprehension.
5. Listen to the dialogue, but this time, repeat each sentence *without* referring to the book.
6. Try translating the English version back into Arabic. Continue until such translation is rapid and confident.
7. Read the "Notes on Grammar and Usage" before attempting the exercises.
8. Make sure that you can do the exercises with confidence before passing on to the next lesson.
9. Though a large amount of revision is included in the course, it will be a good idea to revise as a matter of course three or four lessons before the lesson you are actually engaged on.

Dialogue 1 – *Hiwaár raqm waáHid* (= dialogue number one)

(Ahmed meets Bashir)

'aHmad:

SabaáH al-xayr	*Good morning*
SabaáH	*morning*
'al-xayr	*(of) the good*

bashiír:

SabaáH an-nuur, kayf Haálak?	*Good morning, how are you?*
'an-nuur	*(of) the light*
kayf	*how?*
Haal *pl.* 'aHwaál	*state, condition*
-ak	*your (m.s.) (i.e. to a single human being)*

21

'aHmad:
    mabsuúT, 'al-Hámdu líllaah,   *Well, praise be to God. How are*
      kayf Haálak 'ínta?   *you?*
    mabsuúT   *well, contented*
    Hamd(u)   *praise*
    li/llaah   *to/God*
    'ínta   *you (m.s.)*

bashiir:
    'al-Hámdu líllaah, bixaýr   *Praise be to God, well.*
    bi (xayr)   *in, with (an instrument)*

'aHmad: (leaving)
    bixaáT(i)rak   *Good-bye (lit: in your mind)*
    xaáTir   *mind*
    xaáTrak   *your mind (note the fall of the*
        weak syllable)

bashiir:
    má9a s-salaáma   *Good-bye (said by the one*
        remaining)
    ma9a   *with*
    salaáma   *peace*

'aHmad:
    'állaah yusállimak   *God preserve you!*
    yusállim/ak   *he preserve/you*

Dialogue 2 – *Hiwaár raqm 'ithnáyn* (= dialogue number two)

    (Huda – woman's   name – meets   Samira – another   woman's
name)

húda:
    masaá' al-xayr, ya samiíra   *Good evening, Samira.*
    masaá'   *evening*
    ya   *O! (when addressing someone)*

samiíra:
    masaá' an-nuur, kayf Haálik   *Good evening, how are you?*
    (Haal)-ik   *your (f.s.) (i.e. to a single female*
        human being)

huda:
    mabsuúTa, 'al-Hámdu líllaah   *Well, praise be to God.*
    kayf Haálik, 'ínti?   *How are you?*
    mabsuúT(a)   *-a is the feminine ending for*
        adjectives
    'ínti   *you (f.s.)*

samiira:	
'al-Hámdillaah, bixáyr	Praise be to God, well.
'al-Hámdillaah	(common variant of the more elevated 'al-Hamdu lillaah)
huda:	
bixaáTrik	Good-bye
samiira:	
má9a s-salaáma	Good-bye
huda:	
'állaah yusáll(i)mik	God preserve you
-ik	you (f.s.)

Dialogue 3 – Hiwaar raqm thalaatha (= dialogue number 3)

(Amin goes to see a friend of his called Mahmoud in his office)

'amiín:	
márHaba	Hallo (lit: welcome)
maHmuúd:	
marHabtáyn, kayf aS-SíHHa?	Hello (lit: two helloes). How is the health?
-(t)ayn	(the dual ending used for two of anything)
SíHHa pl. SiHHaát	health
'amiin:	
kuwáyyis, 'al-Hámdu líllaah	Good, praise be to God.
kuwáyyis	good, nice
maHmuud:	
tafáDDal! táshrab qáhwa?	Please sit down! Do you (want to) drink coffee?
tafáDDal	(lit: do yourself the favour of . . .)
táshrab	you drink
qáhwa	coffee
'amiin:	
shúkran, ná9am.	Thank you. Yes.
maHmuud:	
'áhlan wa sáhlan	Welcome! (a very common phrase used to make people welcome)

23

'amiin: (drinks coffee and replaces cup)

dáyma.	*Always* (*i.e. may you always have coffee*)
maHmuud:	
SaHHtáyn.	*Two healths* (*usual reply to above*)

Notes on Grammar and Usage

1. In *SabaáH al-xayr*, *'al-* is the definite article "the". *'al-*, like "the", does not change for masculine, feminine or plural. To indicate the presence of the indefinite article "a/an" in Arabic, it is normally sufficient to use the noun by itself e.g. *'al-bint* = the girl, *bint* = a girl.

2. *SabaáH an-nuur* is the normal reply to *SabaáH al-xayr*. Note the doubling of the "sun" letter *n* in *'an-nuur*, a feature remarked on in the Introduction.

3. *-ak* means "your" when addressing a male human being, *-ik* for a female human being, *-kum* for two or more of either sex.

4. *'inta* = you (when addressing a male human being, *'inti* when addressing a female human being, *'intu* when addressing two or more of either sex.

5. *'al-Hámdu líllaah* – God must be praised for good health, since only He can grant it.

6. The farewells given here are those used in Greater Syria. Though understood everywhere, they may be regarded in some areas as being over elaborate.

7. *yusállim(ak)* – the suffixes *-ak*, *-ik*, *-kum* when added to a verb are translated as "you". It is when these suffixes are attached to a noun (e.g. *Háalak/ik/kum*) that they mean "your".

8. *mabsuúT(a)* – *a* is added to make the feminine of adjectives. All nouns in Arabic are either masculine and feminine and adjectives must agree with them.

   Most masculine nouns end in a consonant (e.g. *Haal, SabaáH*) while most feminine nouns end in *-a* (e.g. *márHaba, salaáma*). There are very few exceptions to this, and these are indicated when encountered. As regards human beings, male sex corresponds with masculine gender and female sex with feminine gender (e.g. *xaliifa* = caliph (masculine despite the *-a* ending), *bint* = girl (feminine despite not ending in *-a*)).

9. *marHabtáyn* – the ending *-ayn* denotes the dual (i.e. two of anything). *márHaba* is a feminine word (as noted above). When endings are attached to a feminine word ending in *-a*, the final *-a* is dropped and a *t* inserted before the ending.

The dual is used here since it is customary to reply to a greeting with a warmer one.

10. *tafáDDal* – this is an imperative (command form of the verb). According to context it can mean "please enter . . . please precede me . . . please sit down . . . please take what I am offering you" etc. It is in constant use.

tafáDDal is used to one male human being (i.e. masculine singular – m.s.), *tafáDDali* to one female human being (i.e. feminine singular – f.s.), *tafáDDalu* to two or more of either sex (i.e. plural – pl.)

11. The stressed syllables in words may vary according to the suffixes added. Consider the following examples: *yusállimak* but *yusallímkum*, *bixaáTrak* but *bixaaTírkum* (see the section on Stress in the Introduction).

Exercises

Translate:
1. Good morning (+ standard reply)
2. Good evening (+ standard reply)
3. How are you? (to a man, woman, several)
4. Well, praise be to God (from a man, a woman)
5. Please sit down! (to a man, woman, several)
6. Good-bye – Go with peace – God keep you (to a man, woman, several)

Answers to Exercises

1. SabaáH al xayr – SabaáH an-nuur
2. masaá' al-xayr – masaá' an-nuur
3. kayf Haálak/ik/kum?
4. mabsuúT, 'al-Hámdu líllaah/ mabsuúTa, 'al . . .
5. tafáDDal! tafáDDali! tafáDDalu!
6. bixaáTrak/ik/bixaaTírkum – ma9a s-salaáma – 'állaah yusáll(i)mak/ik/yusallímkum

SECOND LESSON – *'ad-dars ath-thaani* (the lesson the second)

MORE GREETINGS AND FAREWELLS

Dialogue 1 – *Hiwaár raqm waáHid*

(Ahmed comes upon Hamid, an acquaintance of his)

muHámmad:
'as-salaámu 9aláykum

salaám
9ála

kum

*Peace be upon you (no "be"
equivalent required in Arabic)*
peace
*on (9ála becomes 9aláy before a
pronoun ending)*
*you (pl.) – plural form used for
politeness*

Haámid:
wa 9aláykum as-salaám (wa
ráHmat allaáh wa
barakaátuh)
wa
ráHma
báraka *pl.* barakaát
barakaát/uh

*And on you be peace and the
mercy of God and his blessings*

and
mercy, compassion
blessing
uh = *his, its (final h not
pronounced)*

muHammad:
kayf Haálkum? wa kayf al-
9aá'ila?

kum

9aá'ila *pl.* 9awaá'il

*How are you? And how is the
family (no "are" or "is" required in Arabic)*
*– the plural again used for
politeness.*
family

Haamid:
náshkur 'állaah. kayf Haal al-
'awlaád?

náshkur
wálad *pl.* 'awlaád

*We thank God. How are the
children? (no "are" equivalent
in Arabic)*
we thank
child, boy

muHammad:
'al-Hámdilla mabsuuTiín,
shúkran
-iin

Praise be to God, well, thankyou.

– plural ending for adjectives

Haamid:
'astá'dhin, laázim 'aruúH 9al-
bayt. bixaaTírkum
'astá'dhin
laázim
'aruúH
9a(l)

*Excuse me, I have to go home.
Good-bye.*
I ask leave (to go)
must, have to
I go
to (short for 9ala = on)

bayt *pl.* buyuút	*house*
9al-bayt	*to the house*

muHammad:

má9a s-salaáma	*Good-bye*

Haamid:

'állaah yusallímkum	*God keep you.*

Dialogue 2 – *Hiwaar raqm 'ithnayn*

(Abdullah meets a friend of his, Abdul Khalid)

9abdúllah:

'áhlan	*Hello*

9abd ul-xaálid:

'áhlan fiik	*Hello to you*
fii/k	*in/you (-ak has been reduced to k because of the preceding long vowel)*

9abdullah:

la wayn raáyiH?	*Where are (you) going?*
la/li	*to*
wayn	*where?*
raáyiH	*going*

9abd ul-xaalid:

'ana raáyiH lil-madiína	*I am going to the city*
'ána	*I*
raáyiH	*going (active participle from the same verb as 'aruúH in Dialogue 1)*
li	*to (also 'íla)*
madiína *pl.* múdun	*city, town*

9abdúllah:

'ána kamaán	*I too am going there*
kamaán	*too, also*

9abd ul-xaalid:

ta9aál má9ii. xalliína naruúH sáwa	*Come with me. Let us go together.*
ta9aál!	*come!*
(ma9)ii	*me*
xallii/na	*let/us*
naruúH	*we go*
sáwa	*together*

27

9abdullah:
| fíkra kuwáyyisa | *good idea* |
| fíkra *pl.* 'afkaár | *idea* |

Dialogue 3 – *Hiwaar raqm thalaatha*

(Bashir meets a neighbour, Abdul Karim)

bashiír:
| 'áhlan ya 9abd ul-kariím | *Welcome, Abdul Karim.* |

9abd ul-kariím:
| 'áhlan, 'áhlan, 'áhlan . . . | *Welcome . . . (warmth shown by repetition of greeting)* |

bashiír:
| kayf al-9aá'ila! | *How is the family?* |

9abd ul-kariím:
'al-Hámdilla, bass bintii	*Praise be to God, but my*
mariíDa shwayy	*daughter is a little ill.*
bass	*but, only*
bint *pl.* banaát	*girl, daughter*
mariíD *pl.* márDa/mariiDiín	*sick, ill*
shwayy	*a little*

bashiír:
| salaamátha! | *May she get well soon!* |
| salaáma(t)/ha | *safety/her* |

9abd ul-kariím:
| 'állaah yusállimak | *God keep you* |

Dialogue 4 – *Hiwaar raqm 'arba9a*

(Ahmad meets two friends of his, *dauud* (= David) and Hanna (= John))

dauúd:
| 'áhlan | *Welcome.* |

'aHmad:
bíkum, lawaýn raayHiín,	*Welcome to you. Where are you*
'ínta wa Hanna	*going, you and Hanna?*
la/wayn?	*to where (i.e. whither?)*

dauud:
| níHna raayHiín 9as-siínama, | *We are going to the cinema, and* |
| wa 'int? | *you?* |

28

'aHmad:
'ana mashghuúl shwayy
fil-madiína, ma fiínii 'aruúH
má9kum.
mashghuúl
ma

fii/nii

dauud:
'állaah yu9aafiík, állah

má9a s-salaáma
ya9Tii/k
9aáfya

	I am a little busy in the city, I cannot go with you
	busy, occupied
	– negates verbs and verb-like expressions
	lit: in me i.e. (the ability is not) in me
	God give you good health (for work)
	Good-bye.
	give/you
	(good) health, well-being – the whole expression is to wish success in work.

'aHmad:
'állaah yu9aafiík, 'állaah
yusállimak

God grant you good health, God keep you.

Notes on Grammar and Usage

1. The greeting *'as-salaámu 9aláykum* is used by the one coming upon someone or joining a group. *'áhlan* is used to welcome a newcomer.
   The principle of returning a warmer greeting holds with *wa ráHmat allaáh wa barakaátu*. Except on formal occasions these words would be said in a rapid mutter.
2. *barakaát* is the plural of *báraka*. Most feminine words ending in *-a* have this plural. Also presented is the adjective plural ending *-iin* as in *mabsuuTiin*. The plural of every noun is given because it is usually impossible to predict what the plural of a word will be. It is advisable therefore to learn the plural along with the singular.
3. Social customs vary widely in the Arab World. In some areas it would be a grave fault to ask after a wife. Families are safer, but not entirely without danger.
4. In this lesson we have had bits of the present tense of three verbs. They are: *náshkur* (= we thank), *narúuH* (= we go) – the "we" form is prefixed with *na*.
   'aruúH (= I go) – the "I" form has a prefixed *'a*.
   ("I thank" would be *'áshkur*)

29

We have had several examples of the "he" forms e.g. *yusállim* and (in this lesson) *ya9tiík*. The "he" form, therefore, begins with *ya or yu* (selection between these two forms is not according to whim – the matter will be dealt with later).

5. In dialogues 2 and 4 verb-like expressions have been given e.g. *'ána raáyiH* (= I am going) and *níHna raayHiín* (= we are going). All personal subject pronouns are given below with the appropriate form of the active participle:

Masculine	Feminine	Plural
'ána raáyiH (I)	*'ána raáyHa* (I – woman)	*níHna raayHiín* (we)
'ínta raáyiH (you)	*'ínti raáyHa* (you – woman)	*'íntu raayHiín* (you)
húwa raáyiH (he)	*híya raáyHa* (she)	*hum raayHiín* (they)

6. Here is a complete list of the possessive suffixes:

báyt/ii (= my/house)   *báyt/na* (= our house)
,, /ak (= your/. . .)
,, /ik (= your/. . . woman)   ,, /kum (= your/. . .)
,, /uh = his/. . .)
,, /ha (= her/. . .)   ,, /hum (= their/. . .)

7. Here is a complete list of the pronoun suffixes attached to verbs. Only *-nii* (= me) is different from the possessive endings given above:

yashkúr/nii (= he thanks/me)   *yashkúr/na* (= he thanks/us)
,, /ak (= he thanks/you)
,, /ik (= ,,   ,, /you)   ,, /kum (= ,,   ,, /you)
– a woman.   – two or more.
,, /uh (= ,,   ,, /him)
,, /ha (= ,,   ,, /her)   ,, /hum (= ,,   ,, /them)

N.B. An example of *-nii* was given in *ma fiinii*.

When *-ak* follows a long vowel it is reduced to *k* e.g. *fiik, xalliík*. In these circumstances, *-ik* becomes *ki* e.g. *fiiki, xalliíki*.

8. You should note the absence of any verb "to be" in sentences such as *'ána mashghúul* (= I (am) busy) or *húwa raáyiH* (= he (is) going)

Exercises

Some of the exercises below refer you to the relevant paragraph in "Notes on Grammar and Usage", which you should consult to make sure your answers are correct. However, though space will not permit every answer to be given, those problems which are asterisked have their answers given at the end of the lesson.

1. Give the Arabic greetings and the appropriate replies:

(a) Good Morning . . .   (d) Welcome . . .
(b) Good Evening . . .   (e) Peace be upon you! . . .
(c) Hallo . . . Two Hallos.

2. Give the plurals of the following words (consult the lessons and paragraph 2 of "Notes on Grammar and Usage")

wálad	mabsuúT	bint
Haal	mashghuúl	SíHHa
fíkra	raáyiH	báraka
bayt	9aá'ila	madiína
		mariíD

The following exercises involve substitution. An English sentence is given on the left of the page with a corresponding translation into Arabic. Substitutions and other changes to the original sentence are suggested under the English sentence. It is suggested that you first cover up the right of the page where the Arabic versions are printed. Try to translate the English sentences into Arabic. Check your answers. Then make the substitutions and other modifications suggested, covering up the Arabic version of the sentence you are tackling. Answers including asterisked elements are given at the end of the lesson.

3. *I must go home (to the*   laázim 'aruúH 9al-bayt
   house)
   (*he/*we)
   (to the cinema/the city)

4. *He must go with you*   laázim yaruúH má9ak
   (I/we)
   (with*me/you/him/her/us/
   them) + there (= hunaak),
   home.

5. *I must thank them*   laázim 'ashkúrhum
   (*him/*her/you (m. & f. &
   pl.)) – He must thank*
   me –

6. *I'm going to the city*   'ána raáyiH lil-madiína
   (you/he) + also
   (*she/you (f. s.))
   (*we/they/you (pl.)

7. *Let's go home*   xalliína naruúH 9al-bayt
   (me) + together
   (to the city/cinema)

31

8. *I can go*   fíinii 'aruúH (má9ak)
   (*we*)
   (*with you/them/him/her*)
9. *I can't go with Ahmad*   ma fíinii 'aruúH ma9 'áHmad
   (*we*)
   (*with Mahmoud/Samiira*)

Answers to Exercises

3. láazim yaruúH 9al-bayt – laázim naruúH 9al-bayt
4. laázim yaruúH má9ii
5. laázim 'áshkuruh – laázim 'ashkúrha (*note how the stress shifts*) – laázim yashkúrnii (*note that* nii *translates "me"*)
6. híya raáyHa lil-madiína – níHna raayHiín lil-madiína
8. fíina naruuH

THIRD LESSON – *'ad-dars ath-thaálith*

INTRODUCTIONS

Dialogue 1 – *Hiwaár raqm waáHid*

(John White goes to visit his friend Abdullah, who is giving a party at his home to a considerable gathering)

9abdúllah:
   'áhlan, ya John, 'áhlan   *Hello, John, welcome.*
   wa sáhlan. tafáDDal.   *Please come in.*

John:
   shúkran, ya 9abdúllah   *Thank you, Abdullah.*

9abdullah:
   bíddii 'a9árr(i)fak 9ála   *I want to introduce you to my*
      Sadiiqii Hámad   *friend Hamad*
   bidd/ii   *wish/my*
   'a9árrif/ak   *I introduce/you*
   Sadiíq pl. 'aSdiqaá'   *friend*

9abdullah (continues):
   ya Hámad, haádha Sadiíqii,   *Hamad, this is my friend, John.*
   John.
   haádha   *this (masculine form)*

32

John:
tasharráfna
tashárraf/na

Hamad:
wa 'ílna sh-sháraf
'il (+ pronoun suffix)
na

sháraf

Hamad (continues):
HáDratak min 'ameérka?
HáDrat/ak

min

John:
la, 'ána min 'ingéltera
la

Pleased to meet you.
We/have been honoured

Pleased to meet you
variant of li/la (= *to*)
us (*plural used for greater formality*)
honour (*the whole phrase means "and to us the honour"*)

Are you from America?
your/honour (*polite form of address* = "you")
from

No, I'm from England.
No.

Dialogue 2 – *Hiwaár raqm 'ithnáyn*

(later at the same party)

9abdullah:
ya John, biddii 'a9árrfak 9ála˘
  Sadiíq thaáni min as-
  sifaára l-maSríyya
thaáni
sifaára *pl.* sifaaraát
maSr/máSri

9abdullah (continues):
ya múHsin bíddii 'aqáddimak
  li Sadíiqii John
'aqaddim/ak
li

muHsin:
tasharráfna

John:
wa 'ílna sh-sháraf

John, I want to introduce you to another friend from the Egyptian Embassy.
(*an*)*other, second*
embassy
Egypt/Egyptian (maSríyya *is the feminine form*)

Muhsin, I want to introduce you to my friend John.
I introduce/you
to

Pleased to meet you.

Pleased to meet you.

33

Marcel:
HáDratak min 'ingéltera?   *Are you from England?*

John:
ná9am, 'ána 'ingliízi   *Yes, I am English.*

muHsin:
wayn tashtághil?   *Where do you work?*
wayn?   *where?*
tashtághil   *you work*

John:
'ashtághil fi shárikat nafT   *I work in an oil company.*
'ashtághil   *I work*
fi   *in*
shárika *pl.* sharikaát   *company*
nafT   *oil*

Dialogue 3 – *Hiwaár raqm thalaátha*

(later in the same conversation when both men have become better acquainted)

muHsin:
kayf al-'awlaád?   *How are the children?*
wálad *pl.* 'awlaád   *boy plural often means
                                   "children")*

John:
mabsuuTiín, shúkran   *Well, thank you.*

muHsin:
hum 9aa'ishiín húna má9ak   *Are they living here with you?*
9aá'ish (-iin)   *living*
húna   *here*

John:
la, ma 9aa'ishiín húna, hum   *No, they aren't here. They are
   talaamiídh fi mádrasa fi   pupils at a school in England.*
   'ingéltera
tilmiıdh *pl.* talaamiidh   *pupil, student.*
mádrasa *pl.* madaáris   *school*

9abdullah (returning):
ya John, ya múHsin, shuu   *John, Muhsin, what would you
   t(a)riídu táshrabu?   like to drink?*
shuu?   *what?*

34

| t(a)riídu | you (pl.) wish |
| táshrabu | you (pl.) drink |

(after their decisions)

9abdullah:

| tafáDDalu | Here you are. |

Dialogue 4 – *Hiwaár raqm 'árba9a*

(John prepares to leave)

John:

9an 'ídhnak, 'ismáHlii 'amshi	By your leave. Allow me to go.
9an	from, about (e.g. talk about . . .)
'idhn	permission
9an 'ídhnak	(an apology for disturbing some-one)
'ismáH/l/ii	permit/to/me (a standard for-mula for leave-taking)
'amshi	I go. (for leave-taking)

9abdullah:

líssa bakkiír	It is still early.
líssa	still, up till now.
bakkiír	early

John:

laázim 'aruúH 9al-bayt. búkra 9índii shúghl kathiír	I have to go home. Tomorrow I have a lot of work.
búkra	tomorrow
9ind/ii	I have (lit: with me)
shúghl *pl.* 'ashghaál	work
kathiír	much, many.

Notes on Grammar and Usage

1. Consider the Muslim names for men you have encountered. Several of them have the same consonants $H - m - d$ in common e.g. *'aHmad, muHámmad, maHmuúd, Haámid* and *Hámad*. Because they have the same three letter (triliteral) root, they are related in meaning (the triliteral root $H - m - d$ has to do with praising – *muHámmad* means "greatly praised"). Most Arabic words are based on the triliteral root though some have four (quadriliterals) and a very few have two or five. Variations are worked on the basic root by such means as adding prefixes (*muHámmad,*

maHmuúd), doubling consonants (*muHámmad*), doubling vowels (*maHmuúd*), changing length/quality of vowels (*Haámid, Hámad*). A knowledge of the word derivation system in Arabic is an enormous help to acquiring Arabic vocabulary rapidly and without pain. Just for interest consider the examples of triliteral roots below:

salaáma – yusállim (root = *s – l – m*: basic idea = safety)
tashtághil – mashghuúl (root = *sh – gh – l*: basic idea = occupying)
náshkur – shúkran (root = *sh – k – r*: basic idea = thanking)
tasharráfna – sháraf (root = *sh – r – f*: basic idea = honouring)

One of the main aims of this course is to provide the student with a knowledge of the word formation systems in Arabic.

2. Other Muslim names for men include *9abdúllah, 9abd ul-xaálid* etc. The word *9abd* means "slave". It is then followed by either the word for God as in *9abdúllah* (= slave of God) or by one of the names of God e.g. *9abd ul-xaálid* (= slave of the eternal one), *9abd ul-kariím* (= slave of the generous one).

The way Muslim names are built up will be explained in the next lesson.

3. "This" is expressed in Arabic by *haádha* with masculine nouns and *haádhi* with feminine nouns. Note the differences between:

(a) *haádha Sadiiqii* = this is my friend
haádhi bint = this is a girl
(b) *haádha S-Sadiíq* = this friend
haádhi l-bint = this girl

When *haádha/haádhi* is used as an adjective (examples (b)), a definite article is required on the following noun.

4. *maSr* (= Egypt)/*máSri* (= Egyptian)/*maSriyya* (feminine adjective)/*maSriyyiín* (plural adjective) – on this pattern adjectives can be formed from nouns (note the shift of stress in the feminine and plural forms. e.g. *briiTaánya* (Britain)/*briiTaáni* (British)/*briiTaaniyya* (f.) *briiTaaniyyiín* (pl.)

mádrasa (= school)/*mádrasi* (= scholastic/*madrasíyya* (f)

N.B. -*a* endings are removed from nouns before addition of -*i/íyya* etc.

5. *bíddii:* this is an important way of expressing "want to" in colloquial Arabic (see appendix for some regional alternatives). It can be followed directly by a noun e.g. *bíddii shúghl* = I want work, *bíddak bayt?* = do you want a house? (rising inflection for question).

It can also be followed by a verb in the appropriate person e.g.

bíddii 'a9árrif = I want to introduce . . .

bíddna nashtághil = we want to work

bídduh yaruúH . . . = he wants to go . . .

ma bíddii 'aruúH má9uh = I don't want to go with him (use *ma* to negate *bidd/*-)

6. *mush:* negates nouns, adjectives, adverbs, pronouns, prepositions etc, e.g.

híya mush Sadiíqa = she is not a friend (note feminine for "friend")

níHna mush mabsuuTiín = we are not well

mush húwa, 'ána = not him, me.

húwa mush má9hum = he is not with them

and N.B.

'intu mush raayHiín 'íla l-madiína = you are not going to the city.

7. *ma* negates verbs and verb-like expressions (and occasionally active participles as in *ma 9aa'ishiín* (= not living)) e.g.

ma 'ashtághil fi 9ammaán = I don't work in Amman.

ma bíddna naruúH . . . = we don't want to go . . .

ma 9índii bayt = I don't have a house.

(Note how *bidd*- and *9ind*- are "verb-like", though not really verbs)

Note:

mush Daruúri 'aruúH 9al-bayt = I don't need to go home

laázim ma 'aruúH 9al-bayt = I must not go home

8. Here are the full conjugations in the imperfect of some of the verbs you have met. The "imperfect" tense indicates unfinished actions. It is most often used therefore for the present and future.

áshkur – I thank	*'aruúH* – I go . . .	*'áji* – I come . . .
táshkur – you . . .	*taruúH* – you . . .	*tíji* – you . . .
táshkuri – you (f.s.)	*taruúHi* – you (f.s.)	*tíji* – you (f.s.)
yáshkur – he . . .	*yaruúH* – he . . .	*yíji* – he . . .
táshkur – she . . .	*taruúH* – she . . .	*tíji* – she . . .
náshkur – we . . .	*naruúH* – we . . .	*níji* – we . . .
táshkuru – you (pl.)	*taruúHu* – you (pl.)	*tíju* – you (pl.)
yáshkuru – they . . .	*yaruúHu* – they . . .	*yíju* – they . . .

Exercises (asterisked items have their answers at the end of the lesson)

1. Give the plurals of the following words.

mádrasa	*wálad*	*shárika*
tilmiídh	*bint*	**Sadiíqa* (= woman friend)
Sadiíq	*raáyiH*	**tilmiídha* (= girl pupil)
briiTaáni	*mariíD*	**briiTaaníyya* (British woman)

2. Give the Arabic of the following expressions. Give the formal replies necessary.

Good morning . . .	Good evening . . .
Hello . . .	Peace be upon you . . .
Pleased to meet you . . .	My daughter is a little ill . . .
Please come in . . .	*My son is a little ill . . .
*By your leave, I have to go now . . .	

3. I want to see (= *'ashuúf*) this house	*bíddii 'ashuúf haádha l-bayt.*
+ boy/pupil (masculine words)	
*you (m. & f.)/he/she/we/ you (pl.)/they	
+ this country (*bilaád*)	*haádhi l-bilaád*
school, embassy, company (feminine words)	
4. Does he wish to drink coffee?	*bídduh yáshrab qáhwa?*
she, they/you (m. f. & pl.)	
– No, he doesn't want to drink coffee, he wants to drink tea (= *shaay*)	*la, ma bídduh yáshrab qáhwa, bídduh yáshrab shaay.*

N.B. remember the answers to the "you" questions would begin with "I" or "we" depending on whether the question was singular or plural.

5. I don't have to work in this company	*mush Daruuri 'áshtaghil fi haádhi sh-shárika.*
you/he etc./this country/city/school	
6. You (pl.) must not go together	*laázim ma taruúHu sáwa.*

38

we/they – go home/to
the city
to America/to England
etc.
7. (*a*) This is a friend   *haádha Sadiíq*
    house/boy etc.
   (*b*) This is coffee   *haádhi qáhwa*
    a girl/company/*oil
    company.

Answers

1. *Sadiiqaát, tilmiidhaát, briiTaaniyyaát* (a plural like *talaamiídh*
includes both men and women. When only women are denoted,
then the usual plural for nouns ending in *-a* is used i.e. *-aat*).
2. *'al-wálad mariíD shwayy – salaámtuh!*
'astádhin or *'ismáHlii* (m.s.)/*'ismaHiílii* (f.s.)/*'ismaHuúlii* (pl.)
3. *bíddak tashuúf . . . – bíddik tashuúfi . . .*
7. *haádhi shárikat nafT* (note the *t* added to *shárika*. Compare
with the similar phenomenon in *salaáma – salaamátha.*

FOURTH LESSON – *'ad-dars ar-raabi9*

DIRECTIONS

Dialogue 1 – *Hiwaár raqm waáHid* (– Where is? . . .)

(Sa'ad is looking for the post-office. He asks a stranger for help)

sá9ad:
  'arjuuk, wayn máktab al-   *Please, where is the post-office?*
   bariíd
  'arjuúk/ki/kum   *please* (*from*   raja = *request,*
                         hope)
  máktab *pl.* makaátib   *office*
  ('al)-bariíd   (*of*) (*the*) *post, mail.*

ghariíb (= stranger):
  máktab al-bariíd hunaák,   *The post-office is there opposite*
   muqaábil as-siínama   *the cinema.*
  muqaábil   *opposite*

sa9ad:
  shúkran   *Thank you*

39

'al-ghariib:
la shukr 9ála waájib   *Don't mention it (no thanks for a*
                                         duty)

Dialogue 2 – *Hiwaár raqm 'ithnáyn*

(Sa'ad is now looking for the Grand Hotel (*'al-funduq al-kabiir* = "the hotel the big"))

sá9ad:
min fáDlak, múmkin taquúl   *Please, can you tell me where the*
lii   wayn   al-fúnduq   al-   *Grand Hotel is?*
kabiír?
múmkin   *possible*
taquúl   *you say*
l/ii   *to/me*
kabiír *pl.* kibaár   *big, senior, old (of people)*

'al-ghariib:
muta'ássif, ma bá9rif al-   *I am sorry, I don't know the city.*
madiína
muta'ássif   *sorry*
bá9rif   *I know* (See note 4 in "Notes on
                                 Grammar & Usage")

sa9ad: (to another stranger)
min fáDlak, yúmkin taquúl lii   *Please, can you tell me where the*
wayn al-fúnduq al-kabiír?   *Grand Hotel is?*
yúmkin   *(it is) possible (used like*
                                 múmkin)
fúnduq *pl.* fanaádiq   *hotel*

'al-ghariib:
ná9am, shii basiíT. 'imshi   *Yes, that's easy. Go straight*
dúghri wa ba9adáyn . . .   *ahead and then . . .*
shii *pl.* 'ashyaá'   *thing*
basiíT *pl.* bisaáT   *simple, easy*
'imshi!   *walk! go! (an imperative)*
dúghri   *straight ahead*
ba9adáyn   *afterwards*

sa9ad:
wa ba9adáyn? . . .   *and afterwards? . . .*

'al-ghariib:
wa ba9adáyn, xudh ash-   *and then, take the street on your*
shaári9 9ála yamiínak   *right.*

xudh!	*take! (imperative)*
shaári9 *pl.* shawaári9	*street*
yamiín	*right*
9ála yamiínak	*on your right*

sa9ad:
'al-fúnduq fi haádha sh-shaári9?	*Is the hotel in this street?*

'al-ghariib:
ná9am, raH tashuúf al-fúnduq 9ála shimaálak	*Yes, you'll see the hotel on your left.*
raH	*particle used with the imperfect to indicate the future.*
tashuúf	*you see*
shimaál	*left, north*
9ála shimaálak	*on your left*

sa9ad:
mamnuúnak kathiír	*I'm very grateful to you.*
mamnuún/ak	*grateful/to you*
kathiír	*much, many, very*

'al-ghariib:
'al-9áfu	*Don't mention it.*

Dialogue 3 – *Hiwaár raqm thalaátha*

(On his way to the Grand Hotel, Sa'ad notices a large building and asks a policeman what it is) – policeman = *buliís* pl. *buliisíyya*

sá9ad:
'arjuuk, shuu haádhi l-binaáya?	*Excuse me, what is this building?*
binaáya *pl.* binaayaát	*building*

buliís:
haádhi híya s-sifaára l-'ameerkíyya	*This is the American Embassy*
híya	*she, it* (referring to feminine nouns such as sifaara)

sa9ad:
ya salaám! kabiíra jíddan!	*My word? (It's) very big.*
ya salaám!	*(exclamation of surprise)*
jíddan	*very*

41

buliis:

ná9am, wa jánbha fii bi-naáyat shárikat nafT, ka-maán kabiíra	*Yes, and next to it there is an oil company building. (That's big too)*
janb/ha	*next, near to/it* (ha refers back to the feminine word binaáya)
fii	*there is* (not to be confused with fi = in)
kamaán	*also*

sa9ad:

'ashkúrak	*I thank you*

buliis:

'al-9áfu	*Don't mention it.*

Notes on Grammar and Usage

1. Some further useful vocabulary:

> *ruuH 'íla l-yamiín/yamiínak* – Go to the/your right.
> *ruuH 'íla sh-shimaál/shimaálak* – Go to the/your left.
> *xudh 'áwwal shaári9 9ála l-yamiín/ash-shimaal* – Take the first street on the right/left.
> *xudh ash-shaári9 ath-thaáni/ath-thaálith/ar-raábi9* etc. – Take the second street/third/fourth etc.
> *9ála yamiínak/shimaálak* . . . – on your right/left . . .
> > *quddaám* – in front of
> > *wára* – behind

2. *máktab al-bariíd*: this means "*the* post-office". *máktab bariíd* (without the definite article on *bariíd*) means "*a* post-office". Similarly *shárikat nafT* means "*an* oil company" and *shárikat an-nafT* means "*the* oil company".

3. *'al-fúnduq al-kabiír*: adjectives have to agree with their nouns in definiteness. If the noun is definite, then the adjective too is definite and has the definite article *'al-* prefixed e.g. *'al-bayt al-kabiír* (= the big house), but if the noun is indefinite then the adjective lacks the definite article e.g. *shii basiíT* (= an easy thing).

Adjectives also agree with the noun in gender –

> e.g. *binaáya kabiíra* = a big building
> *bayt kabiir* = a big house
> *'al-binaáya l-kabiira* = the big building
> *'al-bayt al-kabiír* = the big house

42

Sentences such as "the house is big" are expressed by having the noun definite and the adjective indefinite –

e.g. *'al-binaáya kabiíra* = the building is big
'al-bayt kabiír = the house is big

4. *bá9rif*: it is usual in the dialects of Greater Syria and Egypt to prefix the forms of the imperfect you were given in Lesson 3 with *b-*.

There follow the full conjugations of the three verbs fully conjugated in Lesson 3 together with that of *bá9rif*.

báshkur = I thank	*b(a)ruúH* = I go	*báji* = I come	*bá9rif* = I know
btáshkur – you	*bitruúH* – you	*btíji* – you	*btá9rif* – you
btáshkuri – you	*bitruúHi* – you	*btíji* – you	*btá9rifi* – you (fem.)
byáshkur – he	*biruúH* – he	*byíji* – he	*byá9rif* – he
btáshkur – she	*bitruúH* – she	*btíji* – she	*btá9rif* – she
mnáshkur – we	*minruúH* – we	*mníji* – we	*mná9rif* – we
btáshkuru – you	*bitruúHu* – you	*btíju* – you	*btá9rifu* – you (pl)
byáshkuru – they	*biruúHu* – they	*byíju* – they	*byá9rifu* – they

Notes on Forms

(*a*) Since there is no infinitive in the Arabic verb, when Arabs wish to identify a verb they quote the 3rd person masculine singular e.g. *yashkur/byashkur*

(*b*) The "we" forms begin with *m* because of anticipation of the nasal *n*. A *b* beginning can also be heard.

(*c*) The conjugations of *byáshkur* and *byá9rif* resemble each other closely, the only difference being in the vowels before the final consonants. The conjugation of *biruúH* is typical of a "hollow" verb, i.e. a verb with a long middle vowel like *biruúH* or *bishuúf*.
by i ji is idiosyncratic and should be learnt as a separate item.

Notes on Usage

(*a*) In the dialects of Greater Syria and Egypt, the imperfects of verbs carry a *b* prefix when used as independent verbs. When they are dependent on a preceding expression such as *laazim*, *bidd-*, or *mumkin*, imperfects without *b* are used.

e.g. *bá9rif al-madiina* but *bíddii 'á9rif al-madiina*
(= I know the city)   (= I want to know the city)
bitruúH 'íla l-yamiín   *laázim taruúH 'íla l-yamiín*
(= you go to the right)   (= you must go to the right)
byíju búkra   *múmkin yáju/yíju búkra*
(= they are coming   (= they may/can come
tomorrow)   tomorrow)

In this sort of context, the *b*-less forms are similar to the English infinitive in meaning.

The *b*-less forms are also used when expressing wishes e.g. *nash-kur allaah* (= let us thank God)

N.B. In Iraq, Saudi Arabia and Gulf, only the forms without *b* are usual. See appendix A for further details.

5. *Further note on Arab names:* – An Arab's name may be composed of the following elements, written in this order:

(*a*) personal, given name,
(*b*) father's name with or without *bin* (= son (of)),
(*c*) grandfather's name,
(*d*) family name or surname (often derived from a place or profession).

For other than official purposes, an Arab may consider elements (*a*) and (*b*) or (*a*) and (*d*) sufficient to identify himself. The use of elements (*a*) and (*d*) alone is common among Christian Arabs and "westernised" Muslims. The following is an example of a name with the four elements indicated.

(*a*)	(*b*)	(*c*)	(*d*)
muHámmad/*9abd al-xaálid*/		*kariím*	/*bayTaár*
(greatly praised)	(slave of the eternal one)	(generous)	(veterinary surgeon)

Information on how to address men is given in Lesson 6.

Exercises

1. Plurals: what are the plurals of the following words?

máktab	*binaáya*	*buliis*
mádrasa	*sifaára*	*kabiír*
fúnduq	*shárika*	*madiína*

Note the similar vowel patterning in the plurals of the four consonant words in the left-hand column.

2. Form the questions with the elements proposed in part (*a*), answer using the suggestions in part (*b*).

(*a*) Excuse me, where is the post-office? /school/hotel/the Embassy/the American Embassy/the oil company building (= *binaáyat shárikat an-nafT*)   *'arjuúk, wayn máktab al-bariíd?*

(b) It is opposite the cinema behind/the oil company next to/the Embassy in front of/the school etc.

hu/hiya muqaábil as-siínama (remember *hu* for masculine nouns and *hiya* for feminine ones)

3 (a) Excuse me, can you tell me where the cinema/Grand Hotel/French Embassy is?

'arjuúk, múmkin/yúmkin taquúl lii wayn as-siínama?

(b) Yes, take the 1st/2nd/3rd/4th/ street on your left/right and then go straight ahead.

ná9am, xudh 'áwwal shaári9/ash-shaári9 ath-thaáni 9ála shimaálak/yamiínak wa ba9adáyn ruuH dúghri

4 (a) Can you tell me please where the American/British (= *briiTaaniyya*)/Embassy is?

múmkin taquúl lii min fáDlak wayn as-sifaára l'ameerkíyya?

(b) Yes, Go to your right/left and then take the 1st/2nd/3rd/4th street on your right/left.

ná9am, ruuH li yamiínak/ shimaálak wa ba9adáyn xudh 'áwwal shaári9/ash-shaári9 ar-raábi9 9ála yamiínak/ shimaalak

5. (a) I'm very grateful to you (to a man/woman/two or more)

mamnuúnak/ik/kum kathiir

(b) Don't mention it

'al-9áfu/la shukr 9ála waájib

6. Translate: (look at the Arabic only after an unaided attempt)

The big Embassy	*'as-sifaára l-kabiíra*
A big Embassy	*sifaára kabiíra*
The big house	*'al-bayt al-kabiir*
A big house	*bayt kabiir*
The Embassy is big	*'as-sifaára kabiíra*
The house is big	*'al-bayt kabiir*
The children are well	*'al-'awlaád mabsuu'l un*
The girl is well	*'al-bint mabsuúTa*
The big city	*'al-madiina l-kabiíra*
The city is big	*'al madiina kabiíra*
My friend is from America	*Sadíiqii min 'ameérka*
America is a big country	*'ameérka biláad kabiíra*

7. Translate the first English sentence into Arabic. Repeat the sentence but introducing *laázim* (= must). Make the necessary changes to the verb. Do the same for all persons of the verb.

Every day (*kull yawm*) I work in the office	*kull yawm bashtághil fil-máktab*
+ *laázim*	*kull yawm laázim 'ashtághil fil-máktab*
you/he/she/we/you (pl.)/they	

FIFTH LESSON – *'ad-dars al-xaamis*

REVISION LESSON

English sentences are given on the left of the page with a corresponding Arabic translation. Depending on the student's confidence in himself, a start could be made with the Arabic sentences, translating them into English while covering up the solutions, or the English sentences could be translated into Arabic. The aim of the sentences is to cover all the grammar presented so far together with most of the vocabulary. Purely formal phrases are comparatively neglected.

1. How are you? (to a man)	*kayf Haálak?/káyfak?*
(to a woman)	*kayf Haálik?/káyfik?*
(to two or more)	*kayf Haálkum?/káyfkum?*
2. Well, praise be to God (man)	*mabsuúT, 'al Hámdu líllaah*
(woman)	*mabsuúTa, . . .*
(plural)	*mabsuuTíin, . . .*
3. Good-bye – Good-bye – God keep you. (to a man)	*bixaáTrak – ma9a s-salaáma – 'állaah yusállimak.*
(to a woman)	*bixaáTrik . . . 'állaah yusállimik*
(to two or more)	*bixaaTírkum . . . 'állaah yusallímkum*

N.B. Consult Note 11 in Lesson 1 for the stress changes caused by the different endings.

4. I must go home	*laázim 'aruúH 9al-bayt*
5. He wants to go to the cinema	*bídduh yaruúH lis-siínama/9as-siínama*
6. It is possible we go to the city.	*yúmkin/múmkin naruúH 'íla l-madiina*

46

7. My house is big   *báytii kabiír*
8. His daughter is ill   *bíntuh mariiDa*
9. May she get well soon   *salaamátha*
10. Our big house is in the city   *báytna l-kabiír fil-madiina*

N.B. a noun with a possessive suffix is definite.

11. Your house is not big (to woman – to two +)   *báytak mush kabiir (báytik – báytkum)*
12. Their house is also not big   *báyt-hum kamaán mush kabiír*
13. Let them go home together   *xalliíhum yaruúHu 9al-bayt sáwa*
14. I'm living (= *saákin*) in London (feminine)   *'ána saákin fi lúndun (saákina)*
15. We are going to Beirut   *niHna raayHiín 'ila bayruút*
16. She is living in her house   *híya saákina fi báytha*
17. I'm busy today   *'ána mashghuúl al-yawm*
18. God give you strength   *'állaah ya9Tiik al-9aáfya*
19. I can't come with them   *ma fiinii 'áji má9hum*
20. We can't come with you   *ma fiina niji má9ak, ik, kum*
21. Come with me!   *ta9aál má9ii! + ta9aalii (f) ta9aalu (pl)*
22. I want to give you a book (= *kitaáb*)   *bíddii 'a9Tiík/ki/kum kitaáb*
23. I must give them a book   *laázim 'a9Tiíhum kitaáb*
24. They must give us money (= *fuluús*)   *laázim ya9Tuúna fuluús*
25. I don't want to go   *ma bíddii 'aruúH*
26. My friend doesn't want to work (*Sadiiqii ma bídduh . . .*)   *Sadiiqii ma bídduh yashtághil*
27. What would you like to drink   *shuu bitriíd táshrab?*
28. I should like to drink . . .   *bariíd 'áshrab . . .*
29. This is the Egyptian Embassy.   *haádhi híya s-sifaára l-maSríyya*
30. This house is big   *haádha l-bayt kabiir*
31. This is a girl   *haádhi bint*
32. Ahmed is not in the house   *'áHmad mush fil-bayt*
33. The students are not in the school   *'at-talaamiidh mush fil-mádrasa*
34. Excuse me, will you allow me (to leave) (m. f. & pl.)?   *9an 'ídhnak/ik/'idhinkum, 'ismáHlii/'ismaHiílii/ 'ismaHuúlii* or *'astá'dhin*

35. It is still early	*lissa bakkiir*
36. I have a lot of work tomorrow	*9índii shúghl kathiír búkra*
37. Good-bye and thank you	*bixaáTrak wa shúkran*
38. Good-bye	*má9a s-salaáma*
39. God keep you	*'állaah yusállimak*
40. Every day (= *kull yawm*) I see my friend Ahmed	*kull yawm bashuúf Sadiiqii 'áHmad*
41. Every day he goes to his office	*kull yawm biruúH li máktabuh*
42. Every day he says that (= *'in*) he will not go to his office	*kull yawm biquúl 'ínnuh ma raH yaruúH li máktabuh*
43. Every day I drink coffee in the office, but (= *bass*) you drink tea.	*kull yawm báshrab qáhwa fil-máktab bass 'ínta btáshrab shaay*
44. Every day Ahmed comes home from his company	*kull yawm 'áHmad byíji 9al-bayt min shárikatuh*
45. Then his friends come to his house	*wa ba9adáyn 'aSdiqaá'uh byíju li báytuh.*
46. The first house	*'áwwal bayt*
47. The third house	*'al-bayt ath-thaálith*

SIXTH LESSON – *'ad-dars as-saádis*

POSSESSION

Dialogue – *Hiwaár*

'áHmad:

9índak sayyaára?	*Have you a car?*
9ind/ak	*You have* (lit: *with you*)
sayyaára-aat	*car*

kariím:

la, ma 9índii sayyaara	*No, I don't have a car*
9ind/ii	*I have*

'aHmad:

miin SaáHib haádhi s-sayyaára?	*Who is the owner of this car?*
miin?	*Who?* (always question word)
SaáHib *pl.* 'aSHaáb	*owner, friend*

48

kariim:

has-sayyaára tába9 al-mudiír ha

This car belongs to the director.

this (masculine, feminine and plural – most common form when "this" is adjective)

taba9

belonging to (See Note 5 in "Notes on Grammar and Usage")

'aHmad:

ya salaám, híya sayyaára kabiíra!

My word! It's a big car.

hiya

she, it (referring to feminine nouns)

kariim:

ná9am, wa 9índuh kamaán sayyaára thaánya Saghiíra.

9ind/uh

Saghiír *pl.* Sighaár

Yes, and he has another small car too.

he has

small, young

'aHmad:

kull al-muwáZZafiín húna 9indhum sayyaaraát?

kull (+ plural)

muwáZZaf (-iin) 9ind/hum

Have all the officials here got cars?

all (N.B. kull + singular = *every*)

official, employee
they have

kariim:

yá9ni, 'akthárhum 9índhum sayyaaraát

yá9ni

'ákthar

Well, most of them have cars.

according to context = "you mean", "i.e.", "that means" …

more (when defined – as here by the suffixed *hum* – means "most")

'aHmad:

laákin, 'ínta, ma 9índak sayyaára

laákin

But you, you have no car.

but

kariim:

la, laákin záwjatii 9índha sayyaára, wa 'ána 9indii bis-klaat. 'áHsan bikathiír min-shaán aS-SíHHa!

No, but my wife has a car, while I have a bicycle. Much better for the health.

49

záwja-aat	*wife*
bisklaat (-aat)	*bicycle*
9ind/ha – 9índii	*she has – I have*
'áHsan	*better* (compare shape of this word with *'ákthar*)
minshaán	*for*

Questions on Dialogue

There follows a new kind of exercise. Questions in Arabic are printed on the left of the page and the answers (also in Arabic) on the right. You should read both questions and answers through first of all and work out the constructions and meanings of both. Then cover up the answers and read each question aloud. Give the answer to the question, again aloud. You should use the answers given in the book, not because they are the only answers possible but because both questions and answers have been chosen to provide practice in essential new language items.

1. kariím 9índuh sayyaára?	la, ma 9índuh sayyaára
2. miin SaáHib as-sayyaára?	'al-mudiír SaáHib as-sayyaára
3. sayyaárat al-mudiír kabiíra?	ná9am, sayaárat al-mudiír kabiíra
4. 'al-mudiír 9índuh sayyaára thaánya?	ná9am, 9índuh sayyaára thaánya
5. 'as-sayyaára th-thaánya kabiíra?	la, híya mush kabiíra, híya Saghiíra
6. 'ákthar al-muwáZZafiín 9índhum sayyaaraát?	ná9am, 'akthárhum 9índhum sayyaaraát
7. záwjat kariím 9índha sayyaára?	ná9am, 9índha sayyaára
8. kariím shuu 9índuh?	9índuh bisklaát

Narrative – *riwaáya*

The narrative that follows is a new way (for this book) of presenting material, particularly of a narrative or descriptive sort.

1. mudiír ash-shárika 'ísmuh 'as-sáyyid muSTáfa 9abd al-9aziíz	*The name of the director of the company is Mustafa Abd el Aziz*
mudiír *pl.* múdara	*director, manager, administrator*
'ism *pl.* 'asaámii/'asmaá'	*name*
'as-sáyyid	*equivalent to "mister" in westernised Arab countries.*

2. kull yawm byíji l-mudiír lil-máktab fi sayyaártuh — *Every day the director comes to the office in his car.*

kull yawm — *every day* (compare with *kull al-muwaZZafíin* in dialogue above)

sayyaártuh — *his car* (note how the dropping of the weak syllable converts *sayyaáratuh* to *sayyaártuh*. This is normal).

3. sayyaárat al-mudiir fransaawíyya. — *The director's car is French.*

4. máktab al-mudiír fiT-Taábiq al-'áwwal fi binaáya kabiíra janb wizaárat ad-daáxilíyya — *The director's office is on the first floor in a big building next to the Ministry of the Interior.*

Taábiq *pl.* Tawaábiq — *storey, floor*

wizaára-aat — *ministry*

daáxilíyya — *interior* (feminine of *daáxili*)

5. wára l-binaáya fii wizaárat al-xaárijíyya — *Behind the building is the Ministry of Foreign Affairs*

xaárijíyya — *outer* (feminine of *xaáriji*).

6. wa quddaámha fii binaayaát wizaárat al-muwaáSalaát — *And in front of it there are the buildings of the Ministry of Communications*

7. musaá9id al-mudiír 'ísmuh já9far Hámdi — *The assistant of the director is called Ja'afar Hamdi*

musaá9id (-iin) — *assistant, helper*

8. wa fi máktabuh fii Taáwilat kitaába — *and in his office there is a desk (writing table)*

Taáwila-aat — *table, backgammon*

kitaába — *writing*

9. wára T-Taáwila fii kúrsi muriíH — *Behind the table is a comfortable chair*

kúrsi *pl.* karaási — *chair*

muriíH — *comfortable*

10. wa 'amaámha fii thalaath karaási minshaán az-zuwwaár — *and in front of it there are three chairs for visitors*

zaa'ir (zuwwaar) — *visitor*

Questions on Narrative

1. shuu 'ísm mudiir ash-shárika? — 'ísmuh 'as-sáyyid muSTáfa 9abd al-9aziíz

51

2. sayyaárat al-mudiír briiTaaníyya?

la, sayyaárat al-mudiír, fransaawíyya.

3. wayn máktab al-mudiír?

fiT-Taábiq al-'áwwal

4. 'ayy (= *which?*) wizaára janb ash-shárika?

wizaárat ad-daáxilíyya

5. 'ayy wizaára wára sh-shárika?

wizaárat al-xaárijíyya

6. 'ayy wizaára quddaám ash-shárika?

wizaárat al-muwaáSalaát

7. shuu 'ism musaá9id al-mudiír?

'ísmuh já9far Hámdi

8. 9induh Taáwilat kitaába fi máktabuh?

'áywa (= *yes*) fii Taáwilat kitaába fil-máktab

9. shuu fii wára Taáwilat al-kitaába?

fii kúrsi muriíH wára Taáwilat al-kitaába

10. wa 'amaám aT-Taáwila?

fii thalaáth karaási minshaán az-zuwwaár

Notes on Grammar and Usage

1. Arabic does not possess a verb equivalent to the English "to have". Instead prepositions are used plus the appropriate pronoun suffix. The most common preposition used is *9ind*:

e.g. *9índak sayyaára?* (= do you have a car?)
ma 9índii kúrsi (= I don't have a chair)

Another common preposition is *ma9* which is used for small objects actually on the person:

e.g. *má9ak qálam?* (= do you have a pen?)
la, ma má9ii qálam (= No, I don't have a pen (on me))

2. *"Construct"*: in the dialogue and the narrative of this lesson there are several examples of the typical Arabic possessive relationship between two nouns known as the "construct state".

e.g. *mudiír ash-shárika* (= the director of the company)
sayyaárat al-mudiír (= the car of the director i.e. the director's car)

In this construction only the *last* noun of the group may bear the definite article, and yet the preceding noun is definite, made definite by the very fact of a noun following with which it has a possessive relationship.

You should note too that feminine words ending in -*a* like *sayyaára* add -*t* before a noun with which they are in construct.

There may be three nouns (rarely more) in a construct:

e.g. *máktab musaá9id al-mudiir* (= *the* office of *the* assistant of the director)

Here again only the last noun can bear the definite article.

Note: *'áwwal shaári9* in lesson 4 meant "*the* first street" because *'áwwal* is in construct with *shaári9* and made definite by it.

3. *Descriptive Construct:* the type of construct discussed above in note 2 is possessive (the director possesses the car). Another type is the "descriptive" construct where the second word describes the first:

e.g. *shárikat naf T* (= *an* oil company)
Taáwilat kitaába (*a* writing desk)

In such constructs the whole group is made definite by adding the definite article *al-* to the second word:

e.g. *shárikat an-naf T* (= *the* oil company)
Taáwilat al-kitaába (= *the* writing table)

4. *Construct – position of adjectives:* the only words which can come between nouns involved in a construct are the demonstratives *haádha/haádhi* and *ha-*:

e.g. *SaáHib has-sayyaára* (= the owner of this car)

Adjectives come after the whole group even if they refer to the first noun:

e.g. *sayyaárat al-mudiir al-kabiira* (= the director's big car)

kabiira agrees in gender (feminine) and number (singular) with its noun *sayyaára*. It is also marked as definite with *'al-* since *sayyaára* is rendered definite by the following noun.

5. *tába9*: words like *tába9* (consult Appendix A for the regional variants) are used in most dialects firstly to reduce the rigidity of the construct case (and possible ambiguities) and secondly to express "mine" "yours" etc. *tába9* is always in construct with a following noun or a pronoun suffix. It does not change for gender.

An example of ambiguity inherent in the construct case:

e.g. *bayt al-waziír al-kabiir* (= EITHER – the minister's big house OR – the house of the old/great minister)

The ambiguity stems from not knowing which noun *kabiír* refers to. The phrase become clear when expressed as follows:

'al-bayt tába9 al-waziír al-kabiír (= . . . the great/old minister) or *'al-bayt al-kabiír tába9 al-waziír* (= the big house . . .)

some further examples of *tába9*:

haádha tába9ii (= this is mine)
haádha tába9 'áHmad (= this is Ahmed's)
has-sayyaára tába9 'áHmad (= this car is Ahmed's)
tába9 miin haádha? (= whose is this?)

6. *Some forms of address:*
'as-sáyyid – "Mr" in more westernised countries. In other countries it may be an inherited rank or a religious dignity. The feminine is *'as-sáyyida* (= "Mrs").

'al-místir – used for English speaking Europeans.

Exercises

1. Translate:
(*a*) The manager of the Grand Hotel is in his office.
(*b*) Does the manager have a car?
(*c*) No, but his wife has a car.
(*d*) Is the manager's wife's car big?
(*e*) The car belonging to her is very big.
(*f*) Does this house belong to Ahmed?
(*g*) No, this house is Muhammad's.
(*h*) The first street on the left is Beirut street.

Answers:

(*a*) mudiír al-fúnduq al-kabiír fi máktabuh
(*b*) 'al-mudiír 9índuh sayyaára?
(*c*) la, laákin záwjatuh 9índha sayyaára
(*d*) sayyaárat záwjat al-mudiír kabiíra?/'as-sayyaára tába9 záwjat al-mudiír kabiíra?
(*e*) sayyaarátha kabiíra, jíddan/as-sayyaára tába9ha kabiíra jíddan
(*f*) hal-bayt tába9 'áHmad?/hal-bayt bayt 'áHmad?
(*g*) la, hal-bayt tába9 muHámmad/la, hal-bayt bayt muHámmad
(*h*) 'áwwal shaári9 9ála sh-shimaál shaári9 bayruút.

2. Translate the first sentence and then make the suggested substitutions:

Who is the owner of this car?	*miin SaáHib has-sayyaára?*
house/hotel/building/company	*. . . hal-bayt?*

3. He has a bicycle.   *9índuh bisklaát*

    I   have/you   have/we have/she has/you (pl.) have/they have

    a car/a house/a lot of work/a   big   office/a small daughter . . .

4. All the officials have cars   *kull al-muwáZZafíin 9índhum*
    directors/visitors/   *sayyaaraát*
    assistants/police/
    students/Americans

    bicycles/a lot of work/ many friends/desks/ small offices/wives/a lot of money . . .

5. Every official has a car   *kull muwáZZaf 9índuh sayyaára*
    (substitutions as in 4 above)

6. I must thank my friends   *laázim 'áshkur 'aSdiqaá'ii*

You	your
he	his
she	her
we	our
you (pl.)	your
they	their

7. I come to the city every   *báji lil-madiína kull yawm*
    day
    you/he/she/we/you   *btíji . . .*
    (pl.)/they

8. I go to the city every day   *baruúH . . .*
    (substitutions as in 7 above)

SEVENTH LESSON – 'ad-dars as-saábi9

DISCUSSING THE PAST

Dialogue

(Mahmoud asks John about how, where and when he studied Arabic)

maHmuúd:
wayn darást 9árabi, ya John?

darást
9árabi

Where did you study Arabic, John?

you studied
Arabic (language)/Arab (person, thing)

John:
darást al-lúgha fi briiTaánya
darást
lúgha (-aat)

I studied the language in Britain.
I studied
language

maHmuud:
li 'ayy múdda darástha?
múdda *pl.* múdad

(For) how long did you study it?
period

John:
darást li múddat shahráyn faqáT
faqáT

I studied for the period of two months only.
only

maHmuud:
wa ta9allámt miliíH?
ta9allámt
miliiH

Did you learn well?
you learned
well, excellent

John:
'áywa, laákin ta9allámt 'ák-thar ba9d wuSuúlii li húna.
'ákthar
wuSuúl/ii

Yes, but I learned more after my arrival (to) here.
more (comparative of *kathiír*)
my/arrival

maHmuud:
wa 'aSHaábak Peter wa David dárasu fi nafs al-waqt?
SaáHib pl. 'aSHaáb

dárasu
nafs pl. nufuús

Did your friends Peter and David study at the same time?

friend (also "owner" as in Lesson 6)
they studied
soul, same

John:
ná9am, kúllna darásna l-lúgha fi nafs al-waqt wa fi nafs al-makaán.
darásna

Yes, we all studied the language at the same time and in the same place.
we studied

56

| kull/na | all (of) us |
| makaán pl. 'ámkina | place |

maHmuud:
'aZúnn 'in ta9allámtu ku- wáyyis wa btíHku 9árabi miliiH	I think that you have learned well and you speak Arabic well.
'aZúnn	I think ("my opinion is . . .")
ta9allámtu	you (pl) learned
btíHku	you (pl) speak (bíHku = he speaks)

John:
| mush kuwáyyis kathiír, bass maashi l-Haal. | Not very well, but O.K. |
| maashi – Haal | going – state, condition, situation. |

Narrative – *riwaáya*

John dáras 9árabi li múddat shahráyn fi 'ingéltera	John studied Arabic (for a period of) two months in England.
dáras	he studied
wa 'aSHaábuh dárasu má9uh	and his friends studied with him
dárasu	they studied
ta9államu l-Háki wa l-kitaába fi nafs al-waqt	They learned talking and writing at the same time.
ta9államu	they learned
Háki	talking
kitaába	writing
wa ba9d wuSuúlhum 'ila l-9aálam al-9árabi 'ishtághalu fi shárikat nafT.	And after their arrival in the Arab world, they worked in an oil company.
9aálam	world
'ishtághalu	they worked
kull waáHid bya9táqid 'innuh ta9állam 'ákthar ba9d wuSuúluh	Each one believes that he learned more after his arrival.
bya9táqid	he believes
wa hállaq byádrusu qiraá'at al- lúgha l-9arabíyya.	And now they are learning read- ing the Arabic language.
hallaq	now (from hal-waqt = this time)
qiraá'a	reading

Questions on Dialogue and Narrative

(Study question and answer. Then ask the question – aloud. Raise your eyes from the book to give the answer. Check your answer is the one in the book)

1. John dáras 9árabi qabl (= *before*) wuSuúluh 'íla l-9aálam al-9árabi?

   'áywa, dáras 9árabi qabl wuSuúluh.

2. wayn dáras 9árabi?

   dáras fi briiTaánya.

3. dáras wáHduh? (= *alone*)

   la, dáras ma9 'aSHaabuh

4. dáras al-lúgha li 'ayy múdda?

   dáras li múddat shahráyn.

5. dáras al-Háki faqáT?

   la, dáras al-kitaába kamaán.

6. ta9állam miliiH?

   'áywa, ta9állam miliiH/ kuwayyis

7. miin dáras má9uh?

   'aSHaabuh Peter wa David darasu má9uh.

8. 'al-'aSHaáb ta9államu kathiír ba9d wuSuúlhum 'íla l-9aálam al-9árabi?

   ná9am, ta9államu kathiír ba9d wuSuúlhum.

9. wa shuu byádrusu hállaq?

   hállaq byádrusu l-qiraá'a.

Notes on Grammar and Usage

1. In lessons 3 and 4 you were presented with the Imperfect tense and told that this tense was used for incomplete actions and therefore usually referred to the present or the future. This lesson gives examples of the only other tense in Arabic – the Perfect. Since this tense is used for complete actions (hence "perfect"), it normally refers to the past.

Here are the perfects of the three main verbs in the lesson conjugated in full:

dáras (= he studied)	*ta9állam* (= he learned)	*'ishtághal* (= he worked)
darást (= I studied)	*ta9allámt* (= I . . .)	*'ishtaghalt* (= I . . .)
darást (= you studied)	*ta9allámt* (= you . . .)	*'ishtaghált* (= you . . .)
darásti (= you (f.s. . . .)	*ta9allámti* (= you . . .)	*'ishtaghálti* (= you . . .)
dáras (= he studied)	*ta9állam* (= he . . .)	*'ishtághal* (= he . . .)
dárasat (= she studied)	*ta9államat* (= she . . .)	*'ishtághalat* (= she . . .)
darásna (= we studied)	*ta9allámna* (= we . . .)	*'ishtaghálna* (= we . . .)
darástu (= you (pl.) . . .)	*ta9allámtu* (= you . . .)	*'ishtagháltu* (= you . . .)
dárasu (= they studied)	*ta9államu* (= they . . .)	*'ishtághalu* (= they . . .)

N.B. – *darásti* etc. are the forms used to address women.

– *darástu* etc. are the forms used to address more than one person.

2. The Perfect is formed by adding endings while the Imperfect is formed mainly by adding prefixes to the root.

3. The Perfect may be derived from the Imperfect by removing the prefix and inserting vowels after the first and second root consonants (normally *a-a*) e.g. *yádrus* → *drus* → *dáras*.

The Imperfect may be derived from the Perfect of "1st Form verbs" such as *dáras* by dropping the first vowel (*dras*), changing the remaining vowel to the one used for the imperfect of the particular verb – in this case *u*(*drus*) – and then adding the imperfect prefixes '*a-*, *ta-*, *ya-*, *na-* ('*ádrus*, *tádrus*, *yádrus*, *nádrus* etc.). The vowel of the imperfect of "1st form verbs" is always indicated in the glossary e.g. *dáras*(*u*).

4. **Derived Forms:** (what follows is for interest and background information rather than learning – full information on derived forms is to be found in Lessons 20 and 21.)

A peculiarity of Arabic is that verbs may not just come in a simple form based on the unvarnished triliteral root (See Lesson 3, Note 1) but have forms derived from this simple one by the addition of consonants, vowels or whole syllables. The effect is that a verb so modified from the simple (or "1st form") has meanings usually derived from the simple form, though sometimes the meanings are so much changed that the connection is difficult to see.

The forms of the verb are usually numbered 1–10, though no single triliteral root can have all the forms. Examples of the forms are given below together with some explanatory notes. You should note that as well as actual examples of each form, we give the formula used by the Arabs to describe words (in this formula f = 1st consonant, 9 = 2nd consonant, l = 3rd consonant, so that *fá9al* describes words like *dáras*, *shákar* etc. '*af9aál* describes words like '*awlaád*, '*afkaár* etc.).

2nd form – formed by doubling the middle consonant.

Perfect: *9árraf* (= to introduce) – *fá99al*
Imperfect: *yu9árrif*/*bi9àrrif* – *yufá99il*/*bifá99il*

N.B. of the alternative forms given of the imperfect, the first is without *b-* and is nearer the written language norm than the second which has the *b-* prefix and is more colloquial in character.

The meaning of the 2nd form is often causative or intensive:

e.g. *9áraf* (= to know)   *9árraf*(= to make known, to introduce)

kásar (= to break)   *kássar* (= to smash)

Other examples: *sállam* (= to protect, to make safe), used in '*állaah yusállimak!*

59

3rd form – formed by inserting a long *aa* in the first syllable.

Perfect: *kaátab* (= to correspond with) – *faá9al*
Imperfect: *yukaátib/bikaátib* – *yufaá9il/bifaá9il*

The 3rd form often relates the first form meaning to a person:

e.g. *kátab* (= to write) *kaátab* (to correspond with)

4th form – formed by prefixing an *'a-* and removing the vowel between the 1st and 2nd root consonants.

Perfect: *'ámkan* (to make/be possible) – *'áf9al*
Imperfect: *yúmkin/byímkin* – *yúf9il/byíf9il*

The meaning is usually causative.

5th form – like the 2nd form but with a prefixed *ta-*.

Perfect: *ta9állam* (= to learn) – *tafá99al*
Imperfect: *yata9állam/byit9állam* – *yatafá99al/byitfá99al*

The meaning is often the reflexive of the 2nd form:

e.g. *9állam* (= to teach) *ta9állam* (= to teach oneself, learn)

Other examples: *tashárraf* (= to be honoured) as in *tasharráfna!*
  tafáDDal (= to do oneself the favour)

6th form – like the 3rd form but with a prefixed *ta-*.

Perfect: *takaátab* (= to correspond with one another) – *tafaá9al*
Imperfect: *yatakaátab/byitkaátab* – *yatafaá9al/byitfaá9al*

The meaning is often that of the reciprocal of the 3rd form:

e.g. *takaátabu* (= they corresponded with each other)

7th form – formed by prefixing *'in* to the perfect – only a prefixed *n-* remains in the imperfect.

Perfect: *'inkásar* (= to be broken) – *'infá9al*
Imperfect: *yankásir/binkásir* – *yanfá9il/binfá9il*

The 7th form is the passive of the 1st form:

e.g. *kásar* (= to break (some- *'inkásar* (= to break/be broken)
  thing))
qaal (= he said) *'inqaál* (= it was said)

8th form – formed by prefixing *'i* and inserting *t* after the first root consonant – the inserted *t* stands alone in the imperfect.

Perfect: *'ishtághal* (= to work) – *'iftá9al*
Imperfect: *yashtághil/bishtághil* – *yaftá9il/biftá9il*

A specific meaning for the 8th form is difficult to pin down.
9th form – only used for colours and bodily deformities and rather rare in spoken Arabic:

e.g. *'iHmárr* (= to be or become red, to blush)

10th form – formed by prefixing *'ista* to the perfect – *sta* to the imperfect – and by removing the vowel after the first root consonant.

Perfect: *'istá9lam* (= to enquire) – *'istáf9al*
Imperfect: *yastá9lim/bistá9lim* – *yastáf9il/bistáf9il*

The 10th form sometimes means "to wish for …", but it is impossible to be specific about meanings.
Further example: *'istashaár* (= to wish for advice, consult)

Notes:

1. It will be noticed on consulting the English – Arabic Glossary that where a derived form verb appears, the imperfect (and verbal noun) are given in full. There is therefore no difficulty about finding the correct form.
2. Derived forms of verbs take the same endings as the simple 1st form verbs in the perfect (see Note 1 for the examples of *ta9állam* and *'ishtághal*). With the slight necessary changes in vowelling, the prefixes of the imperfect also remain the same as for the 1st form verbs.

5. Numerals 1–12:
   1 – *waáHid* (m.) *waáHida* (f.) – an adjective which follows the noun
   2 – *'ithnáyn* (m.) *thintáyn* (f.) – the noun dual usually suffices
   3 – *thalaátha*
   4 – *'árba9a*
   5 – *xámsa*
   6 – *sítta*
   7 – *sáb9a*   Notes on usage for other than telling the
   8 – *thamaánya*   time appear in the next lesson
   9 – *tís9a*
   10 – *9áshara*
   11 – *Hidá9sh*
   12 – *'ithná9sh*

N.B. Zero is indicated by dot · not a circle. It is called *Sifr*.

In telling the time, one uses *'as-saá9a* (= the hour) followed by the numeral required:

e.g. *'as-saá9a waáHida* = one o'clock (*waáHida* used with feminine *saá9a*)
'as-saá9a 'ithnayn = two o'clock (*thintáyn* also possible)
'as-saá9a thalaátha = three o'clock
'as-saá9a 'ithna9sh = twelve o'clock

Exercises

1. I studied Arabic from (*min*) 8 o'clock till (*Hátta*) 10. (substitute whole range of times in this sentence framework) + he/she/you/they
darást 9árabi min as-saá9a thamaánya Hátta as-saá9a 9áshara

2. Answer the following questions in the affirmative.

Question	*Answer*
SaHíiH (= correct) *ta9allámt kathiír qabl wuSuúlak?*	*'áywa, ta9allámt kathiír qabl wuSuúlii.*
SaHíiH ta9államat kathiír qabl wuSuúlha?	*'áywa, ta9államat kathiír qabl wuSuúlha.*

+ he/you f. & pl./they/we
+ *ba9d*

N.B. remember to add the correct possessive endings to *wuSuúl!*

3. Translate question and answer. Compare with model translation, then make the suggested changes.

– Do you work every day in the office?
btashtághil kull yawm fil-máktab?

– No, but I worked yesterday in the office.
la, laákin 'ishtaghált 'umbaáriH fil-máktab.

+ he/she/we/they/you m., f. & pl./ + school/embassy/ministry/company/hotel/city.

EIGHTH LESSON – *'ad-dars ath-thaámin*
FURTHER DISCUSSION OF THE PAST
Dialogue (conversation between teacher and pupil)
mu9állim:

qaaluúlii 'ínnak ta9allámt 9árabi shwayy fi 'ingéltera.
They told me (i.e. I have been told) that you learned a little Arabic in England.

qaáluu/lii	*they said/to me (i.e. they told me)*
'inn/ak	*that/you*

tilmiidh:

ná9am, darást li múddat 'árba9t ásh-hur	*Yes, I studied for a period of four months.*
shahr *pl.* 'ásh-hur/shuhuúr	*month* (note two possible plurals)

mu9allim:

kam saá9a fil-yawm	*How many hours a day?*
kam?	*How much/many?* (always followed by singular!)

tilmiidh:

thalaáth saa9aát faqáT	*Three hours only.*
thalaáth(a)	*3* (note dropping of final -*a* when followed by a noun beginning with a consonant)
faqát	*only*

mu9allim:

kunt táqDi kull hal-waqt fi ghúrfat aS-Saff?	*Did you spend all this time in the classroom?*
kunt	*you were* (see Grammar Notes)
qáDa (yáqDi/byáqDi)	*spend (time)*
ghúrfa *pl.* ghùraf	*room*
Saff *pl.* Sufuúf	*row, class*

tilmiidh:

la, kúnna náqDi saá9a waáHida faqaT fi ghúrfat aS-Saff.	*We spent one hour only in the classroom.*

mu9allim:

yá9ni, kaan laázim tádrus xaárij ghúrfat aS-Saff kamaán?	*You mean, it was necessary (for you) to study outside the classroom also?*
kaan (yakuún/bikuún)	*was* (Imperfect of *kaan* has future meaning, not present)
xaárij	*outside*

tilmiidh:

ma9luúm, kaan laázim nashtághil saa9atáyn xaárij al-mádrasa	*Certainly, it was necessary (for us) to work two hours outside the class.*
ma9luúm	*of course, certainly*

mu9allim:
wa kuntu taHku kathiir 'ath-
naa' as-saá9a fi ghúrfat aS-
Saff?

Did you speak a lot during the hour in the classroom?

Háka (yáHki/byíHki)
talk, speak
'athnaá'
during

tilmiidh:
ma kunna naHki kathiir
fil-bidaaya.

We did not speak a lot in the beginning.

bidaáya (-aat)
beginning
fil-bidaáya
in the beginning

mu9allim:
laákin ba9dáyn?

But afterwards?

tilmiidh:
ba9d   xámsat   asaabii9
taqriíban

After five weeks approximately.

'usbuú9 *pl.* 'asaabii9
week
taqriíban
about, approximately (always placed after expression refer-red to)

xámsat
(Note how the numeral ends in a *t* when followed by a word beginning with a vowel)

mu9allim:
bada'tu táHku . . .
You began to speak . . .
bada' (yabda'/byabda')
begin

tilmiidh:
wa ba9d 9ásharat asaabii9,
kúnna náHki Tuul al-waqt

And after ten weeks, we were speaking all the time.

9ásharat
(Note the *t* ending before the vowel)

kúnna
we were (from kaan)
Tuul
throughout

mu9allim:
kam kaan 9ádad at-
talaamiídh fiS-Saff?

How much was the number of students in the class?

9ádad *pl.* 'a9daád
number

64

tilmiidh:

fil-bidaáya, kaan 9ádad-hum   *In the beginning their number*
tís9a wa fin-nihaáya Saáru   *(was) nine and in the end seven*
sáb9a faqáT   *only.*
nihaáya(-aat)   *end*
fin-nihaáya   *in the end, finally*
Saáru   *they became* (Saar (yaSiir/biSiir)

mu9allim:

ya   salaám,   'ishtagháltu   *Good heavens, you (pl.) worked*
kathiír! wa hállaq btíHki   *hard! And now you speak*
9árabi miliíH.   *Arabic well.*

tilmiidh:

yá9ni . . . mush baTTaál.   *Well . . . not bad.*
baTTaál   *bad*

mu9allim:

wa ba9dáyn jiit rá'san 'íla   *And afterwards you came*
l-xaliíj?   *straight to the Gulf?*
jiit   *you came (from 'ája (yíji/byiji)*
rá'san   *straight away, immediately*
xaliíj *pl.* xuljaán   *gulf, bay*

tilmiidh:

la, qabl wuSuúlii, ruHt 'íla   *No, before my arrival, I went to*
'ameérka wa baqayt tha-   *America and stayed eight*
maanyat asaabií9 hunaák.   *weeks there.*
ruHt   *I went (from raaH = he went)*
baqayt   *I stayed (from baqa (yabqa/*
                                   byabqa))

Questions on the Dialogue

1. 'at-tilmiídh ta9állam 9árabi   ná9am, ta9állam 9árabi fi
   fi 'ingéltera?   'ingéltera.
2. li 'ayy múdda dáras?   dáras li múddat 'árba9t áshhur.
3. kam saá9a dáras fil-yawm?   dáras thalaáth saa9aát fil-
                                    yawm.
4. kaan yáqDi kull hal-waqt fi   la, saá9a waáHda fiS-Saff bass
   ghúrfat aS-Saff?   (bass = *only*).
5. kaan laázim yádrus xaárij   'áywa, kaan laázim yádrus xaá-
   al-mádrasa?   rij al-mádrasa.
6. qaddáysh   dáras   xaárij   dáras saa9atáyn.
   ghúrfat aS-Saff? (qad-
   daysh = *how much/long?*)

7. 'at-talaamiídh kaánu yáHku kathiír 'athnaá' ad-dars?

ma kaánu yáHku kathiír fil-bidaáya laákin ba9dáyn kaánu yáHku kathiír.

8. wa ba9d 9ásharat asaabíí9?

kaánu yáHku Tuul al-waqt.

9. kam kaan 9ádad at-talaamiídh fiS-Saff?

fil-bidaáya, kaanu tís9a.

10. wa fin-nihaáya?

fin-nihaáya kaan fii sab9 talaamiídh faqáT.

11. 'at-talaamiídh byíHku 9árabi miliíH?

ná9am, byíHku 9árabi miliíH kathiír.

12. 'at-tilmiídh raaH rá'san 'ila l-xaliíj?

la, kaan laázim yaruúH 'ila 'ameérka 'áwwalan (= *firstly*).

13. qaddáysh báqa fi 'ameérka?

qaDa thamaán shuhuúr fi 'ameérka.

14. wa ba9dáyn 'ája 'ila l-xaliíj?

'áywa, 'ája 'ila l-xaliíj ba9dáyn.

Notes on Grammar and Usage

1. In Lesson 7 you were given the numerals 3 to 10 in the form they have when standing alone i.e. with final -a: e.g. *thalaátha*

(*a*) Before nouns beginning with consonants, the numerals drop the -a:

e.g. *thalaátha* but *thalaáth saa9aát*
sáb9a but *sab9 talaamiidh*

(*b*) Before noun plurals beginning with a vowel, the numerals 3–10 add a -t, rather like feminine nouns adding a -t when in construct:

e.g. *thamaányat asaabíí9*
'árba9t ásh-hur

Note: The numerals 11 and 12 are followed by nouns in the SINGULAR. They also add -ar when followed by counted nouns:

e.g. *Hidá9shar wálad* = 11 children
'ithná9shar bint = 12 girls

2. Perfect of Hollow Verbs

"Hollow" verbs are those which have a weak radical *w* or *y* in their middles. This weak radical becomes *aa* in the third persons: e.g. *raaH, raáHat, raáHu*. In the case of hollow verbs with a notional *w* in the middle, the other persons have a short *u* vowel: e.g. *ruHt* (= I went), *rúHna* (= we went). There follow the complete conjugations in both Perfect and Imperfect of two very common verbs.

raaH (yaruúH/biruúH)

Perfect	Imperfect
ruHt (= I went)	*'aruúH/baruúH*
ruHt (= you went)	*taruúH/bitruúH*
rúHti (= you went – f.s.)	*taruúHi/bitruúHi*
raaH (= he went)	*yaruúH/biruúH*
raáHat (= she went)	*taruúH/bitruúH*
rúHna (= we went)	*naruúH/minruúH*
rúHtu (you went – pl.)	*taruúHu/bitruúHu*
raáHu (= they went)	*yaruúHu/biruúHu*

kaan (yakuún/bikuún)

Perfect	Imperfect
kunt (= I was)	*'akuún/bakuún*
kunt (= you were)	*takuún/bitkuún*
kunti (= you were)	*takuúni/bitkuúni*
kaan (= he was)	*yakuún/bikuún*
kaánat (= she was)	*takuún/bitkuún*
kúnna (= we were)	*nakuún/minkuún*
kúntu (= you were)	*takuúnu/bitkuúnu*
kaánu (= they were)	*yakuúnu/bikuúnu*

N.B. 1. The Imperfect of *kaan* refers to the future NOT to the present.

2. Verbs with *y* are conjugated like *baa9* (= he sold), *bi9t* (= I sold), *'abii9* (= I sell)

3. Perfect of Defective Verbs

"Defective" verbs are verbs having a weak radical *w* or *y* as their final radical. The perfects of three very common verbs of this type follow:

qáDa (= spend time)	*Háka* (= talk)	*'ibtáda* (= begin)
qaDáyt (= I spent)	*Hakáyt*	*'ibtadáyt*
qaDáyt (= you spent)	*Hakáyt*	*'ibtadáyt*
qaDáyti (= you spent – f.s.)	*Hakáyti*	*'ibtadáyti*
qáDa (= he spent)	*Háka*	*'ibtáda*
qáDat (= she spent)	*Hákat*	*'ibtádat*
qaDáyna (= we spent)	*Hakáyna*	*'ibtadáyna*
qaDáytu (you spent – pl.)	*Hakáytu*	*'ibtadáytu*
qáDu (= they spent)	*Háku*	*'ibtádu*

67

4. The Verb *'ája* (*yíji/byíji*) = to come

Perfect	Imperfect
jiit (= I came)	*'áji/báji*
jiit (= you came)	*tíji/btíji*
jiíti (= you came – f.s.)	*tíji/btíji*
'ája (= he came)	*yíji/byíji*
'ájat (= she came)	*tíji/btíji*
jiína (= we came)	*níji/mníji*
jiítu (= you came – pl.)	*tíju/btíju*
'áju (= they came)	*yíju/byíju*

Notes: just as with the hollow verbs, the third persons of the perfect (i.e. "he", "she" and "they" forms) stand apart from the others

– the imperative "come!" is expressed by *ta9aál!* (+ -*i* for feminine and + -*u* for plural)

Exercises

1. Write down English versions of the following Arabic numerals. The answers are given at the end of the lesson.

'árba9a   thamaánya   tís9a   sáb9a   sítta   xámsa

2. Translate (answers given at the end of the lesson)
(*a*) I went to America and spent five months there.
(*b*) We studied Arabic for four hours a day.
(*c*) They spent eight weeks in France.
(*d*) We had to speak Arabic all day.
(*e*) I was in the house when (= *lamma*) he came.
(*f*) I told him that you had gone home.
(*g*) I had a big car when I was in America.
(*h*) I was working in the office when he came.

3. Translate the model sentence and then make the suggested substitutions.

He went to America	*raaH 'ila 'ameérka*
(I/you/she/we/you – pl./ they	*ruHt . . .*
+ to France, Britain, the Gulf	
to the city, home	
4. He spent five months in Egypt.	*qáDa xámsat úsh-hur fi máSr.*
+ France/America/England	*qaDáyt . . .*
+ I/you/she/we/you (pl)/they	

68

5. I had to speak Arabic all day	*kaan laázim 'áHki 9árabi kull al-yawm.*
+ you/they/she/he	*kaan laázim tíHki . . .*
	kaan laázim yíHku . . .
+ 3 hours a day/4/5/6	
+ in the class/outside the class	
6. When he came, I was working.	*lámma 'ája, kunt bashtághil.*
+ you came/they came	*lámma jiit . . .*
+ you were working/they etc.	*kunt btashtághil*
7. He believes that you came yesterday.	*bya9táqid 'ínnak jiit 'umbaáriH*
+ that he/that we/that they	*'ínnuh 'ája/ 'ínna jiína/ 'ínhum 'áju*

Answers

1. four, eight, nine, seven, six, five.
2. (a) ruHt 'ila 'ameérka wa qaDáyt xámsat úsh-hur hunaák.
   (b) darásna 9árabi 'árba9 saa9aát kull yawm.
   (c) qáDu thammaányat asaabii9 fi fránsa.
   (d) kaan laázim naHki 9árabi kull al-yawm.
   (e) kunt fil-bayt lámma 'ája.
   (f) qult luh 'ínnak ruHt 9al-bayt.
   (g) kaan 9índii sayyaára kabiíra lámma kunt fi 'ameérka.
   (h) kunt bashtághil fil-máktab lámma 'ája.

NINTH LESSON – *'ad-dars at-taási9*

A STORY SET IN THE PAST

Narrative – *riwaáya*

lámma kunt tilmiídh fil-mádrasa, kaan 9índii zamiíl 'ismuh bashiír.	*When I was a pupil at school, I had a friend called (his name) Bashir.*
lámma	*when* (not for questions: *when?* = 'aymta?)
zamiíl *pl.* zumalaá'	*colleague, comrade.*

márra, 9addáyna kull al-buyuút fil-qárya.	*Once, we counted all the houses in the village.*
márra (-aat)	*time* (in the sense of *"occasion"*)
9addáyna	*we counted from* 9add (ya9údd/bya9údd)
qárya *pl.* qúra	*village*
9addáyt, 'ána, tis9 buyuút, laá- kin húwa 9add 9áshar buyuút.	I *counted nine houses, but* he *counted ten houses.*
fi hal-láHZa 'ája 'ábii wa 'áxii l-kabiír.	*At this moment came my father and my older brother.*
laHZa (-aat)	*moment*
'ab	*father*
'ax	*brother*
wa sa'alnaáhum kam 9ádad al- buyuút fil-qárya	*And we asked them what was the number of houses in the village.*
sá'al (yás'al/byás'al)	*ask (a question)*
sa'alnaáhum	*we asked them* (note the leng- thening of -*na* before the pro- noun ending)
9ádad *pl.* 'a9daád	*number (quantity)*
'ábii HaTT shánTatuh 9ála l-'arD wa sa'álna 9an má9na s-su'aál.	*My father put his bag (case) on the ground and asked us about the meaning of the question.*
HaTT (yaHúTT/byaHúTT)	*put*
shánTa *pl.* shúnaT	*case, bag*
'arD *pl.* 'araáDi	*earth, ground, floor* (feminine!) (pl.) = *lands, territory.*
má9na *pl.* ma9aáni	*meaning (related to* yá9ni*) (masculine!)*
su'aál *pl.* 'ás'ila	*question* (of interrogative type)
wa ba9d ma fáhim, DáHik wa qaal lii . . .	*And after he understood, he laughed and said to me . . .*
ba9d ma	*after* (note now *ma* is added to *ba9d* before a verb)
fáhim (yáfham/byáfham)	*understand*
DáHik (yáDHak/byáDHak)	*laugh*
'ya bunaáy, 'al-Haqq ma9 bashiír wa 'inta múxTi'	*O my little son!* (affectionate mode of address for son) *Bashir is right and you are wrong.*

Haqq *pl.* Huquúq	right, correctness, legal claim
múxTi'	mistaken
fii 9áshar buyuút fil-qárya, 'ínta nisiít báytna!	There are ten houses in the village. You have forgotten our house!
nisiít	you forgot – from nísi (yánsa/byánsa)

Questions on the Narrative

1. shuu kaan 'ism aS-Sadiíq? — 'ísmuh bashiír.
2. 'al-'awlaád, shuu 9ámalu márra? — 9áddu l-buyuút fil-qárya.
   9ámal (yá9mal/byá9mal) = do.
3. kam bayt 9add bashiír? — 9add 9áshar buyuút.
4. 'ar-raáwi 9add kam bayt? — 9add tis9 buyuút.
   raáwi = *narrator*
5. miin 'ája fi hal-láHZa? — 'ábu r-raáwi 'ája. ⎤ *N.B. when*
6. miin 'ája ma9 al-waálid? — 'áxu r-raáwi 'ája. ⎦ *in construct,*
   waálid *pl.* waalidiín = ⎡ 'ab *and* 'ax
   father ⎦ *add* u.

7. wayn HaTT al-waálid shánTatuh? — HaTTha 9ala l-'arD.
8. shuu 9ámal al-waálid qabl ma jaáwab? — qabl ma jaawab, DaHik.
   qabl ma – ma *necessary before a verb just as with* ba9d ma.
   jaáwab (yujaáwib bijaáwib) = *answer*
9. miin kaan 9ála Sawaáb? — bashiír kaan 9ála Sawaáb.
   9ala Sawaáb = *right*
10. miin kaan múxTi'? — 'ar-raawi kaan muxTi'.

Notes on Grammar and Usage

1. Perfects of Doubled Verbs – "doubled" verbs are those verbs with the same second and third root consonants e.g. 9add, HaTT. Their perfects closely resemble those of defective verbs.

HaTT (yaHúTT/biHúTT)	*9add (ya9udd bi9udd)*
HaTTáyt (= I put)	*9addáyt* (= I counted)
HaTTáyt (= you put)	*9addáyt* (= you counted)
HaTTáyti (= you put – f.s.)	*9addáyti* (= you counted – f.s.)
Hatt (= he put)	*9add* (= he counted)

71

HáTTat (= she put)	*9áddat* (= she counted)
HaTTáyna (= we put)	*9addáyna* (= we counted)
HaTTáytu (= you put – pl.)	*9addáytu* (you counted – pl.)
HáTTu (= they put)	*9áddu* (= they counted)

Other common doubled verbs are *Zann* (*yaZúnn*/*biZúnn*) = think, suppose (fleetingly introduced in Lesson 7) and *Habb* (*yaHíbb*/*biHíbb*) = love, like.

2. Perfect of the Defective Verb *nisi* (*yansa*/*byansa*) = forget:

nisíit (= I forgot)	*nisíina* (= we forgot)
nisíit (= you forgot)	
nisíiti (= you forgot – f.s.)	*nisíitu* (= you forgot – pl.)
nísi (= he forgot)	
nísiyat (= she forgot)	*nísiyu* (= they forgot)

Note particularly the *y* introduced into the 3rd person feminine singular (the "she" form) and the 3rd person plural (the "they" form).

3. Plurals of Nouns and Adjectives

A variety of plurals have been presented so far and the time has come to make some generalisations about plurals in Arabic.

Plurals of nouns and adjectives fall into two groups: "sound" and "broken".

Plurals are "sound" when the internal structure of the word is not disturbed but an ending added, *-iin* for masculine words and *-aat* for feminines:

e.g. *-iin: mabsuuTíin – raayHíin – maSriyyíin*
     -aat: Sadiiqaát – banaát – marraát

The masculine sound plural ending (*-iin*) is only used for a limited number of nouns and adjectives applying to male human beings.

The feminine sound plural ending (*-aat*) is much more widely used. It is not only used for most feminine nouns but also to form plurals of some masculine words (including foreign words):

e.g. *'ijtimaá9* (= meeting) pl. *'ijtimaa9aát*
     ford (= a Ford)   pl. *fordaát*

Plurals are "broken" when the plural idea is indicated not by adding an ending but by breaking the word and reshaping it internally, though its root consonants remain in the same order. The following are nouns:

72

e.g. *shughl* (= work)   pl. *'ashghaál*
     bayt (= house)   pl. *buyuút*
     tilmiidh (= pupil)   pl. *talaamiidh*
     maktab (= office)   pl. *makaátib*

But adjectives too can have broken plurals, especially the very common ones:

e.g. *kabiír* (= big, old)   pl. *kibaár*
     kathiír (= many)   pl. *kithaár*
     Tawiíl (= tall)   pl. *Tiwaál*
     qaSiír (= short)   pl. *qiSaár*
     and *mariiD* (= ill)   pl. *márDa* (or the sound
                                 plural *mariiDiín*)

4. Note the important meanings stress can carry:

sá'al = he asked   *sa'álna* = he asked us
sa'álna = we asked   *sa'alnaáhum* = we asked them
sá'alu = they asked   *sa'aluúhum* = they asked them
sá'aluh = he asked him
sa'aluúh = they asked him (shift of stress to the last syllable pro-
            vides sufficient indication that there is a pronoun
            ending)

Exercises

1. Translate into Arabic. Answers at the end of the lesson.
(a) I put the money on the ground and counted it. (money =
    fuluús)   (N.B. *fuluús* is feminine)
(b) We liked Ahmed's father (*'ábu*).
(c) The girl loved Bashir's brother.
(d) They forgot their Arabic books.
(e) We asked them why they had come.
(f) They asked us the number of students in the school.
(g) He asked them whether they had forgotten their brother.
    whether = *'idha*   their brother = *'axuúhum*
(h) They asked him whether he had counted all the money.

2. Translate the model sentence and then make the suggested variations.

I put everything into my bag +   *HaTTáyt kull shii fi shánTatii.*
   you/he/she/we/you -- pl./they   *HáTTu kull shii fi shanTáthum*
   + your/his/her/our/your   –   (note the shift in stress when
pl./their   possessive ending begins with
   + room/on to . . . table/on to   a consonant)
. . . chair
   N.B. "my chair = *kursíyya*

73

3. We liked Mahmoud's brother very much.   *Habbáyna 'áxu maHmuúd kathíir.*

+ I/he/she/they
+ Mahmoud's father/   *. . . 'ábu maHmuúd.*
Samiira's brother negative

4. He forgot the name of his visitor.   *nísi 'ism zaá'iruh.*

+ I/you/she/we/you – pl. they
+ my visitor/your/her/our/ your – pl./their.
+ visitors/Ahmed's brother/ Bashir's colleague/the pupil/the teacher/the senior official.

5. This exercise concerns stress. Consult the Introduction and the examples given in section 3 of the Notes on Grammar and Usage in this lesson.

(*a*) He asked us whether we want to come.   *sa'álna 'idha minriid níji.*

They asked . . .   *sa'aluúna . . .*
+ to see the film (= *fiilm*)/ speak Arabic/study Arabic/ learn Arabic.

(*b*) He asked him whether he wants to go.   *sá'aluh 'idha bídduh yaruúH.*

They asked . . .   *sa'aluúh . . .*
+ drink coffee/tea (= shaay)/has to go to the city.

(*c*) I asked him why he was working.   *sa'áltuh laysh kaan 9am yashtághil.*

You (m.s.)   *sa'áltuh . . .*
You (f.s.)   *sa'altiíh . . .*
You (pl.)   *sa'altuúh . . .*
+ after six o'clock/7/8 etc.   N.B. *9am* emphasises con-
+ where he was working.   tinuity.
+ yesterday.

Answers to Translation Exercise

(*a*) HaTTáyt al-fuluús 9ála l-'arD wa 9addáytha.
(*b*) Habbáyna 'ábu 'áHmad.
(*c*) 'al-bint Hábbat 'áxu bashiír.
(*d*) nísiyu kutúbhum al-9arabíyya.

(*e*) sa'alnaáhum laysh 'áju.

(*f*) sa'aluúna kam 9ádad at-talaamiídh fil-mádrasa.

(*g*) sá'alhum 'ídha nísiyu 'axuúhum.

(*h*) sa'aluúh 'ídha 9add kull al-fuluús.

TENTH LESSON – '*ad-dars al-9aáshir*

NUMBERS

1. This is a reference lesson. It is convenient to give most essential information relating to numbers in one place for easy reference. The lesson presents the information in chunks separated by "exercises" and "tests". Answers to the exercises will be found in the facing column on the same page – this is to facilitate rapid switching from one to another and so build fluency. Answers to the tests are given at the end of the lesson – this is to help the student prove to his/her own satisfaction that the material has been mastered.

It is not necessary to master all the material at once, but a good command of the numbers of the foreign language is a great asset quite early on in one's studies.

2. Here are the numbers 1–10:

| 1. *waáHid* (m.) | *waáH*(*i*) *da* (f.) |
| 2. *'ithnáyn* (m.) | *thintáyn* (f.) |

Isolated forms	+ plural noun with initial consonant	+ plural noun with initial vowel
3. *thalaátha*	*thalaáth*	*thalaáthat*
4. *'árba9a*	*'árba9*	*'árba9t*
5. *xámsa*	*xáms*	*xámsat*
6. *sítta*	*sítt*	*síttat*
7. *sáb9a*	*sáb9*	*sáb9at*
8. *thamaánya*	*thamaán*	*thamaányat*
9. *tis9a*	*tís9*	*tís9at*
10. *9áshara*	*9áshar*	*9ásharat*

N.B. *Sifr* is 'zero' (c.f. 'cypher'). It is written with a dot.

Exercise I

[*a*] one boy	*wálad waáHid*
(*b*) one girl	*bint waáH*(*i*)*da*
(*c*) two cars	*sayyaáratáyn* (*thintáyn*)

75

(d) two pupils	*tilmiidháyn ('ithnáyn)*
(e) four days	*'árba9t ayyaám*
(f) eight companies	*thamaán sharikaát*
(g) There are nine	*fii tís9a*
(h) One, two, three, four ...	*waáHid, 'ithnáyn, thalaátha, 'árba9a ...*
(i) For ten weeks	*li múddat 9ásharat asaabií9*

N.B. The numbers for 1–10 have been treated in lessons 7 and 8. The student should refer to these chapters for more explicit notes on usage.

3. The numbers 11–20 are as follows:

Isolated forms	Followed by counted noun in SINGULAR
11. *'iHdá9sh/Hidá9sh*	*'iHdá9shar/Hidá9shar*
12. *'ithná9sh*	*'ithná9shar*
13. *thalaathtá9sh*	*thalaathtá9shar*
14. *'arba9tá9sh*	*'arba9tá9shar*
15. *xamstá9sh*	*xamstá9shar*
16. *sittá9sh*	*sittá9shar*
17. *saba9tá9sh*	*saba9tá9shar*
18. *thamaantá9sh*	*thamaantá9shar*
19. *tis9atá9sh*	*tis9atá9shar*
20. *9ishriín*	*9ishriín* (no change)

Notes: (i) The numbers from 11 to 20 (as indeed all numbers apart from 3–10 are followed by SINGULAR nouns.

e.g. *'iHdá9shar muwáZZaf* (= 11 officials)
sittá9shar bint (= 16 girls)

(ii) Note the addition of *-ar* when the numbers 11–19 are followed by the noun they are counting.

Exercise II

(a) 20 storeys	*9ishriín Taábiq*
(b) 19 visitors	*tis9atá9shar zaá'ir*
(c) 16 chairs	*sittá9shar kúrsi*
(d) 12 embassies	*'ithná9shar sifaára*
(e) 13, 14, 15 etc.	*thalaathtá9sh, 'arba9tá9sh, xamstá9sh ...*

Test I

(a) 5 schools (b) 11 cities (c) 15 months (d) 12 villages (e) 8, 9, 10, 11, 12, 13, 14, 15 etc ...

4. Here are the numbers 20–100:

20 – *9ishriín*	70 – *sab9iín*
30 – *thalaathiín*	80 – *thamaaniín*
40 – *'arba9iín*	90 – *tis9iín*
50 – *xamsiín*	100 – *míyya* (*miít* when in con-
60 – *sittiín*	struct with following noun)

Note: the above too are followed by singulars –

e.g. *xamsiín qárya* (= 50 villages)
 miít bayt (= 100 houses)

5. To express numbers like 21, 22, 23 etc., we put the units first followed by the tens:

e.g. 21 – *waáHid wa 9ishriín* (i.e. 'one and twenty')
 22 – *'ithnáyn wa 9ishriín*
 38 – *thamaánya wa thalaathiín*

Such numbers are again followed by singular nouns:

e.g. *sítta wa xamsiín mariíD* (= 56 sick people)
 tís9a wa tis9iín wálad (= 99 boys)
 miít fransaáwi (= 100 Frenchmen)

Exercise III

(*a*) 35 countries	*xámsa wa thalaathiín bálad.*
(*b*) 74 Englishmen	*'árba9a wa sab9iín 'ingliízi*
(*c*) 86 pupils	*sítta wa thamaaniín tilmiídh*
(*d*) 14 directors	*'arba9tá9shar mudiír*
(*e*) 8 schools	*thamaán madaáris*
(*f*) 100 days	*miít yawm*
(*g*) 97, 98, 99, 100	*sáb9a wa tis9iín, thamaánya wa*
	tis9iín, tís9a wa tis9iín, míyya.

Test II

(*a*) 4 offices. (*b*) 9 hotels. (*c*) 13 streets. (*d*) 23 buildings. (*e*) 2 embassies. (*f*) one car. (*g*) 40 officials. (*h*) 9 ministries. (*i*) 8 days. (*j*) 100 visitors.

6. To express numbers between 101 and 110, the following are used:

 101 – *míyya wa waáHid*
 (101 dinars = *miít diinaár wa diinaár* (other variants used))

102 – *míyya wa 'ithnáyn*
(102 dinars = *míyya wa diinaarayn*
103 – *míyya wa thalaátha*
(103 dinars = *míyya wa thalaáth danaaniír*)

N.B. a plural noun is used in this last example because the noun is immediately preceded by a numeral between 3 and 10.

110 – *míyya wa 9áshara*
(110 days = *míyya wa 9ásharat ayyaám*)

Exercise IV

(*a*)	101 chairs	*miit kúrsi wa kúrsi*
(*b*)	102 books	*míyya wa kitaabayn*
(*c*)	105 tables	*míyya wa xams Taawilaát*
(*d*)	108 days	*míyya wa thamaányat ayyaám*

Test III

(*a*) 100 hotels. (*b*) 101 hours. (*c*) 107 weeks. (*d*) 102 months.

7. Numbers from 111 to 120 are expressed as follows:

115 books = *míyya wa xamstá9shar kitaáb*
119 villages = *míyya wa tis9atá9shar qárya*

N.B. the counted noun is once more in the singular because it is immediately preceded by a number greater than 10.

8. Numbers from 121 to 199 would be expressed as follows:

121 girls = *míyya wa waáHid wa 9ishriín bint*
167 officials = *míyya wa sáb9a wa sittiín muwáZZaf*

N.B. in the first example no agreement is necessary between *waáHid* and *bint*. Elements of the numeral are linked with *wa*.

9. The forms of the hundreds are the following:

200 *miitáyn* (a dual form of *míyya*)
300 *thalaáth míyya* (*míyya* is the one exception to the rule that numerals 3–10 are followed by plurals)

400 *'árba9 míyya*	700 *sáb9 míyya*
500 *xams míyya*	800 *thamaán míyya*
600 *sitt míyya*	900 *tis9 míyya*
	1000 *'alf*

Here are some examples of numerals using the information given above:

206 *miitayn wa sítta* (note the obligatory *wa* for linking the parts of the whole numeral)

517 *xams míyya wa sab9atá9sh* (*sab9atá9shar* if noun follows)
694 *sitt míyya wa 'árba9a wa tis9iín*
902 boys – *tis9 míyya wa waladáyn*

Exercise V

(*a*) 972 boys	*tis9 míyya wa 'ithnáyn wa sab9iín wálad* (remember singular noun!)
(*b*) 802 girls	*thamaán míyya wa bintáyn*
(*c*) 301 languages	*thalaáth miit lúgha wa lúgha*
(*d*) 717 cities	*sáb9a míyya wa sab9atá9shar madiina* (remember -*ar* ending of 'teens')
(*e*) 493 houses	*'árba9a míyya wa thalaátha wa tis9iín bayt*
(*f*) 508 dinars	*xams míyya wa thamaán danaaniir* (remember plural noun after numeral between 3 and 10)
(*g*) 608 days	*sitt míyya wa thamaányat ayyaám* (Note -*t* before word beginning with vowel)

Test IV (use glossary for nouns you do not know)

(*a*) 5 Arabs. (*b*) 24 camels. (*c*) 100 tanks. (*d*) 101 men. (*e*) 102 hours. (*f*) 308 days. (*g*) 207 dogs. (*h*) 512 elephants. (*i*) 942 donkeys.

10. Numbers from a thousand upwards are given below:
1000 *'alf*
2000 *'alfáyn*
3000 *thalaáthat aalaáf* (note the -*t* ending of the numeral)
4000 *'arbá9t aalaáf* (note the -*t* ending of the numeral, used because *aalaaf* begins with a vowel)
1200 *'ithná9shar 'alf* (singular used because it comes after a numeral exceeding 10)
milyáwn (= million)   *milyawnáyn* (= 2 million)
thalaáth malaayiín (3 million) etc.
sittá9shar milyáwn (singular after *sittá9shar*) etc.
bilyáwn/milyaár (= 1 thousand million)

Exercise VI (use glossary for unknown words)

(*a*) 2341 soldiers	*'alfáyn wa thalaáth míyya wa waáHid wa 'arba9iín júndi*

79

| (b) 9217 pounds (money) | tís9at aalaáf wa miitáyn wa sab9atá9shar junáyh (c.f. "guinea") |
| (c) 6,500,000 dinars | sitt malaayiín wa xams miit 'alf diinaár. |

Answers to Tests

Test I:

(a) *xams madaáris.* (b) *'iHdá9shar madiina.* (c) *xamstá9shar shahr.* (d) *'ithná9shar qárya.* (e) *thamaánya, tís9a, 9áshara, 'iHdá9sh* etc.

Test II:

(a) *'árba9 makaátib.* (b) *tis9 fanaádiq.* (c) *thalaathtá9shar shaári9.* (d) *thalaátha wa 9ishriín binaáya.* (e) *sifaar(a)táyn.* (f) *sayyaára (waáHida).* (g) *'arba9iín muwáZZaf.* (h) *tis9 wizaaraát.* (i) *thamaányat ayyaám.* (j) *miit zaá'ir/zaáyir.*

Test III:

(a) *miit fúnduq.* (b) *miit saá9a wa saá9a.* (c) *míyya wa sáb9at asaabii9.* (d) *míyya wa shahráyn.*

Test IV:

(a) *xamst 9árab.* (b) *'árba9a wa 9ishriín jámal.* (c) *miit dabbaába.* (d) *miit rájul wa rájul.* (e) *míyya wa saa9atáyn.* (f) *thalaáth míyya wa thamaányat ayyaám.* (g) *miitáyn wa sab9 kilaáb.* (h) *xams míyya wa 'ithná9shar fiil.* (i) *tis9 míyya wa 'ithnáyn wa 'arba9iín Himaár.*

ELEVENTH LESSON – 'ad-dars raqm 'iHda9sh

NOUN PLURALS

Revision Lesson

A. Give the plurals and meanings of the following words (the Glossary will give the correct answers – but test your memory before resorting to it).

Haal	bayt	Sadiiq	mádrasa
SiHHa	madiína	sifaára	shughl
báraka	fíkra	shárika	'ingliízi
9aá'ila	bint	bilaád	Sadiiqa
wálad	mariiD	tilmiídh	tilmiídha

80

máktab	fúnduq	shaári9	binaáya
buliís	sayyaára	SaáHib	Saghiír
bisklaát	mudiír	'ism	Taábiq
wizaára	musaá9id	Taáwila	kúrsi
zaá'ir	múdda	nafs	makaán
shahr	'usbuú9	Saff	láHZa
9ádad	shánTa	'arD	má9na
su'aál	xaliíj		

B. Translate the following sentences. The answers are to be found at the end of the lesson.

1. We're going to the school.
2. She's living in London.
3. We must see him.
4. Let me go to the office.
5. She's very busy.
6. This is her friend (lady friend).
7. This girl is our friend.
8. I want work.
9. They want to thank them.
10. He's not my friend.
11. We're ill.
12. I don't want to go home.
13. The post-office is in Beirut street.
14. Take the first street on the right.
15. The oil company building is in front of the Ministry of the Interior.
16. I know the city very well.
17. Go straight ahead!
18. My friend's house is not very big.
19. Her big house is near the Ministry.
20. Every day I have to work in the office.
21. I have a large bag.
22. She doesn't have any money.
23. Whose house is this?
24. I studied Arabic in England for a period of 9 months.
25. We did not work a lot.
26. It's five o'clock.
27. We studied Arabic from 10 o'clock to 12 o'clock.
28. I went to London for two months.
29. We spent three hours in Yuusif's office.
30. There were 352 pupils in the school.

C. *Polite formula revision:* – you will have noticed that polite formulae in Arabic are both elaborate and much used. For social confidence it is essential to know both the initial remark and the appropriate rejoinder of a range of common expressions. The following material has the following aims:

(*a*) to list the polite formulae already presented;
(*b*) to add a few extra items;
(*c*) to provide a format for practice in using and recalling the formulae.

Suggestion – Find the first part of the exchange from the translation and/or context description whilst covering up the Arabic. Give the reply to the first part of the exchange whilst covering up the right hand side of the page where the replies appear.

N.B. * marks those expressions which have not yet appeared.

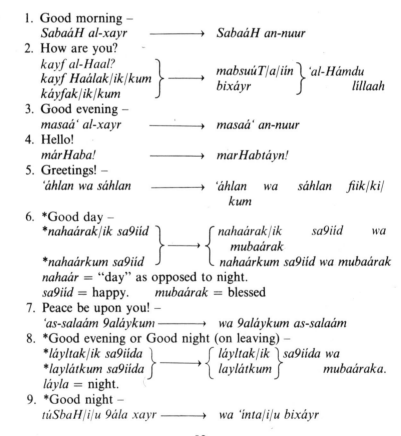

1. Good morning –
   SabaáH al-xayr ⟶ *SabaáH an-nuur*
2. How are you?
   kayf al-Haal?
   kayf Haálak/ik/kum ⟶ *mabsuúT/a/iin* ⟩ '*al-Hámdu*
   káyfak/ik/kum *bixáyr* ∫ *líllaah*
3. Good evening –
   masaá' al-xayr ⟶ *masaá' an-nuur*
4. Hello!
   márHaba! ⟶ *marHabtáyn!*
5. Greetings! –
   '*áhlan wa sáhlan* ⟶ '*áhlan wa sáhlan fiik/ki/kum*
6. *Good day –
   **nahaárak/ik sa9iíd*
   ⟶ { *nahaárak/ik sa9iíd wa mubaárak*
   **nahaárkum sa9iíd* *nahaárkum sa9iíd wa mubaárak*
   nahaár = "day" as opposed to night.
   sa9iíd = happy.   *mubaárak* = blessed
7. Peace be upon you! –
   '*as-saláam 9aláykum* ⟶ *wa 9aláykum as-saláam*
8. *Good evening or Good night (on leaving) –
   **láyltak/ik sa9iída*
   ⟶ { *láyltak/ik* ⟩ *sa9iída wa*
   **laylátkum sa9iída* *laylátkum* ∫ *mubaáraka.*
   láyla = night.
9. *Good night –
   túSbaH/i/u 9ála xayr ⟶ *wa 'ínta/i/u bixáyr*

10. Good-bye –
bixaáTrak/ik/bixaaTírkum ⟶ *ma9 as-salaáma*
⟶ *'allaah yusállimak/ik/yusallímkum*

11. *Good-bye (particularly in the Arabian peninsula and Gulf) –
fi 'amaán allaáh ⟶ *fi 'amaán allaáh (ma9 as-salaáma)*
'amaán = protection

12. *Au revoir –
'íla l-liqaá' ⟶ *'íla l-liqaá'*
liqaá' = meeting

13. Please come in/accept this etc. –
tafáDDal/i/u ⟶ *shúkran*

14. Thank you –
shúkran
'ashkúrak/ik/kum ⟶ *la shukr 9ála waájib* (= no thanks for a duty)
*mutashákkir/a/iin
mamnuúnak/ik/kum ⟶ *'al-9áfu/'áhlan wa sáhlan*

15. On being introduced –
tasharráfna ⟶ *'ash-sháraf lána/líyya* (= to me)

16. After drinking coffee –
dáyma ⟶ *SaHHtáyn* (= two healths)

17. *Congratulations –
mabruúk ⟶ *'állaah yubaárik fiik/ki/kum*

18. To someone working hard –
'állaah ya9Tiik al-9aáfya ⟶ *'állaah yu9aafiik/ki/kum*

19. *To someone who is ill –
salaámtak/ik/salaamátkum ⟶ *állah yusállimak/ik/yusallímkum*

20. To someone who tells you a relative is ill –
salaámtuh
salaamátha ⟶ *'állaah yusállimak/ik*

21. *Congratulations on festival or birthday –
*kull sána wa 'int bixáyr ⟶ *wa 'int bixáyr*

22. *To a beggar when refusing alms –
'állaah ya9Tiik
*/'állaah kariím ⟶ · · ·
kariím = generous

23. Taking leave –
'astá'dhin ⟶ *líssa bakkiír/*ba9d bakkiír*

24. *Excuse me, may I pass –
9an 'idhnak/ik/ídhinkum ⟶ *tafáDDal/i/u*

83

1. níHna raayHiín lil-mádrasa/9al-mádrasa.
2. híya saákina fi lúndun.
3. laázim nashuúfuh.
4. xalliíni 'aruúH lil-máktab/9al-maktab.
5. híya mashghuúla kathiír.
6. haádhi Sadiiqát-ha.
7. hal-bint Sadiiqátna.
8. bíddii shughl.
9. bíddhum yashkuruúhum.
10. húwa mush Sadiíqii.
11. níHna mariiDiín/marDa.
12. ma bíddii 'aruúH 9al-bayt.
13. máktab al-bariíd fi shaári9 bayruút.
14. xudh 'áwwal shaári9 9ála l-yamiín.
15. binaáyat shárikat nafT quddaám wizaárat ad-daaxilíyya.
16. bá9rif al-madiína kuwáyyis kathiír.
17. ruuH dúghri.
18. bayt Sadiíqii mush kabiír kathiír.
19. báyt-ha l-kabiír janb al-wizaára (or) qariíb min al-wizaára.
20. kull yawm, laázim 'ashtághil fil-máktab.
21. 9índii shánTa kabiíra.
22. ma 9índha fuluús.
23. hal-bayt tába9 miin?/la miin hal-bayt?
24. darást 9árabi fi 'ingéltera li múddat tís9at ásh-hur.
25. ma 'ishtaghálna kathiír.
26. 'as-saá9a xámsa.
27. darásna 9árabi min as-saá9a 9áshara Hátta s-saá9a 'ithná9sh.
28. ruHt 'íla lúndun li múddat shahráyn.
29. qaDáyna thalaáth saa9aát fi máktab yuúsif.
30. kaan fii thalaáth míyya wa 'ithnáyn wa xamsiín tilmiídh fil-mádrasa.

TWELFTH LESSON – *'ad-dars raqm 'ithná9sh*

DAILY ROUTINE

Dialogue (*Hiwaár bayn mu9állim wa tilmiídh*)

mu9állim:

quul lii shuu 9amált	*Tell me what you did yesterday*
'umbaáriH aS-SubH	*in the morning!*

84

quul!	*say! tell! . . .(imperative from qaal (yaquúl/biquúl))*
SubH	*morning*

tilmiídh:

'ams, qumt min an-nawm as-saá9a sítta wa nuSS. — *Yesterday, I woke up at half past six.*

'ams	*yesterday*
qumt	*I rose (from qaam (yaquúm/ biquúm) = rise up, stand up, get up*
nawm	*sleep*
nuSS *pl.* 'anSaáS	*half*

mu9allim:

sharíbt shaay fi l-firaásh? — *Did you drink tea in bed?*

sharíbt	*you drank (from shárib (yáshrab/byáshrab) = drink)*
shaay	*tea*
firaásh *pl.* fúrush	*bed*

tilmiidh:

ná9am, wa ba9adáyn qumt wa ruHt lil-Hammaám. — *Yes, and then I got up and went to the bathroom.*

Hammaám(-aat) — *bath(room)*

mu9allim:

fi 'ayy saá9a? — *At what time?*

tilmiidh:

'aZúnn 'inn as-saá9a kaanat sáb9a 'illa rub9 biZ-ZábT. — *I think that the time was a quarter to seven exactly.*

'illa	*except, save for*
sáb9a 'illa rúb9	*seven except a quarter (= 6.45)*
biZ-ZabT	*with precision (= exactly)*

mu9állim:

shuu 9amált bil-'áwwal? — *What did you do at first?*

bil-'áwwal — *at first, first of all*

tilmiidh:

bil-'áwwal ghasált wájhii wa 'iidáyya. — *First of all, I washed my face and hands.*

ghásal (yághsal/byághsal)	*wash (v. tr.)*
wajh *pl.* wujuùh	*face, aspect.*

85

'iid *pl.* 'ayaádi

hand (feminine because it is a part of the body coming in a pair)

'iidáyn→'iidáy→'iidáyya

my two hands (c.f. kursíyya = *my chair*)

tilmiidh:
 wa ba9adáyn naDDáft 'as-naánii wa Haláqt

And then I cleaned my teeth and shaved.

 náDDaf (yunáDDif/ bináDDif)

clean

 sinn *pl.* 'asnaán

tooth

 Halaq (yaHliq/byaHliq)

shave

mu9allim:
 qaddáysh 'axádht waqt?

How long did you take?

 qaddáysh?

how long?

 'áxadh (yaáxudh/byaáxudh)

take

 waqt *pl.* 'awqaat

time

tilmiidh:
 9áshar daqaáyiq bass.

Ten minutes only.

 daqiiqa *pl.* daqaáyiq.

minute

mu9allim:
 wa taHammamt?

Did you have a bath?

 taHámmam (yataHam-mam/byatHámmam)

take a bath (or 'axádht Hammaám?)

tilmiidh:
 ma9luúm, batHámmam kull yawm aS-SubH, wa ba9d ma taHammámt, labíst thiyaábi.

Of course, I have a bath every morning, and after I had bathed, I put my clothes on.

 lábis (yálbas/byálbas)

wear

 thawb *pl.* thiyaáb

garment (pl. = *clothes*)

mu9allim:
 'afTárt fi 'ayy saá9a?

You breakfasted at what time?

 'áfTar (yúfTir/bífTir)

breakfast

tilmiidh:
 'afTárna, 'ána wa záwjatii, 'as-saá9a sáb9a wa 9áshara.

My wife and I breakfasted at ten past seven.

mu9allim:

qaráyt al-jariída?   *Did you read the newspaper?*
qára (yáqra/byáqra)   *read*
jariída pl. jaraáyid   *newspaper*

tilmiidh:

ná9am, 'ána qaráyt al-jariída   *Yes, I read the newspaper before*
    qabl   al-fuTuúr   wa   *and during breakfast while my*
    'athnaá'uh   wa   záwjatii   *wife read it after breakfast.*
    qarát-ha ba9d al-fuTuúr.

mu9allim:

wa 'áymta tarákt al-bayt   *When did you leave the house to*
    Hátta taruúH lil-máktab?   *go to the office?*
tárak (yátruk/byátruk)   *leave*
Hátta   *so that (+ imperfect tense)*

tilmiidh:

'as-saá9a   thamaánya   'illa   *At twenty to eight.*
    thulth.
thulth pl. 'athlaáth   *third (as a fraction)*

Questions on the Dialogue

1. 'áymta   qaam   at-tilmiídh   qaam min an-nawm as-saá9a
    min an-nawm?   sítta wa nuSS.
2. shárib shaay fil-firaásh?   ná9am, shárib shaay fil-firaásh.
3. shuu 9ámal ba9d ma shárib   qaam wa raaH lil-Hammaám.
    shaay?
4. fi 'ayy saá9a raaH lil-   raaH lil-Hammaám as-saá9a
    Hammaám?   sáb9a 'illa rub9.
5. shuu 9ámal bil-'áwwal?   ghásal wájhuh wa 'iidáyh.
6. wa ba9dáyn?   náDDaf 'asnaánuh wa Hálaq.
7. qaddáysh 'áxadh waqt?   'áxadh 9áshar daqaáyiq.
8. wa taHámmam?/'áxadh   'áywa, taHámmam/'áxadh
    Hammaám?   Hammaám.
9. byatHámmam kull yawm   ná9am, byatHámmam kull
    aS-SubH?   yawm.
10. shuu   9ámal   ba9d   ma   ba9d ma taHámmam lábis
    taHámmam?   thiyaábuh.
11. 'áfTarat záwjatuh má9uh?   ná9am, híya 'áfTarat má9uh.
12. fi 'ayy saá9a 'áfTaru?   'áfTaru s-saá9a sáb9a wa
                                           9áshara.
13. 'áymta tárak al-bayt?   tárak al-bayt as-saá9a tha-
                                           maánya 'illa thulth.

14. qára l-jariída?
15. wa záwjatuh?

'áywa, qára l-jariída.
híya qárat al-jariída kamaán.

Narrative (new vocabulary is listed after the text)
   kull yawm ('ílla yawm al-júm9a) báSHa min an-nawm as-saá9a
sítta wa thulth. ba9d xams daqaáyiq, yá9ni s-saá9a sítta wa nuSS
'illa xámsa, baquúm min al-firaásh wa bátruk ghúrfat an-nawm wa
baruuH lil-Hammaám. fil-Hammaám bághsal wájhii wa 'iidáyya,
báHliq wa batHámmam. 9aádatan báqDi rub9 saá9a fil-
Hammaám. wa ba9dáyn bárji9 'ila ghúrfat an-nawm wa bálbas
thiyaábii wa báfTir wáHdii. bil-fuTuúr, baákul xubz wa bayD wa
báshrab shaay 'aw qáHwa. 'athnaá' al-fuTuúr báqra l-jariída. bátruk al-bayt as-saá9a sáb9a wa nuSS wa xámsa wa batawájjah lil-
máktab.

Vocabulary

(yawm) al-jum9a: *Friday* (= *the day of assembly*) – *Friday is a*
   holiday in Muslim countries.
báSHa (min an-nawm): *I wake up* (*from* SiHi (yáSha/
   byáSHa) = *to wake up*).
'as-saá9a sítta wa nuSS 'illa xámsa: *6. 25* (*i.e. six and a half less five*).
ghúrfat nawm: *bedroom* (ghúrfat an-nawm = the *bedroom*).
mayy: *water.*
rája9 (yárji9/byárji9): *return.*
wáHdii: (*I*) *alone* – wáHduh: (*he*) *alone* – wáHdha: (*she*) *alone etc.*
xubz: *bread.*
bayD: *eggs* (bayD *is the collective* – báyDa = *egg*).
bat(a)wájjah: *I go* (*from* tawájjah (yatawájjah/byatwájjah) = *to go*).

   N.B. tawájjah = *turn one's face towards* (wajh = *face*)

Questions on the Narrative (answer the narrator's questions)

1. báSHa fi 'ayy saá9a?
2. fi 'ayy saá9a baquúm min
   al-firaásh?
3. la wayn baruúH bil-'áwwal?
4. shuu bá9mal fil-Hammaám?

5. qaddáysh baáxudh waqt fil-
   Hammaám?
6. báfTir wáHdii?
7. shuu baákul bil-fuTuúr?

btáSHa s-saá9a sítta wa thulth.
bitquúm min al-firaásh as-saá9a
   sítta wa nuSS 'illa xámsa.
bitruúH lil-Hammaám.
btághsal wájhak wa 'iídayk,
   btáHliq wa btatHámmam.
btaáxudh rub9 saá9a 9aádatan.

ná9am, btifTir wáHdak.
btaákul xubz wa bayD.

88

8. shuu báshrab?   btáshrab shaay 'aw qáhwa.
9. shuu bá9mal 'athnaá' al-   btáqra l-jariída.
     fuTuúr?
10. 'áymta bátruk al-bayt?   btátruk al-bayt as-saá9a sáb9a
     wa nuSS wa xámsa.
11. bátruk al-bayt la wayn?   btátruk al-bayt Hátta taruúH
     'íla l-máktab.

Notes on Grammar and Usage

1. *Ordinals* – "first", "second", "third" etc. are as follows:

'áwwal – first (f. = *'uúla*)	*thaáni* – second (other)
thaálith – third	*raábi9* – fourth
xaámis – fifth	*saádis* – sixth
saábi9 – seventh	*thaámin* – eighth
taási9 – ninth	*9aáshir* – tenth

The above behave like normal adjectives as regards feminine and plural agreements:

e.g. *'awlaád thaanyiín* = other children
     'al-bint as-saábi9a = the seventh girl

When an ordinal from "eleventh" upwards is required, the ordinary numeral is used prefixed with the definite article:

e.g. *'ad-dars al-'ithná9sh* = the twelfth lesson
     'al-yawm al-9ishriín = the twentieth day
     'al-márra s-sítta wa xamsiín = the fifty-sixth time

Ordinals 11th to 19th can be expressed by (noun) + raqm + numeral. See the lesson titles of this book for examples. (*raqm* = number)

2. *Fractions* – the fractions from "half" to "tenth" are as follows:

nuSS pl. *'anSaáS* = half	*thulth* pl. *'athlaáth* = third
rub9 pl. *'arbaá9* = quarter	*xums* pl. *'axmaás* = fifth
suds pl. *'asdaás* = sixth	*sub9* pl. *'asbaá9* = seventh
thumn pl. *'athmaán* = eighth	
tus9 pl. *'atsaá9* = ninth	*9ushr* pl. *'a9shaár* = tenth

The singular is of the *fu9l* pattern and the plural *'af9aál*.
Fractions above "tenth" are expressed with ordinary numerals as follows:

waáHid min/9ála 9ishriín = one from/over twenty
'iHdá9sh min/9ála sítta wa 'arba9iín = eleven forty-sixths

3. Telling the Time – to ask the time one says *qaddáysh as-saá9a?* or *'as-saá9a kam?* Possible replies are:

'as-saá9a waáHida wa xámsa (daqaáyiq)	=	1·05
'as-saá9a waáHida wa 9áshara	=	1·10
'as-saá9a waáHida wa rub9	=	1·15 (i.e. "and a quarter")
'as-saá9a waáHida wa thulth	=	1·20 (i.e. "and a third")
'as-saá9a waáHida wa nuSS 'illa xámsa	=	1.25 (i.e. "and a half except five")
'as-saá9a waáHida wa nuSS	=	1·30
'as-saá9a waáHida wa nuSS wa xámsa	=	1·35 (i.e. "and a half and five")
'as-saá9a 'ithnáyn 'illa rub9	=	1·45
'as-saá9a 'ithnáyn 'illa xámsa	=	1·55
'as-saá9a thalaátha 'illa thulth	=	2·40

4. Imperfects of Defective Verbs – most defective verbs have imperfects ending in *-i* (the endings are identical with those of *yíji* = he comes).

e.g.
'áqDi (= I spend (time))	*naqDi* (= we spend)
táqDi (= you spend)	*taqDu* (= you spend (pl.))
táqDi (= you spend (f.s.))	
yáqDi (= he spends)	*yaqDu* (= they spend)
táqDi (= she spends)	

Some defective verbs have imperfects ending in *-a*.

e.g. *qara* (*'yáqra/byáqra*) = read
'áqra (= I read)	*náqra* (= we read)
táqra (= you read)	*táqru* (= you read (pl.))
táqri (= you read (f.s.))	
yáqra (= he reads)	*yáqru* (= they read)
táqra (= she reads)	

Notes:

(i) other verbs on this pattern are *yánsa* = he forgets (from *nísi* (*yánsa/byánsa*)) and *yáSHa* = he wakes up (from *SiHi* (*yáSHa/byáSha*)).

The important verb *rája* (*yárju/byárju*) has an imperfect ending in *-u* which remains unchanged throughout the conjugation:

e.g. *'arjuúk, 'a9Tiinii l-kitaáb* = I beg you (please), give me the book.

nárju 'innuh raH yíji búkra = we hope that he will come tomorrow.

5. Imperfects of Verbs beginning with ' – verbs like *'ákal* (= eat) and *'áxadh* (= take) have long *aa* in the first syllable of the imperfect:

e.g. *'áxadh ⟶ yaáxudh*   *'ákal ⟶ yaákul*

Exercises

1. Translate (answers at the end of the lesson)

(a) The first villages were very pleasant (= *laTiif*).
(b) The other girl was not in the house.
(c) I spent three quarters of an hour in the bathroom.
(d) The time was 5.20 when he came.
(e) At 8.35 in the morning exactly we woke up.
(f) They read the Arabic newspapers every day.
(g) We read a lot but we forget everything.
(h) Please (I beg you), come to our house today.

2. Give the following times in Arabic:

2.00 2.15 2.30 2.45 3.00 5.05 5.25 5.20 5.35 5.50
8.03 8.20 8.25 8.35 8.55.

ba9d aD-Dúhur = (in) the afternoon. i.e. = p.m.
'aS-SubH = in the morning i.e. = a.m.

2.00 a.m.   3.15 p.m.   5.25 p.m.   6.35 a.m.   11.00 a.m.
10.10 a.m.   11.35 p.m.   12.20 p.m.

noon, midday = *'aD-Dúhur*
midnight = *nuSS al-layl*

3. Translate the key sentence, then make the suggested substitutions.

– I read an Arabic newspaper every day.   *báqra jariída 9arabíyya kull yawm*

+ you/you-f.s./he/she/we/ you – pl./they
+ French newspaper/ English/American (= *'ameerkíyya*)

91

4. I forget everything after I read it.

+ they/you/he/she/you – pl.

bánsa kull shii ba9d ma 'aqraáh.

byánsu kull shii ba9d ma yaqruúh.

N.B. "Notes on Grammar and Usage" – Lesson 9 – Note 4. – Object pronouns and stress.

5. The student should give an account of the early part of his/her day, mentioning precise times and using all the verbs presented in the lesson.

Then a similar account of a friend's programme – so using "he" or "she" forms.

Then an account of a couple's programme or that of a group – so using "they" forms.

These "accounts" should be spoken, to be written down later if required.

Answers

1. (a) *'al-qúra l-'uúla kaánat laTiifa kathiir.*
   (b) *'al-bint at-thaánya ma kaánat fil-bayt.*
   (c) *qaDáyt thalaáthat arbaá9 saá9a fil-Hammaám.*
   (d) *kaánat as-saá9a xámsa wa thulth lámma 'ája.*
   (e) *fis-saá9a thamaánya wa nuSS wa xámsa biZ-ZabT qúmna min an-nawm.*
   (f) *byáqru l-jaraáyid l-9arabíyya kull yawm.*
   (g) *mnáqra kathiir laákin mnánsa kull shii.*
   (h) *'arjuúk, tafáDDal 9a báytna l-yawm.*

THIRTEENTH LESSON – *'ad-dars raqm thalaathtá9sh*

THE DAILY ROUTINE (contd.)

Narrative

rashiíd byátruk al-bayt as-saá9a sáb9a wa nuSS wa xámsa Hátta yaruúH lil-máktab.

Rashid leaves the house at seven thirty-five to go to the office.

9aádatan bisuúq sayyaártuh laákin 'aHyaánan Sadiíquh biwáSSiluh lil-máktab fi sayyaártuh.

Usually he drives his car but sometimes his friend takes him to the office in his car.

rashiíd byuúSal li máktabuh as-saá9a thamaánya.

Rashid arrives at his office at eight o'clock.

92

9aádatan, 'áwwal shii byá9mal ba9d wuSuúluh qiraáyat ar-rasaá'il.

wa ba9dáyn byimli makaatiíb 9ála sekratáyratuh.

marraat kathiira byitghadda fi maT9am Saghiír mush ba9iíd 9an al-máktab.

ba9d al-gháda 9índuh 9aádatan mawaa9iíd wa laázim yáHDar 'ijtimaa9aát.

daá'iman ba9d ash-shughl al-yáwmi byásh9ur bit-ta9ab wa byárji9 9al-bayt bi-súr9a wa byirtaaH wa byit9áshsha.

Usually, the first thing he does after his arrival is reading the letters (post).
And then he dictates letters to his secretary.
He lunches often in a small restaurant not far from the office.
After lunch, he usually has appointments and he has to attend meetings.
Always after the daily work he feels tired (feels tiredness) and returns home quickly (with speed) and rests and has dinner.

Vocabulary

bisuúq: *he drives (from* saaq (yasuúq/bisuúq), *which is conjugated like* raaH *and* kaan)

'aHyaánan: *sometimes (notice how adverbs frequently end in* -an)

biwáSSil: *he takes i.e. "he makes to arrive" (from* wáSSal (yuwáSSil/biwáSSil))

yuúSal: *he arrives (from* wáSal (yuúSal/byuúSal) = *arrive)*

risaála *pl.* rasaá'il: *letter. pl. = post*

byimli: *he dictates (from* 'ámla (yúmli/byímli) = *dictate* (9ála = *to))*

maktuúb *pl.* makaatiíb: *letter (passive participle from* kátab = *write)*

byitghádda: *he lunches (from* taghádda (yataghádda/byitghádda))

marraát kathiíra: *often*

máT9am *pl.* maTaá9im: *restaurant*

ba9iíd: *far* (9an = *from*)

gháda: *lunch*

9aádatan: *usually*

máw9id *pl.* mawaa9iíd: *appointment*

yáHDar: *he attends (from* HáDar (yáHDar/byáHDar))

'ijtimaá9 (-aat): *meeting*

daá'iman: *always*

yáwmi: *daily*

byásh9ur + bi: *he feels . . . (from* shá9ar (yásh9ur/byásh9ur))

byásh9ur bin-na9s = *he feels sleepy* (na9saán = *sleepy*)
byásh9ur bil-9aTsh = *he feels thirsty* (9aTshaán = *thirsty*)
byásh9ur bil-juu9 = *he feels hungry* (jaw9aán = *hungry*)

bi-súr9a: *with speed i.e. quickly*
byirtaáH: *he rests* (*from* 'irtaáH (yartaáH/byirtaáH) = *to rest*)
byit9áshsha: *he dines* (*from* ta9áshsha (yata9áshsha/byit9áshsha)
(9ásha = *dinner*))

Questions on the Narrative (answer the narrator's questions)

1. 'áymta bátruk al-bayt?

btátruk al-bayt as-saá9a sáb9a wa nuSS wa xámsa.

2. bátruk al-bayt fi hassaá9a Hátta 'aruúH li máT9am?

la, btátruk al-bayt Hátta taruúH lil-máktab.

3. kayf baruúH 9aádatan lil-máktab?

bitsuúq sayyaártak.

4. miin biwaSSílnii 'aHyaánan li máktabii?

'aHyaánan Sadiíqak biwáSSilak li máktabak.

5. shuu bá9mal 'áwwal shii ba9d wuSuúlii lil-máktab?

btáqra r-rasaá'il.

6. shuu bámli 9ála sekratáyratii?

btímli makaatiíb 9ála sekratáyratak.

7. wayn batghádda?

btitghádda fi máT9am.

8. al-máT9am qariíb 'aw ba9iíd 9an al-máktab?

'al-máT9am qariíb min al-máktab.

9. 9índii shughl kathiír ba9d al-gháda?

ná9am, 9índak shughl kathiír ba9d aD-Dúhur.

10. shuu shúghlii ba9d aD-Dúhur?

9índak mawaa9iíd wa 'ijtimaa9aát.

11. kayf básh9ur ba9d ash-shughl?

btásh9ur bi tá9ab.

12. shuu bá9mal ba9d ash-shughl?

btárji9 9al-bayt wa btirtaaH wa btit9áshsha.

Dialogue

'áHmad:
shuu 9amált fil-máktab 'umbaáriH?

What did you do yesterday in the office?

bashiir:

'áwwal shii qaráyt ar-rasaá'il wa 'amláyt makaatiíb 9ála sekratáyratii.

First I read the post and dictated letters to my secretary.

'aHmad:

'áymta taghaddáyt?

When did you lunch?

bashiir:

taghaddáyt as-saá9a 'ithná9sh wa nuSS wa rajá9t lil-máktab as-saá9a waáHida wa rub9.

I lunched at half past twelve and returned to the office at a quarter past one.

'aHmad:

yá9ni, qaDáyt thalaátht ar- baá9 saá9a xaárij al- máktab?

So, you spent three quarters of an hour outside the office.

bashiir:

ná9am, wa ba9d al-gháda kaan 9índii mawaa9iíd kathiira.

Yes, and after lunch I had many appointments.

'aHmad:

al-muqaabalaát bitduúm mú- dda Tawiíla 'aw qaSiíra?

(Did) the interviews last a long time or a short (time)?

bashiir:

9aádatan, 'al-muqaabalaát bitduúm múdda qaSiíra, wa bin-naádir bitduúm mú- dda Tawiíla.

Usually the interviews last a short time, they rarely last a long time.

'aHmad:

wa fi 'aáxir an-nahaár, shuu 9amált?

And at the end of the day, what did you do?

bashiir:

ba9d ash-shughl rajá9t 9al- bayt wa 'istaráHt wa ba9dáyn ta9ashsháyt wáHdii.

After work, I returned home and had a rest, then I had dinner alone.

Vocabulary

kathiira: *feminine singular adjectives are frequently used with the plurals of nouns denoting things.*

muqaábala (-aát): *interview, discussion, audience (with royalty).*

Tawiíl *pl.* Tiwaál: *long, tall* (Tiwaál *is the plural to be used with human beings.* Tawiíla (*f.s.*) *is the agreement often used when the adjective describes objects*).

qaSiír *pl.* qiSaár: *short* (*the remarks on agreement made for* Tawiíl *apply also to* qaSiír).

bitduúm: (*they*) *last* (*from* daam (yaduúm/biduúm) = *last*). *Note that just as adjectives describing plural things are often in the feminine singular* (*e.g.* kathiíra, Tawiíla *and* qaSiíra) *so a verb with the plural of something non-human as its subject is often feminine singular. Hence* bitduúm *and not* biduúmu.

bin-naádir: *rarely.*

'aáxir: *end* (*especially "end of . . ."*).

nahaár: *day* (*as opposed to "night"* – yawm = *24 hour day*).

'istaráHt: *I rested* (*from* 'istaraáH (yastariíH/byastariíH) = *rest*).

ta9ashsháyt: *I dined* (*from* ta9áshsha (yata9áshsha/byit9áshsha) = *dine*).

Questions on the Dialogue

1. shuu 9ámal bashiír 'áwwal shii fil-máktab 'ams?
   qára r-rasaá'il.

2. 'áymta taghádda?
   taghádda s-saá9a 'ithná9sh wa nuSS.

3. 'áymta rája9 lil-máktab?
   rája9 lil-máktab as-saá9a waáHida wa rub9.

4. kam waqt qáDa xaárij al-máktab?
   qáDa thalaáthat arbaá9 saá9a xaárij al-máktab.

5. shuu 9ámal ba9d al-gháda?
   ba9d al-gháda kaan 9índuh mawaa9iíd kathiíra.

6. 'al-muqaabalaát Tawiíla 'aw qaSiíra?
   9aádatan bitduúm al-muqaabalaát múdda qaSiíra.

7. shuu 9ámal bashiír ba9d ash-shúghl?
   rája9 9al-bayt.

8. ta9áshsha ma9 Háda?
   Háda = *anyone*
   la, ta9áshsha wáHduh.

Notes on Grammar and Usage

1. In Lesson 7, Note 4 of the "Notes on Grammar and Usage" gave some preliminary notions on the derived forms of the verb. The present note is merely to take some of the derived forms in the lesson and illustrate any points of interest in their conjugations.

   (*a*) *wáSSal* (*yuwáSSil/biwáSSil*) = *take, transport* (*'ila/li* = *to*). This is a 2nd form verb derived from *wáSal* (*yuúSal/*

byuúSal) = arrive (*'ila/li* = at). It has the typical causative meaning of the 2nd form, meaning "make to arrive".

The first of the two imperfects given is that of the literary language, is ultra correct and cannot be wrong (it is also the one given in the English–Arabic Glossary). The second is more colloquial and has the *b-* prefix. It is probably wiser to use the first variant since it is part of an Arabic which is understood all over the Arab World.

(*b*) *'ámla* (*yúmli/byímli*) = dictate (*9ála* = to). This is a 4th form verb. Because its characteristic vowel system tends to be lost in colloquial Arabic, the 4th form moves towards absorption in the 1st form.

(*c*) *taghádda* (*yataghádda/byitghádda*) = have lunch.
ta9áshsha (*yata9áshsha/byit9áshsha*) = have dinner.

These two verbs are 5th forms. Of the two imperfects given, the first will always be correct, the second is a typical colloquial variant. Being defective verbs they are conjugated like *qára* (*yáqra/byáqra*):

e.g. *ta9ashsháyna* = we dined   *yata9áshsha* = he dines
    tagháddu = they lunched   *tatagháddu* = you (pl.) lunch

(*d*) *'istaraáH* (*yastariíH/byastariíH*) = rest. This is a 10th form verb derived from *raaH* and with the perfect bearing the typical *'ista-* prefix. It is also a hollow verb (like *raaH* itself), but in derived forms of hollow verbs the *aa* vowel of the root is merely shortened to *a* when endings beginning with a consonant are added: e.g. *'istaraáHu* = they rested but *'istaráHna* = we rested.

2. Agreement of Adjectives – in colloquial Arabic the following agreements are usual:

(*a*) masculine singular noun + masculine singular adjective

e.g. *wálad Saghiir* = a small boy
    'al-muwáZZaf al-kabiir = the senior official

(*b*) feminine singular noun + feminine singular adjective

e.g. *bint jamiíla* = a beautiful girl
    'al-bint aS-Saghiíra = the small girl

(*c*) masculine plural noun (referring to human beings)
    + masculine sound plural adjective or broken plural adjective (if such exists)

N.B. See Lesson 9, Note 3 for "sound" and "broken" plurals.

> e.g. *rijaál Tiwaál* = tall men
> *talaamiidh mabsuuTiin* = contented students

(*d*) feminine plural nouns (referring to human beings)
   + broken plural adjective (if such exists) or masculine sound plural

> e.g. *banaát Hilwiin* = beautiful girls
> *tilmiidhaát Sighaár* = young (girl) pupils

(*e*) plural nouns (referring to non-human things and animals)
   + feminine singular adjective or (possibly) broken plural adjective

> e.g. *muqaabalaát qaSiira* = short interviews
> *'ijtimaa9aát Tawiila* = long meetings

(*f*) dual nouns (masculine) + plural adjective
   dual nouns (feminine) + masculine or feminine plural adjective

> e.g. *'al-baytáyn al-kibaár* = the two big houses
> *'al-madras(a)táyn al-jidaád/al-jadiidaát* = the two new schools

3. **Agreements of Verbs and Pronouns** – like adjectives, verbs and pronouns are feminine singular when referring to plural nouns denoting non-human things:

> e.g. *'al-muqaabalaát bitduúm waqt Tawiíl* = the interviews last a
> long time.
> *haádhi l-makaatiib híya min . . .* = these letters (they)
> are from . . .

Exercises

1. Translate into Arabic (answers at the end of the lesson):
(*a*) I drove my friend's car to the Embassy.
(*b*) Yesterday we lunched in a small restaurant near the ministry.
(*c*) Usually we have dinner together but sometimes he eats alone.
(*d*) After I've worked for three or four hours, I always feel thirsty.
(*e*) Ahmed's wife cleans the house by herself.
(*f*) I rested for a long time in the afternoon yesterday.
(*g*) In the morning I leave the house at twenty to eight.
(*h*) They were all hungry and thirsty and very tired.

(i) The embassies are near numerous schools.

(j) The big restaurants are all in the middle (*wasT*) of the city.

2. Adjective agreement: supply the correct form of adjective chosen from those proposed. Answers are given at the end of the lesson. An additional exercise would be to translate the English equivalents on the right of the page into Arabic, checking your answers against the Arabic appearing on the left.

(a) *banaát* (*mabsuuTiín* (m. pl.) *mabsuúTa* (f.s.))   happy girls

(b) *'aHwaál* (*kuwayyisaát* (f.pl.) *kuwáyyisa* (f.s.))   good conditions

(c) *SíHHa* (*kuwáyyis* (m.s.) *kuwáyyisa* (f.s.))   good health

(d) *'ashghaál* (*laazimaát* (f.pl.) *laázima* (f.s.))   necessary works

(e) *'al-9aa'ilaat* (*raayiH* (m.s.) *raayHiín* (m.pl.))   the families are going

(f) *'al-'awlaád* (*mariíD* (m.s.) *mariidiín* (m.pl.))   the boys are sick

(g) *'al-buuliís* (*mashghuúl* (m.s.) *mashghuúla* (f.s.))   the policeman is busy

(h) *'as-sayyaaraat* (*kabiir/kabiira*)   the cars are big

(i) *'al-waladáyn* (*kabiír/kibaár*)   the boys (2) are big

(j) *'al-bintáyn* (*Hilwatayn/Hilwiin*)   the girls (2) are beautiful

(k) *'al-madiina* (*Saghiir/Saghiira*)   the city is small

3. Agreements of Adjectives, Verbs and Pronouns: put the sentences on the left of the page into the plural. The answers are given on the right of the page, but cover these up when making your first attempt. Afterwards, you can alter the sentences on the right to the singular.

(a) 'al-máT9am qariíb min al-madiína.   'al-maTaá9im qariíba min al-múdun.

(b) hal-bint Tawiíla jíddan.   hal-banaát Tiwaál jíddan.

(c) has-sayyaára btímshi (*goes*) kuwáyyis.   has-sayyaaraát btímshi kuwáyyis.

(d) haádhi shánTat al-mudiír?   haádhi shúnaT al-múdara?

(e) hal-bayt, hu bayt Sadiíq.   hal-buyuút, híya buyuút 'aSdiqaá'.

(f) 'as-sayyaára 'ájat min al-mádrasa.	'as-sayyaaraát 'ájat ɪnin al-madaáris.
(g) 'az-zaá'ir raaH lil-fúnduq.	'az-zuwwaár raáHu lil-fanaádiq.
(h) 'al-xaliíj mush Tawiíl, húwa qaSiír.	'al-xuljaán mush Tawiíla, híya qaSiíra.
(i) 'ash-shárika tá9mal fi l-madiína l-kabiíra.	'ash-sharikaát tá9mal fi l-múdun al-kabiíra.
(j) hal-mádrasa, híya mádⁱrasa kuwáyyisa.	hal-madaáris, híya madaáris kuwáyyisa.
(k) 'al-wálad mashghuúl.	'al-'awlaád mashghuuliín.
(l) 'az-záwja 'ájat bakkiír.	'az-zawiaát 'áju bakkiír.

4. The Dual: put the sentences on the left of the page into the dual. (Remember that pronouns, adjectives and verbs are in the plural when associated with dual nouns.)

(a) 'al-mudiír 'ája.	'al-mudiiráyn 'áju.
(b) 'al-fúnduq al-kabiír janb al-wizaára.	'al-funduqáyn al-kibaár janb al-wizaaratáyn.
(c) 'az-zamiíl saákiin fi wasT al-madiína.	'az-zamiiláyn saakiniín fi wasT al-madiinatáyn.
(d) 'as-safiír hunaák, húwa min 'uruúpa (*Europe*).	'as-safiiráyn hunaák, hum min 'uruúpa.

Answers

1. (a) suqt sayyaárat Sadiíqii lis-sifaára.

(b) 'umbaáriH, taghaddáyna fi máT9am Saghiír qariíb min al-wizaára.

(c) 9aádatan, mnit9áshsha sáwa laákin 'aHyaánan byaákul wáHduh.

(d) ba9d ma bashtághil li múddat thalaáthat árbaa9 saa9aát, daá'iman básh9ur bil-9aTsh.

(e) zawjat 'áHmad bitnáDDif al-bayt wáHdha.

(f) 'istaráHt waqt Tawiil ba9d aD-Dúhur 'umbaáriH.

(g) 'aS-SubH, bátruk al-bayt as-saá9a thamaánya 'ílla thulth.

(h) kúllhum kaánu jaw9aaniín wa 9aTshaaniín wa ta9baaniín kathiír.

(i) 'as-sifaaraát qariíba min madaáris kathiíra.

(j) 'al-maTaa9im al-kabiíra kúllha fi wasT al-madiína.

2. (a) mabsuuTiín. (b) kuwáyyisa. (c) kuwáyyisa. (d) laázima. (e) raayHiín. (f) mariiDiín. (g) mashghuúl. (h) kabiíra. (i) kibaár. (j) Hilwiín. (k) Saghiíra.

COMPARISONS AND RELATIVES

Narrative

9índii Sadíiq 'ísmuh saálim bya-shtághil fi nafs ash-shárika 'ílli 'ána bashtághil fíiha.

I've a friend Salim who works in the same company that I work in.

níHna saakníin fi buyuút fi nafs al-Hayy min al-madíina.

We live in houses in the same quarter of the town.

'ídha qaaránna al-baytáyn min-laáqi 'inn bayt saálim 'ákbar min báytna bi shwayy laákin ghúrafuh 'aqáll.

If we compared the two houses, we would find that Salim's house is slightly bigger than our house but its rooms are fewer.

máthalan, fi báytuh fii thalaáth ghúraf nawm bass laákin fi báytna fii 'árba9a.

For example, in his house there are three bedrooms only while in our house there are four.

ba9táqid 'inn báytna 'ájmal min bayt saálim laákin saHíiH 'inn báytuh 'ájdad min báytna bi kathíir.

I think that our house is more beautiful than Salim's but (it is) true that his house is newer than ours by far.

Hawl bayt saálim fii HayT wa fil-HayT fii bawwaába zárqa.

Around Salim's house is a wall and in the wall is a blue gate.

wa 'ídha daxált Hawsh al-bayt bitlaáqi xams shajaraát kabíira btíHmil fawaákih Hámra.

And if you enter the house's courtyard, you'll find in it five big trees bearing red fruit.

wa hash-shajaraát 'á9la min sáTeH al-bayt.

And these trees are higher than the roof of the house.

'ámma báytna, 'íluh HayT mi-thl bayt Sadíiqna laákin lawn al-bawwaába 'axDar.

As for our house, it has a wall like our friend's house but the colour of the gate is green.

Háwshna 'áSghar laákin fíih zuhuúr jamíila mithl az-zuhuúr 9ind saálim.

Our courtyard's smaller but in it are flowers as beautiful as the flowers at Saalim's house.

haz-zuhuúr min kull al-'alwaán, 'ábyaD, 'áHmar, wa 'ázraq níHna minHíbb kathíir

These flowers are of all (the) colours, white, red and blue.

Hadiiqátna wa marraát kathíir níHna mnaq9ud fíiha.

We like our garden very much and often we sit in it.

Vocabulary

'illi: *who, which, that, he who, that which* (*the relative pronoun – see Notes on Grammar and Usage for full explanations*).

Hayy *pl.* 'aHyaá': *quarter* (*of town*).

qaaránna: *we compared* (*from* qaáran (yuqaárin/biqaárin) = *to compare. The use of a perfect in a conditional sentence after* 'idha *is usual.*

minlaáqi: *we find* (*from* láqa (yulaáqi/bilaáqi) = *to find*).

'ákbar: *bigger* (*from* kabiir = *big*).

bi shwayy: *by a little i.e. "slightly".*

'aqáll: *fewer* (*from* qaliíl).

'ájmal: *more beautiful* (*from* jamiíl = *beautiful*).

'ajdad: *newer* (*from* jadiid = *new*).

bi kathiír: *by far.*

Hawl: *around, about* (Háku Hawl . . . = *they spoke about . . .*).

HayT *pl.* HiiTaán: *wall.*

bawwaába (-aát): *gate.*

zárqa: *blue* (*the feminine form of* 'ázraq = *blue. See Notes on Grammar and Usage*).

daxált: *you entered* (*from* dáxal (yádxul/byádxul) = *to enter*).

Hawsh *pl.* 'aHwaásh: *courtyard.*

bitlaáqi: *you find* (*from* láqa (yulaáqi/bilaáqi) = *to find*). *This verb is peculiar in that the 1st form is used in the perfect and the 3rd form in the imperfect* (*see Lessons 7 and 20 for details on forms*).

shajaraát: *trees* (shájara = *tree* (*one*), shájar = *trees* (*in general and viewed as a group*), shajaraát *is used when trees are counted* (*3 to 10*). *See Lesson 17 for further details on collectives*).

'á9la: *higher* (*from* 9aáli = *high*).

sáTeH *pl.* suTuúH: *roof, surface.*

btíHmil: *it carries* (*from* Hámal (yáHmil/byíHmil) = *to carry, bear*).

'ilha: *they have* (ha *refers to the plural of a non-human thing*).

'il: *is a variant of* li/la *used before object pronouns. It can be used to indicate a possessive relationship for both people and things.*

9ind *can only be used with people.*

faákiha *pl.* fawaákih: *fruit.*

Hámra: *red* (*feminine of* 'áHmar = *red. See Notes on Grammar and Usage*).

'ámma . . .: *as for . . .*

mithl: *like.*

lawn *pl.* 'alwaán: *colour.*

'áxDar: *green.*

záhra *pl.* zuhuúr: *flower.*
'ábyaD: *white.*
minHíbb: *we like, love* (*from* Habb (yaHíbb/byaHíbb) = *to love*).
mináq9ud: *we sit* (*from* qá9ad (yáq9ud/byáq9ud) = *to sit*).

Questions on Narrative (answer for the narrator)

1.	shuu 'ism aS-Sadiíq?	'ismuh saálim
2.	wayn byashtághil aS-Sadiíq?	byashtághil fi nafs ash-shárika 'ílli 'ána bashtághil fiíha.
3.	bayt saálim 'ákbar min báytak wálla/'aw 'áSghar mínnuh?	bayt saálim 'ákbar min báytna.
4.	fi bayt saálim fii ghúraf 'aqáll 'aw ghúraf 'ákthar min báytak?	fii ghúraf 'aqáll bi bayt saálim.
5.	baytak 'ájdad min bayt saálim 'aw 'áqdam mínnuh?	báytuh 'ájdad min báytna. N.B. 'áqdam = *older.*
6.	'ayy bayt 'ájmal min ath-thaáni?	ba9táqid báytna 'ájmal min bayt saálim.
7.	shuu lawn bawwaábat bayt saálim?	láwnha 'áxDar.
8.	shuu bitlaáqi fi Hawsh báytuh?	bitlaáqi xams shajaraát Tawiíla.
9.	'ash-shajaraát 'á9la min al-bayt 'aw 'áqSar mínnuh?	híya 'á9la min al-bayt. N.B. 'áqSar = *shorter.*
10.	shuu lawn fawaákih ash-shajaraát.	láwnha 'áHmar.
11.	shuu lawn bawwaábat báytak.	láwnha 'ázraq.
12.	zuhuúrak jamiíla mithl zuhuúr saálim?	ná9am, híya jamiíla míthlha.
13.	btáq9udu fil-Hadiíqa?	ná9am, mináq9ud fiíha marraát kathiira.

Dialogue (Hamad asks John where he lives)

Hamad:
'ínta naázil fi fúnduq 'aw saákin fi bayt?

Are you staying at a hotel or living in a house?

John:
níHna, yá9ni 'ána wa záwjatii, saakniín fi bayt.

We, that is, my wife and I, are living in a house.

103

Hamad:

laákin kúntu naazliín fi fúnduq qabl mudda, mush
hayk? 'al-fúnduq ma kaan
kuwáyyis?

*But you were staying at a hotel a
little while ago, weren't you?
The hotel wasn't good?*

John:

kaan kuwáyyis, laákin bayt
'áHsan min fúnduq bi
kathiír.

*It was good, but a house is better
than a hotel by far.*

Hamad:

wa l-bayt 'illi 9índkum hállaq
kabiír?

*And the house which you have
now is big?*

John:

ná9am, 'ákbar min báytna fi
briiTaánya.

*Yes, bigger than our house in
Britain.*

Hamad:

bass laázim takuun al-ghuraf
kabiira bi sabab aT-Taqs
'illi huwa Haarr 'akthar mi-
nhu fi 'ingeltera. 'al-bayt
qariib min al-maktab?

*But the rooms need to be big be-
cause of the weather which is
hotter than it is in England. Is
the house near the office?*

John:

ná9am, húwa 'áqrab lil-
máktab min al-fúnduq 'illi
kúnna naazliín fiih.

*Yes, it's nearer than the hotel
which we were staying in.*

Vocabulary

naázil: *staying* (fi = *at*) (*from* názal (yánzal/byánzal) = *to descend*,
(+ min) *get down off* (*a steed*), *get out of* (*vehicle*) (+ fi) *stay at*
(*hotel*).)

saákin: *dwelling* (*from* sákan (yáskun/byáskun) = *to dwell*).

qabl múdda: *a short time ago* (qabl + *unit of time* = '*ago*' *e.g.* qabl
sána = *a year ago*).

mush hayk?: *weren't you?* (*like* "*n'est-ce pas*" *in French represents
all the many question tags that exist in English e.g.* "*isn't it?*",
"*aren't you?*" *etc.*) *A common alternative is* mush kida?

'áHsan: *better.*

bi sábab: *because* (*of*).

Taqs: *weather.*

Haarr: *hot.*

mínhu: *than it* (*is*) . . . (*see Notes on Grammar and Usage*).

Notes on Grammar and Usage

1. Relative Clauses

(*a*) the relative pronoun in colloquial Arabic is *'illi*. This does not change for feminine or plural. It is "invariable". Its English translation could be any of: – who, which, that, whose etc. It is only used when its antecedent (the noun to which it refers) is definite. Here are some examples:

haádha húwa l-wálad 'illi 'ája	*this is the boy who came*
'al-mu9állima 'illi tataghádda...	*the teacher who is lunching ...*

(Note that the English 'who' is subject of the relative clauses in the above sentences)

haádha húwa l-wálad 'illi bá9rifuh	*this is the boy – who – I know him*
haádhi híya sh-shárika 'illi byashtághil fiíha	*this is the company – which – he works in it (i.e. in which he ...)*
haádhi híya sh-shárika 'illi ra'iísha Sadiíqii	*this is the company – which – its president is my friend (whose ...)*

(In the above sentences, the English relative is either the object of a verb or preposition, or is a possessive relative like "whose" or "of which". Since *'illi* cannot itself be the object of a preposition or a verb, suitable pronouns and possessives have to be inserted – attached to a verb when the relative is object (*'illi bá9rifuh*), attached to a preposition when the relative is object of a preposition (*'illi byashtághil fiíha*) and attached to a noun where a possessive is intended (*'illi ra'iísha Sadiíqii*).)

(*b*) When the antecedent is indefinite, *'illi* is not used but apart from that the sentence construction remains unchanged:

e.g. *fil-Hawsh shájara 9aláyha fawaákih láwnha 'áHmar*	in the courtyard is a tree on which there are fruits whose colour is red.
shuft wálad ma bá9rifuh	I saw a boy (whom) I do not know him.

(*c*) *'illi* can also mean "he who", "that which" etc.

e.g. *'illi bídduh yaákul, laázim yashtághil.*	he who wishes to eat, must work.
kaan yás'al 9an kull 'illi bishuúfuh	he asked about all that he saw.

N.B. In an English sentence such as "This is the man whom I saw", "whom" may be omitted since it is the object of the relative clause. *'illi*, however, cannot be dropped for such a reason.

2. Comparison of Adjectives
   (*a*) the comparative of many adjectives is formed on the pattern *áf9al*. This is another invariable form like *'illi*.

e.g.	*kabiir* (big, old)	*'ákbar* (bigger, older)
	jamiil (beautiful)	*'ájmal* (more beautiful)
	qariib (near)	*'áqrab* (nearer)
	qadiim (old)	*'áqdam* (older) – *qadiim for things, kabiir* for people
	qabiiH (ugly)	*'áqbaH* (uglier)
	qaSiir (short)	*'áqSar* (shorter)
	Tawiil (tall, long)	*'áTwal* (taller, longer)
		'aHsan (better)

(*b*) comparatives derived from adjectives whose 2nd and 3rd root consonants are the same have the two consonants pronounced together:

e.g. *jadiid* (new)   *'ajadd* (newer)   *qaliil* (few)   *'aqáll* (fewer)
      (or *'ájdad*)

(*c*) adjectives ending in vowels yield comparatives ending in -*a*:

e.g. *9aáli* (high)   *'á9la* (higher)
      Hílu (sweet, nice, pretty)   *'áHla* (sweeter etc.)

(*d*) 1st form passive participles (*maf9uúl* pattern e.g. *mabsuúT*), adjectives from derived forms or verbs and relative adjectives form their comparatives by the placing of *'ákthar* (more) or *'aqáll* (less) after them:

e.g. *húwa mabsuúT 'ákthar/'aqáll mínnii*
      = He's more/less contented than I
      híya muta9állima 'ákthar/'aqáll mínna
      = She's more/less educated than we (are)

(*e*) when a clause follows the comparative, it is introduced by *mímma* (= *min* + *ma*):

e.g. *húwa 'ákbar mímma Zannáyt* = he is older than I thought

(*f*) In English a sentence such as "the weather here is hotter than the weather in England" may have a pronoun in the place of the second "weather". Hence "the weather here is hotter than (it is)

106

in England". A similar process occurs in Arabic when *Taqs* (= weather) is replaced by *hu* (= it):

e.g. *'aT-Taqs húna Haarr 'ákthar mínhu fi 'ingéltera*

3. The Superlative

(*a*) the superlative ("the biggest" etc.) is usually expressed by placing the comparative form of the adjective before a singular indefinite noun or a plural definite noun. The comparative adjective is made definite by the fact of being in construct with the following noun:

e.g. *húwa 'áTwal tilmiidh fiS-Saff*
   = He's the tallest pupil in the class
   húwa 'áTwal at-talaamiidh fi S-Saff
   = He's the tallest of the pupils in the class

(*b*) The superlative is occasionally rendered by putting the comparative after the noun, the adjective being made definite by addition of the definite article:

e.g. *'al-bayt al-'áqbaH fil-madiina*
   = the ugliest house in the city
   'al-mádrasa l-'ákbar fil-madiina
   = the biggest school in the city

4. Colour Adjectives
Colour adjectives (and those for bodily deformities e.g. "blind") are in their masculine forms identical with the comparative form for adjectives.

	Masculine	Feminine	Plural	Remarks
pattern	*'áf9al*	*fá9la*	*fu9l*	
black	*'áswad*	*sáwda*	*suud*	*'as-suudaán* = country of blacks
white	*'ábyaD*	*báyDa*	*biiD*	the White House = *'al-bayt al-'ábyaD*
red	*'áHmar*	*Hámra*	*Humr*	the 'Alhambra'
green	*'áxDar*	*xáDra*	*xuDr*	*jábal 'áxDar* = Green Mountain
blue	*'ázraq*	*zárqa*	*zurq*	azure (?)
yellow	*'áSfar*	*Sáfra*	*Sufr*	cf. "saffron"

– comparatives with *'ákthar-'aqáll* e.g. *'áswad 'ákthar* = more black

107

– plurals of colour adjectives can normally only refer to human beings. Hence *'al-biiD* = the whites as opposed to *'as-suud* = the blacks.

– feminine singulars are used with plurals of objects:

e.g. *zuhuúr Hámra* = red flowers

most other colour adjectives are relative adjectives and so a matter of vocabulary not one of grammar. An example is *ramaádi* (= grey) from *ramaád* (= ashes).

Exercises

1. Translate into Arabic (answers at the end of the lesson):

(*a*) The restaurant in which I dined was full of (*malyaán bi*) people (*naas*).

(*b*) Anyone who arrives after 11 o'clock will find the door closed (*maq fuúl* or *musákkar*).

(*c*) I'm taller than my brother.

(*d*) My house is nearer to the city than Salim's.

(*e*) The director of the company is lazier (*kaslaán* = lazy, *'áksal* = lazier) than I thought.

(*f*) He's the oldest man in the village.

(*g*) This fruit is redder than that (*haadhiík*) fruit.

(*h*) There are more blacks in this country than whites.

2. (*a*) Translate the key sentence, then make the suggested substitutions.

This house is bigger than that	*hal-bayt 'ákbar min haadhaák*
This school is bigger than that	*hal-mádrasa 'ákbar min haadhiík*

+ courtyard/wall/tree/village/place
+ smaller/higher/older/better/uglier/more beautiful

(*b*) Put in the plural –

e.g. These walls are higher than those	*hal-HiiTaán 'á9la min haadhiík*

N.B. feminine singular agreements with plural of things.

(*c*) These boys are taller than those.	*hal/haadháwl al-'awlaád 'áTwal min haadhawlaák.*

108

+ girls/officials/pupils/assist-
ants
+ younger/shorter/nearer/
older
3. thirsty = *9aTshaán*, hungry = *jaw9aán*, tired = *ta9baán*.
Comparatives on the model – *9aTshaán 'ákthar*

I'm thirstier than I thought	*'ána 9aTshaán 'ákthar mímma Zannáyt*
+ you(m.,f.&pl.)/he/she/we/ they	(*hum 9aTshaaniín 'ákthar mímma Zánnu*)
+ hungrier/more tired/nearer	
4. (*a*) He's the tallest boy in the school.	*húwa 'áTwal wálad fil-mádrasa.*
She's the oldest girl . . .	
He's the youngest pupil . . .	
She's the prettiest girl . . .	
(*b*) He's the shortest man.	*húwa 'áqSar rájul.*
He's the best . . .	
He's the first . . .	*húwa 'áwwal rájul.*
He's the second . . .	*huwa thaáni rájul.*
5. I've a red book	*9índii kitaáb 'áHmar*
+ green/blue/white/black/ yellow	
+ bag	*9índii shánTa xáDra* etc.

Put into the plural remembering the rule for agreements with the plurals of things.

6. This is the hotel I'm stay- ing at.	*haádha húwa l-fúnduq 'illi 'ána naázil fiih.*
+ he is/she is/we are/they are	*haádha húwa l-fúnduq 'illi níHna naazliín fiih.*
7. I'm reading the book you read a week ago.	*'ána 9am báqra l-kitaáb 'illi qa- ráytuh 'inta qabl 'usbuú9.*
+ she read/he read/they read	
+ letter (= risaala)	*'ána 9am báqra r-risaála 'illi qa- ruúha hum qabl 'usbuu9áyn*
+ two weeks ago/three weeks ago/a month ago/a year ago . . .	

Now repeat the exercise but with "a book" and "a letter".
Remember nothing changes except the omission of *'illi*.

Answers to Exercise 1

(*a*) 'al-máT9am 'ílli ta9ashsháyt fiih kaan malyaán bi naas.
(*b*) 'ílli byuúSal ba9d as-saá9a 'iHdá9sh raH yulaáqi l-baab musákkar.
(*c*) 'ána 'áTwal min 'áxii/'axuúy/'axuúya.
(*d*) báytii 'áqrab lil-madiína min bayt saálim.
(*e*) mudiír ash-shárika 'áksal mímma Zannáyt.
(*f*) húwa 'ákbar rájul fil-qárya.
(*g*) haádhi l-faákiha Hámra 'ákthar min haadhiík al-faákiha.
(*h*) fi hal-bilaád fii suud 'ákthar min al-biiD.

FIFTEENTH LESSON – *'ad-dars raqm xamstá9sh*

IN THE BANK

Dialogue (Rashid asks John where he is going)

Rashid:

'áhlan, ya John, la wayn raáyiH?

Hallo John, where (to where) are you going?

John:

'ahlan fiik. 'ana raáyiH 9al-bank. mustá9jil li-ánnii muta'áxxir shwayy.

Hallo to you. I'm going to the bank. I'm in a hurry because I'm a bit late.

Rashid:

xalliina naruúH sáwa. biddii 'ána kamaán 'ásHab fuluús.

Let us go together. I also want to withdraw money.

John:

'áhlan wa sáhlan.

Welcome (i.e. O.K.)

In the bank – fil-bank

Rashid:

ya xasaára! 'ána nisiít dáftar shakkaát taba9ii!

O dear! I've forgotten my cheque book!

John:

wayn nisiítuh? fil-bayt 'aw ... ?

Where did you forget it? In the house or ... ?

Rashid:
yúmkin fil-bayt... ya sa-laám! la! hayyaáh fi jáybii!

Perhaps in the house... Good heavens! No! Here it is in my pocket!

John:
wa hállaq laázim 'ás'al qad-dáysh 9índii fuluús fi Hisaábii qabl ma 'ámDi shakk!

And now I have to ask how much money I have in my account before I sign a cheque.

At the Post-Office – fi máktab al-bariíd

(*John buys stamps and sends an air-letter to the U.S.A.*)
(*He speaks to the official* = muwáZZaf (-iin))

John:
min fáDlak, bíddii 'ashtári thamaán Tawaábi9 'ábu 9áshar quruúsh.

Please. I want to buy eight ten piastre stamps.

muwáZZaf:
'aásif. ma 9índii thamaán Tawaábi9 tába9 9áshar qu-ruúsh. bíddak taáxud sítta bi 9áshar quruúsh wa 'árba9a bi xams quruúsh? 'ínta faáhim?

(*I am*) *sorry. I don't have eight ten piastre stamps. Would you take six ten piastre ones and four five piastre ones? Do you understand?*

John:
la, mush faáhim tamaám. má-rra thaánya min fáDlak. laákin shwayy shwayy.

No, (*I*) *didn't understand completely. Once again please. But slowly.*

muwáZZaf:
ba9Tiík sitt Tawaábi9 'ábu 9áshar quruúsh wa 'árba9a 'ábu xams quruúsh. mafhuúm?

I give you six ten piastre stamps and four five piastre ones. Understood?

John:
Táyyib. min fáDlak, 'a9Tiínii 'iyyaáha... shúkran.
wa bíddii kamaán 'ársil har-risaála 'íla l-wilaayaát al-muttáHida.

Good. Please, give me them... thank you.
And I also want to send this let-ter to the United States.

111

muwáZZaf:
bil-bariíd al-9aádi 'aw bil-
bariíd al-jáwwi?

By ordinary post or by air-mail.

John:
bil-bariíd al-jáwwi.

By air-mail.

muwáZZaf:
'a9Tiínii 'iyyaáha. laázim
'awzínha. baHúTTha fil-
miizaán wa . . . 'aa! wáznha
. . . laázim tádfa9 xamsiín
qirsh.

Give it to me. I have to weigh it.
I put it on the scales and . . .
Ah! Its weight is . . . You
have to pay fifty piastres.

John:
haádhi liíra.

This is a pound.

muwáZZaf:
hayy al-kamaála, xamsiín
qirsh

Here's the change, 50 piastres.

Vocabulary

mustá9jil: *in a hurry.*
bank *pl.* bunuúk: *bank.*
li'án: *because* (li'ánnii = *because I,* li'ánnak = *because you . . .*)
muta'áxxir: *late.*
'ásHab: *I withdraw* (*from* sáHab (yásHab/byásHab) = *to withdraw*
    (*something*)).
dáftar shakkaát *pl.* dafaátir shakkaát: *cheque book* (dáftar
    = *notebook,* shakk = *cheque*).
ya xasaára: *lit: O loss!* (*an exclamation of dismay*)
ya salaám: *lit: O peace!* (*an exclamation of surprise and admiration*)
hayyaáh: *here it is!* (hayyaá + *pronoun suffix, but* hayy + *noun*
    e.g. hayy al-kamaála = *here's the change*).
jayb *pl.* juyuúb: *pocket*
Hisaáb (-aát): (*bank*) *account, bill.*
'ámDi: *I sign* (*from* 'ámDa (yúmDi/byímDi) = *to sign*)
'ashtári: *I buy* (*from* 'ishtára (yashtári/byashtári) = *to buy*)
Taábi9 *pl.* Tawaábi9: *stamp* (*postage*)
'ábu: here = *of* ('ábu *is often used in phrases assigning a particular*
    quality to their subject:

e.g. 'ábu n-nawm = *the poppy* (*lit: father of sleep*)
    'ábu l-hawl = *the Sphinx* (*lit: the father of terror*)

112

faáhim: *have understood* (*from* fáhim (yáfham/byáfham) = *to understand*)

tamaám: *completely*

márra thaanya: *once again* (*also* thaáni márra)

shwayy shwayy: *slowly*

malfhuúm: *understood*

'iyyaáha: ('*íyyaa is a dummy word to which object pronouns can be attached when there are two with the same verb. This occurs particularly with verbs involving giving:*

e.g. *Give them it* = 'a9Tiíhum 'iyyaáh (*or* 'a9Tiíh 'ílhum)

'ársil: *send* (*from* 'ársal (yúrsil/byársil) = *to send*)

jáwwi: *air* (*adjective from* jaww = *air, atmosphere*)

'al-wilaayaát al-muttáHida: *the United States* (*from* wilaáya = *state and* muttáHid = *united*)

'áwzin: *I weigh* (*from* wázan (yáwzin/byáwzin) = *to weigh*)

miizaán *pl.* mayaaziín: *scales*

wazn *pl.* 'awzaán: *weight* (*Note the similarities between the consonants of the last three words*)

tádfa9: *you pay* (*from* dáfa9 (yádfa9/byádfa9) = *to pay* (*or*) *to push*)

liíra (-aát): "*pound*" (*currency used in Lebanon and Syria*)

qirsh *pl.* quruúsh: *piastre* (*1/100 of Lebanese, Syrian and Egyptian pounds*)

kamaála: *change* (*i.e. money returned to one*) *N.B.* furaáTa = *small change.*

Questions on the Dialogue

1. laysh John mustá9jil?
   li'ánnuh muta'áxxir shwayy.

2. lawáyn raáyiH?
   raáyiH 9al-bank.

3. miin bídduh yaruúH 9al-bank má9uh?
   rashiíd bídduh yaruúH ma9 John

4. laysh rashiíd bídduh yaruúH 9al-bank?
   bídduh yás-Hab fuluús.

5. bya9táqid rashiíd 'innuh nísi shii?
   ná9am, bya9táqid 'innuh nísi dáftar shakkaát tába9uh.

6. láqa d-dáftar wílla la?
   láqa dáftar shakkaátuh fi jáybuh.

7. shuu laázim yá9mal, John, qabl ma yámDi shakk?
   laázim yás'al qaddáysh 9índuh fuluús fi Hisaábuh.

8. kam Taábi9 bídduh yashtári?
   bídduh yashtári thamaán Tawaábi9

9. min 'ayy fí'a? (fi'a = *group*)

10. 'al-muwáZZaf, fii 9índuh thamaan Tawaábi9 min hal-qiíma? (= *value*)

11. 'al-muwáZZaf, shuu qaal bídduh yá9Ti John?

12. John fáhim?

13. shuu Tálab John min al-muwáZZaf? (Talab = *ask for*, min *before the person asked*)

14. kayf bídduh John yársil ri-saálatuh 'íla l-wilaayaát al-muttáHida?

15. 'al-muwáZZaf shuu laázim yá9mal?

16. qaddáysh laázim yádfa9, John? qaddáysh = *how much?*

17. John, 'á9Ta l-muwáZZaf liíra?

min fí'at la-9áshar quruúsh.

la, fii 9índuh sítta bass.

qaal bídduh ya9tiíh sitt Tawaábi9 bi 9áshar quruúsh wa 'árba9a bi xams quruúsh.

la, húwa ma fáhim tamaám?

Tálab min al-muwáZZaf yáHki shwayy shwayy.

bídduh yarsílha bil-bariíd al-jáwwi.

laázim yáwzin ar-risaála.

laázim yádfa9 xamsiín qirsh.

'áywa, 'a9Taáh 'iyyaáha.

Notes on Grammar and Usage

1. Active Participle (1st form verb)

(*a*) the active participle of a 1st form regular verb is formed on the model *faá9il* i.e. a long *aa* between 1st and 2nd root consonants with *i* between the 2nd and 3rd:

e.g. *fáhim* (= understand) ⟶ *faáhim*
sákan (= dwell) ⟶ *saákin*

(*b*) Its meaning depends on the kind of verb it is derived from. In verbs that denote processes e.g. "going", "dwelling", the active participle is like the English present participle (-ing form):

e.g. 'ána saákin fi l-kuwáyt = *I'm living in Kuwait.*

(*c*) Participles derived from transitive verbs denoting activities of limited duration are equivalent to the present perfect tense in English ("have done"):

e.g. *húwa kaátib al-maktuúb* = he has written the letter
NOT "He's writing the letter" (= *húwa 9am byáktub al-maktuúb*)

114

AND NOT "he wrote the letter" (= *húwa kátab al-maktuúb*)

Further examples:
húwa faáhim as-su'aál = he's understood the question.
hum laabisiin thiyaábhum = they've put on their clothes.
hiya ghaásila kull shii = she's washed everything.

(*d*) Active participles of hollow verbs have *y* or ' inserted to replace the missing middle consonant:

e.g. *raaH* (= go) ⟶ *raáyiH*   *9aash* (= live) ⟶ *9aá'ish*

Active participles of defective verbs lack a final consonant:

e.g. *nísi* (= forget) ⟶ *naási* (= has forgotten)
qára (= read) ⟶ *qaári* (= has read)
máDa (= pass (of time)) ⟶ *maáDi* (= past, last e.g. *'as-sána l-maáD(i) ya* = last year   *fil-maáDi* = in the past)

Active participles of doubled verbs are regular:

e.g. *Zann* (= think, suppose) ⟶ *Zaánin*

(*e*) Active participles with an adjective or verbal meaning have adjective plurals:

e.g. *'ana raáyiH . . . hiya raáy(i)Ha . . . hum raay(i)Hiín*

but when they are used as nouns they often use a different plural, usually of the *fu99aál* pattern:

e.g. *saákin* (= inhabitant) pl. *sukkaán*
kaátib (= clerk, writer) pl. *kuttaáb*
zaá'ir (= visitor) pl. *zuwwaár*

2. Passive Participle (1st form verb)
(*a*) passive participles of regular 1st form verbs are formed on the pattern *maf9uúl*:

e.g. *fáhim* ⟶ *mafhuúm* (understood)   *wájad* ⟶ *mawjuúd* (found, existing)   *shághal* ⟶ *mashghuúl* (occupied)
dáfa9 ⟶ *madfuú9* (paid)

the passive participle of doubled verbs is formed regularly:

e.g. *Habb* (love, like) ⟶ *maHbuúb* (loved, liked, popular)

passive participles of hollow verbs are very rare. 7th form participles (See Lesson 21) are sometimes used:

e.g. *qaal* ⟶ *munqaál* (= said)

115

the passive participle of most defective verbs ends in -*i*:

e.g. *qára* (read) ⟶ *máqri* (read) *nísi* (forget) ⟶ *mánsi* (forgotten)

BUT *rája* (hope, request) ⟶ *márju* (hoped, requested)

N.B. feminine forms would be *mansíyya* and *marjúwwa*

(*b*) It should be noted that the passive participle can only be used to describe a state not an action. The sentence "the door was broken" can be rendered *'al-baab kaan maksuúr* if we are talking of a state, but if we are concerned with an action, then the 7th form of the verb (see Lesson 21) would be used:

e.g. *'inkásar al-baab*

An English passive sentence where the agent is mentioned is best made active in Arabic:

e.g. "the door was broken by Ahmed" = *'áHmad kásar al-baab* (Ahmed broke the door)

Another common English passive phrase like "it is said" would be made active – *biquúlu* . . . (= they say)

(*c*) You should note as vocabulary items the following very common passive participles:

maksuúr (broken)	*maftuúH* (open)	*maqfuúl* (shut)
mamnuú9 (forbidden)	*masmuúH* (permitted)	*ma9quúl* (sensible)
mas'uúl (responsible)		*majnuún* (mad, "possessed by jinn")

Exercises

1. Translate the following into Arabic (answers at end of lesson):
The wall is broken – The broken flower – The money (that has been) paid – The gate is open – The door is shut – An opened letter – The restaurant is closed – Is the letter written? This is permitted but that is forbidden – Permitted clothes – Reading this book is forbidden – This idea is sensible – She's insane – The official was responsible for (= *9an*) our company – She's forgotten her book – They've written the story – We're returning – We're writing the story.

2. Supply the active or passive participle required (answers at the end of the lesson):

(*a*) Active participle from *qáDa* meaning' judge' . . .

(*b*) Active participle from *9ámal* meaning "worker" . . . Give the plural also.

(c) Passive participle from *9áraf* meaning "known" . . .
(d) Passive participle from *9add* meaning "counted" . . .
(e) Active participle from *dáfa9* meaning "motive" . . .
(f) Passive participle from *HaTT* meaning "lying" . . .
(g) Active participle from *názal* meaning "descending" . . .
(h) Active participle from *shaaf* meaning "you see" . . .

3. Translate the key sentence, then make the suggested substitutions.

I'm going to visit him because he's ill	*'ána raáyiH 'azuúruh li'ánnuh mariiD.*
+ her because she/them because they/you because you	
+ we're going to visit them because they're ill.	*níHna raayHiín nazuúrhum li'ánhum mariiDiín/márDa*
+ you (pl)/they	
+ they're going to visit you because you . . ./they . . . us	
4. Last year I was living in Syria	*'as-sána l-maáD(i)ya kunt saákin fi suúriya.*

you	Lebanon	*lubnaán*
we	Jordan	*'al-'úrdun*
she	Egypt	*maSr*
they	Iraq	*'al-9iraáq*
he	Saudi-Arabia	*'as-sa9uudíyya*

Next week he is going to Damascus.	*'al-'usbuú9 al-jaay húwa raáyiH 'ila sh-shaam.*
Cairo	*'al-qaáhira*
Riyadh	*'ar-riyaáD*

N.B. *jaay* is the active participle from *'ája* (= come) The active participle may combine with *kaan* to form a past continuous tense, or by itself, with suitable adverbs, imply the future.

5. Translate the key sentence into Arabic. Answer the resulting question saying that the first alternative is correct.

(*waáqif* = standing, *qaá9id* = sitting, *mutamáddid* = lying)

Is Samira standing or sitting?	*samiíra waáqfa wálla qaá9ida?*
She's standing.	*híya waáqfa.*
Is the gate open or closed? . . .	
Is this permitted or forbidden? . . .	

Was the question understood or
not understood? . . .

Has the book been read or not   *máqri*
read? . . .

Is he sitting or lying on the bed?

Has the question been forgotten   *mánsi*
or not forgotten? . . .

Are   we   going   there   or
returning?

6. Translate the following into Arabic (answers at the end of the
lesson):

(a) I   want   to   send   this   telegram   to   America,   please.
(telegram = *barqíyya*)

(b) This   parcel   weighs   (*wáznuh*)   3   kilos   and   a   half.
(parcel = *Tard* pl. *Turuúd*)

(c) They always weigh parcels in the post-office before they send
them.

(d) We are in a hurry because we're a bit late.

(e) She wants to draw all her money out of the bank today.

(f) These parcels all weigh 2 kilos. Give them to me!

(g) We've seen Ahmed today. He was standing in the street outside the cinema.

(h) Next week, we're going to Paris, if God wills (*'in shaa' 'allaah*).

(i) I want to come and visit your new house, but I'm very busy
this week.

(j) The director was responsible for the school.

7. Translate question and answer according to the model. Then
make the suggested substitutions.

Has he washed his clothes?   *húwa gḥáasil thiyaábuh.*
– Yes he washed them yesterday   – *ná9am, ghasálhum 'umbaáriH.*
+ Has she . . . her . . .?
– Yes, she washed . . .   N.B. *ghasálhum – hum* not *ha*
                                                                 because the mental picture is
                                                                 of many separate items.

+ Have they written the letter?
– Yes they . . .
+ Have you studied the lesson?   *'inta daaris ad-dars?*
– Yes, I/we . . .   – *ná9am, darást ad-dars*
                                                               'umbaáriH.

(Use all three 'you's, m.s., f.s., & pl.)

118

Answers

1. 'al-HayT maksuúr – 'az-záhra l-maksuúra – 'al-fuluús al-madfuú9a. – 'al-bawwaába maftuúHa – 'al-baab maqfuúl/musákkar – risaála maftuúHa/maktuúb maftuúH – 'almáT9am maqfuúl/musákkar – 'ar-risaála maktuúba? – haádha masmuúH laákin haadhaák mamnuú9 – thiyaáb masmuúHa – qiraáyat hal-kitaáb mamnuú9a – hal-fíkra ma9quúla – híya majnuúna – 'al-muwáZZaf kaan mas'uúl 9an sharikátna – híya naasya kitaábha – hum kaatibiin ar-riwaáya – níHna raaji9iín – níHna 9am náktub ar-riwaáya.

2. (a) qaáDi (b) 9aámil (c) ma9ruúf (d) ma9duúd (e) daáfi9 (f) maHTuúT (g) naázil (h) shaáyif

6. (a) bíddii 'ársil hal-barqíyya 'íla 'ameérka, min fáDlak.

(b) haT-Tard wáznuh thalaáth kiílu wa nuSS/kiiluwaát wa nuSS.

(c) daá'iman byáwzinu T-Turuúd fi máktab al-bariíd qabl ma yarsiluúha.

(d) niHna musta9jiliín li'ánna muta'axxiriín shwayy.

(e) bíddha tásHab kull fuluúsha min al-bank al-yawm.

(f) haT-Turuúd, wazn kull waáHid mínha 'ithnáyn kiílu. 'a9Tiínii 'iyyaáha!

(g) níHna shúfna 'áHmad al-yawm. kaan waáqif fi sh-shaári9 xaárij as-siínama.

(h) 'al-'usbuú9 al-jaay, níHna raayHiín li baariís, 'in shaa' 'allaáh.

(i) bíddíi 'áji 'azuúr báytak al-jadiíd, laakínnii mashghuúl jíddan hal-'usbuú9.

(j) kaan al-mudiír mas'uúl 9an al-mádrasa.

SIXTEENTH LESSON – *'ad-dars raqm sittá9sh*
ORDERS TO A SERVANT

Dialogue (John gives orders to his servant Kamal)

John:

ta9aál ya kamaál! bíddii 'akállimak.	Come here, Kamal! I want to speak to you.

Kamal:

HaáDir, ya siídii	At your orders, sir.

John:

bakuún fil-máktab al-yawm laHátta s-saá9a 'árba9a ba9d aD-Duhur.	I shall be in the office today until 4 o'clock in the afternoon.

bi ghiyaábii náDDif kull al-bayt, kánnis 'arD al-máTbax, wa kánnisuh miniíH!

In my absence, clean the whole house, sweep the floor of the kitchen, and sweep it well!

ghássil aS-SuHuún wal-malaábis!

Wash the dishes and the clothes!

wa ba9dáyn sáwwi l-fúrush!

and then make the beds!

wa ba9d aD-Dúhur, HáDDir aT-Taáwila fi ghúrfat al-'akl li shaxSáyn – fii Sadiíq jaay yata9áshsha 9índna l-láyla.

In the afternoon, lay the table in the dining room for two people – a friend is coming to dine here this evening.

wa la tánsa shii muhímm, la táftaH ash-shabaabiík!

And don't forget something important, don't open the windows!

Kamal:
múmkin 'astá9mil míknasat al-huúver?

May I use the Hoover?

John:
la, la tasta9mílha! li suu' al-HaZZ, híya xarbaána.

No, don't use it! Unfortunately, it's out of order.

laázim 'aaxúdh-ha li sh-shárika 9alashaán yuSalliHuúha.

I have to take it to the company so that they may repair it.

Kamal:
'ash-shárika ba9iída? fíinii 'aaxudh-ha 'ána.

Is the company far? I can take it myself.

John:
la, mush ba9iída, fikra ku-wáyyisa. xúdh-ha lish-shárika wa 'ána baktúblak wáraqa lil-mudiír.

No, not far, good idea. Take it to the company and I will write for you a note for the director.

John:
ya kamaál, yálla, 9ajjil! ruuH lis-suuq wa jiib sagaáyir. fii 9índna Háfla l-láyla wa ma fii sagaáyir fil-bayt 'ábadan.

Kamal, come on, be quick! Go to the market and bring cigarettes! We've a party tonight here and there are no cigarettes at all in the house.

Kamal:
Táyyib, bárji9 bi daqiíqa.

Right, I'll be back in a minute.

(In a cafe – with two friends)

John:
shuu bitriíd táshrab, ya saálim?

What would you like to drink, Salim?

Saálim:
finjaán qáhwa, min fáDlak, wa kubbaáyat mayy.

A cup of coffee, please, and a glass of water.

John:
wa 'ínta, ya nabiíl?

And you Nabil?

Nabiíl:
'ana bafáDDil "pépsi", 'aT-Taqs Haarr al-yawm

I prefer a "pepsi", it's hot today.

John:
(*to waiter*) min fáDlak, haat qahwatáyn wa waáHid pépsi!

Please, bring two coffees and a pepsi!

Vocabulary

'akállimak: *I speak to you* (*from* kállam (yukállim/ bikállim) = *speak to.*)

Haádir: *present, at your orders.*

Hátta: *until.*

ghiyaáb: *absence* (*verbal noun from* ghaab (yaghiíb/bighiíb) = *be absent*).

náDDif: *clean!* (*from* náDDaf (yunáDDif/bináDDif) = *to clean*).

kánnis: *sweep!* (*from* kánnas (yukánnis/bikánnis) = *to sweep*).

'arD pl. 'araáDi: *land, floor, ground* (*a feminine word!*).

máTbax pl. maTaábix: *kitchen.*

ghássil *wash* (*from* ghással (yughássil/bighássil) = *to wash*).

SaHn pl. SuHuún: *plate.*

málbas pl. malaábis: *garment pl. = clothes.*

sáwwi: *make, do* (*from* sáwwa (yusáwwi/bisáwwi) = *make, do, settle*).

HáDDir: *prepare* (*from* HáDDar (yuHáDDir/biHáDDir) – *to prepare*).

'astá9mil: *I use* (*from* 'istá9mal (yastá9mil/byastá9mil) = *to use.*)

míknasa pl. makaánis: *broom, sweeper.*

li suu' al-HaZZ: *unfortunately* (suu' = *evil*, HaZZ = *fortune*).

xarbaán: *out of order, broken down.*

yuSalliHuúha: *they repair it* (*from* SállaH (yusálliH/biSálliH) = *to repair*).

121

báktub: *I write* (*from* kátab (yáktub/byáktub) = *to write*).
wáraqa: *a piece of paper, note, bank-note, playing card* (wáraq *is the collective* = *paper*).
yálla: *get on with it!*
9ájjil!: *hurry!* (*from* 9ájjal (yu9ájjil/bi9ájjil) = *to hurry*).
jiib: *bring!* (*from* jaab/yajiíb/bijiíb) = *to bring*).
sigaára *pl.* sagaáyir: *cigarette*
Háfla (-aat): *party*
'al-láyla: *tonight*
'ábadan: *at all, never* (ma shúftuh 'ábadan = *I've never seen him*).
finjaán *pl.* fanaajiín: *cup.*
kubbaáya (-aát): *tumbler.*
bafáDDil: *I prefer* (*from* fáDDal (yufáDDil/bifáDDil) = *to prefer*).
haat!: *bring!* (*no verb as origin*).

Questions on the Dialogues

(*servant* = xaádim *pl.* xuddaám)

1. 'al-xaádim, shuu laázim yá9mal bi ghiyaáb John?

laázim yunáDDif al-bayt wa yukánnis 'arD al-máTbax wa yughássil aS-SuHuún wal-malaábis.

2. wa ba9dáyn?

laázim yusáwwi l-fúrush.

3. shuu laázim yá9mal ba9d aD-Dúhur?

laázim yuHáDDir aT-Taáwila li shaxSáyn.

3. laysh?

li'án fii Sadiíq jaay yata9áshsha 9índhum.

4. 'al-xaádim, shuu laázim ma yánsa?

mush laázim yáftaH ash-shabaabiík.

5. laysh mush múmkin 'in al-xaádim yastá9mil al-huúver?

li'ánha xarbaána.

6. laysh laázim yaaxudhuúha lish-shárika?

9alashaán yuSalliHuúha.

7. 'al-xaádim byáqdir húwa yaáxudh al-huúver?

ná9am, húwa byáqdir yaaxúdh-ha

8. shuu byáktub luh John?

byáktub luh wáraqa li mudiír ash-shárika.

9. 'al-xaádim, shuu laázim yashtári min as-suuq?

laázim yashtári sagaáyir.

10. fii sagaáyir fil-bayt?

la, ma fii sagaáyir 'ábadan.

11. shuu biriíd yáshrab saálim?

biriíd yáshrab finjaán qáhwa.

12. shuu bifáDDil nabiíl?   bifáDDil pépsi.
13. John, shuu biquúl lil-   haat/jiib qahwatáyn wa waáHid
    gaarsón? (= waiter)   pépsi!

Notes on Grammar and Usage

1. The Imperative

(*a*) The imperative (command form of the verb) is derived from the 2nd persons ("you" forms) of the imperfect by dropping the *t* + vowel prefix:

e.g. *taruúH* (= you go)   *ruuH!* (= go!)
     taruúHi (f.s.)   *ruúHi!*
     taruúHu (pl.)   *ruúHu!*

Similarly –

     tu/náDDif/i/u   *naDDif/i/u!* (clean!)

(*b*) If dropping the *t* + vowel prefix results in two consonants clustering at the beginning of the word, the glottal stop ' + helping vowel is prefixed:

e.g. *tá9mal* (= you do) ⟶ *9mal* ⟶ *'i9mal!*
     tastá9mil (= use) ⟶ *sta9mil* ⟶ *istá9mil!*

(*c*) If the vowel of the imperfect is *u*, then the prefixed helping vowel may be *u* instead of *i* (dialectal variants exist):

e.g. *tádrus* (you study) ⟶ *drus* ⟶ *'údrus!*

(*d*) The student will already have noticed the rather odd imperatives *haat* (=bring!) and *ta9aál!* (= come!), which have no obvious verb as their origin.

(*e*) There follow a few more sample imperatives chosen (with occasional notes) from verbs that have already appeared in the course:

Perfect	Imperfect	Imperative
shárib (= drink)	*yáshrab*	*'íshrab!*
HaTT (= put)	*yaHúTT*	*HuTT!*
Háka (= speak)	*yáHki*	*'íHki!*
nísi (= forget)	*yánsa*	*'ínsa!*
qaal (= say)	*yaquúl*	*quul!*
qáddam (= present)	*yuqáddim*	*qáddim!*
'áfTar (= breakfast)	*yúfTir*	*'áfTir!*

(N.B. imperatives of 4th form verbs like *'áfTar* may begin with *'a*)

123

'ákal (= eat)	*yaákul*	*kul!*
'áxadh (= take)	*yaáxudh*	*xudh!*
wáSal (= arrive)	*yuúSal*	*'uúSal!*

(N.B. imperatives of verbs beginning with *w* follow the example of *wáSal*)

The student should use the above list as an exercise, covering up the imperatives column while deriving the correct imperative from the imperfects.

2. Negative Commands

A prohibition is formed with the ordinary imperfect negated by *la* (or sometimes *ma*):

e.g. *la tasta9mílha* = don't use it!
la táshrabi = don't drink (to a woman)
la tujaáwibu = don't answer! (to two or more)

3. Reported Commands

Sentences such as "I told him to go" are rendered by the verb of ordering + an ordinary imperfect without *b*-:

e.g. *qult luh yaruúH* = I told him to go.
qaálat lii 'aruúH = she told me to go.

4. Nouns of Place and Instrument

(*a*) Nouns beginning with *ma-* often indicate the place where the activity designated by the root is carried on:

e.g. *mádrasa* (= school) – "a place of study" from *dáras* = to study.
máktab (= office) – "a place of writing" from *kátab* = to write.
máT9am (= restaurant) – "a place of eating" (*Ta9aám* = food)
máTbax (= kitchen) – "a place of cooking" from *Tábax* = to cook.

(*b*) Nouns beginning with *mi-* often indicate the instrument:

e.g. *míknasa* (= broom) from *kánnas* = to sweep
miizaán (= scales) from *wázan* = to weigh

(*c*) The names of many machines are given names on the *fa99aála* pattern:

124

e.g. *thallaája* (= refrigerator) – "that which makes *thalj* (= ice)".
barraáda (= refrigerator) – "that which creates *bard* (= cold)".
ghassaála (= washing machine) – from *ghással* (= to wash)

Exercises

1. Translate into Arabic (answers at the end of the chapter).

(*a*) Drive me to the Ministry of Communications!

(*b*) Take a bath before you leave the house!

(*c*) Put your new clothes on and don't forget the money!

(*d*) Don't eat now! We'll have dinner at Ahmed's house (to a woman).

(*e*) Come in! Sit down (*'istariiHu*)! What would you like to drink? (speaking to several)

(*f*) Go to the post-office and buy some stamps for me!

(*g*) Drive the car to the garage and ask the director about repairing it!

(*h*) I told the servant to clean the house and to wash the windows.

(*i*) Unfortunately, the washing machine has broken down. They must repair it.

(*j*) Bring me a cup of coffee and put it on the table!

2. Answer the questions below in accordance with the model.

laázim 'anáDDif al-bayt kúlluh? (Must I clean the whole house?)	*ma9luúm? wa náDDifuh kuwáyyis!* (Certainly! and clean it well!)
laázim 'aghássil ash-shabaabiik?	*ma9luúm wa ghassílha kuwáyyis!*
laázim 'akánnis ghúraf an-nawm?	*ma9luúm! wa kannis-ha kuwáyyis!*
laázim 'aghássil aS-SuHuún?	*ma9luúm! wa ghassílha kuwáyyis!*
laázim 'asáwwi l-fúrush?	*ma9luúm! wa sawwiíha kuwáyyis!*
laázim 'aHáDDir aT-Taáwila?	*ma9luúm! wa HaDDírha kuwáyyis!*

– Now give the answers in the feminine e.g. *naDDifiíh, ghassiliíha* etc. Note the lengthening of the final vowel before an object pronoun.

– Now change question and answer to the plural:

e.g. *laázim nughássil ash-shabaabiik?* – *ma9luúm, ghassiluúha kuwáyyis!*

You should again note the lengthening of the final vowels before the object pronouns.

3. Answer the questions below in accordance with the model.

laázim 'áktub al-maktuúb al-yawm?	*la, la táktubuh l-yawm, 'úktubuh búkra!*
(Do I have to write the letter today?)	(No, don't write it today, write it tomorrow!)
laázim 'akállim 'áHmad 'al-yawm?	*la, la tukállimuh l-yawm, kállimuh búkra!*
laázim 'aSálliH ath-thallaája l-yawm?	*la, . . .*
laázim 'akánnis ghúrfat aT-Ta9aám al-yawm?	*la, . . .*
laázim 'ajiíb as-sagaáyir al-yawm?	*la, . . .*

– Now give the answers in the feminine e.g. *la, la taktubiíh l-yawm, 'uktubiíh búkra!* etc. Note the lengthening of final vowels.

– Now put questions and answers into the plural:

e.g. *laázim nukállim 'áHmad al-yawm? – la, la tukallimuúh l-yawm, kallimuúh bukra!*

4. Translate the following short phrases into Arabic (answers at the end of the lesson).

Pay the money! – Weigh the parcel! – Sign the cheque! – Send the telegram! – Buy this car! – Go into the house! – Sit down! – Read the letter, please! – Get dressed! – Dictate the letters! – Stand up! – Come back in an hour! – Eat the bread! – Put the book down! – Make the beds! – Count the buildings! – Learn English! – Tell me what you have learned!

– Repeat the exercise giving feminine and plural forms.

– Then give negative commands e.g. *la tádfa9 al-fuluús!*

Answers

1. (*a*) waSSílnii 'íla wizaárat al-muwaaSalaát!

(*b*) taHámmam qabl ma tátruk al-bayt!/xudh Hammaám . . .!

(*c*) 'ílbas thiyaábak al-jadiída wa la tánsa l-fuluús!

(*d*) la taákuli hallaq! raH nata9áshsha 9ind 'áHmad.

(*e*) tafáDDalu! 'istariíHu! shuu bitriídu táshrabu?

(*f*) ruuH li (máktab) l-bariíd w-ishtári lii Tawaábi9.

(*g*) suuq as-sayyaára lil-karaáj wa 'is'al al-mudiír 9an taSliíHha!

(*h*) qult lil-xaádim yunáDDif al-bayt wa yughássil ash-shabaabiík.

126

(i) li suu' al-HaZZ, 'al-ghassaála xarbaána. laázim yuSalli-Huúha.

(j) jiib/haat lii finjaán qáhwa wa HúTTuh 9ála T-Taáwila!

4. 'ídfa9/i/u l-fuluús! – 'uúzin aT-Tard! – 'ámDi sh-shakk! (4th form verb) – 'ársil al-barqíyya! (4th form verb) – 'ishtári has-sayyaára! – 'údxul al-bayt! – 'istariíH!/'íjlis! – 'íqra l-maktuúb/ r-risaála, min fáDlak! – 'ílbas malaábisak! – 'ámli l-makaatiíb! – r-rasaá'il! – quum! – 'írja9 bi saá9a! – kul al-xubz! – Hutt al-kitaáb! – sáwwi l-fúrush – 9udd al-binaayaát-ta9állam 'ingliízi! – quul lii shuu ta9allámt!

SEVENTEENTH LESSON – *'ad-dars raqm saba9tá9sh*

SHOPPING FOR FOOD

Buying Vegetables

(John goes to the market and buys vegetables and meat)

John:
SabaáH al-xayr, ya 'ábu bakr.

Good morning, Abu Bakr.

'ábu bakr:
SabaáH an-nuur, ya místir John. kayf al-Haal?

Good morning, Mr John. How are you?

John:
kuwáyyis, 'al-Hámdu líllaah. wa kayf Haálak, 'ínta?

Well, praise be to God. And how are you?

'ábu bakr:
náshkur 'állaah, bi-xayr.

We thank God, well.

John:
laazímnii l-yawm malfuúf wa baTaáTa.

I need today cabbages and potatoes.

'ábu bakr:
kam malfuúfa bitriíd?

How many cabbages do you want?

John:
malfuuftáyn kibaár wa tha-laáth kiílu baTaáTa.

Two big cabbages and three kilos of potatoes.

127

'ábu bakr:
bitriíd shii thaáni?

Do you want anything else?

John:
'a9Tiínii min fáDlak kii-
luwáyn ruzz.

Give me please two kilos of rice.

'ábu bakr:
tíkram.

With pleasure.

John:
shúkran, kam bitriíd mínnii?

Thank you. How much do you want from me?

'ábu bakr:
thalaáth danaaniír.

Three dinars.

At the butcher's – *fi dukkaán al-laHHaám* (*qaSSaáb* in Iraq and Gulf *jazzaár* in Egypt)

John:
'as-salaámu 9aláykum.

Peace be upon you.

'al-laHHaám:
wa 9aláykum as-salaám.
ná9am, ya 'ustaádh, shuu
bitriíd?

And on you be peace. Yes, sir, what would you like?

John:
shuu 9índak kuwáyyis al-
yawm?

What do you have today that's good?

'al-laHHaám:
9índna laHm min muxtálif
al-'anwaá9. kúlluh Taáza
jíddan. shuu bitfáDDil?
laHm xaruúf, laHm
báqar . . ?

We have meat of various kinds. All of them very fresh. What do you prefer? Lamb, beef . . ?

John:
baáxudh nuSS kiílu laHm
9íjil, nuSS kiílu laHm xaruúf biduún shaHm.

I'll take a half kilo of veal, a half kilo of lamb without fat.

'al-laHHaám:
tafáDDal, ya 'ustaádh.

Here you are, sir.

128

John:
qaddáysh bíddak mínnii?

How much do you want from me?

'al-laHHaám:
xams danaaniír.

Five dinars.

John:
haádhi wáraqat 9ishriín
diinaár.

Here's a twenty dinar note.

'al-laHHaám:
wa tafáDDal xamastá9shar
diinaár kamaála.

And I give you fifteen dinars change.

In the market – *'al-mufaáSala* (= bargaining)

(John is buying a carved chest. He bargains with the shop-keeper = *SaáHib ad-dukkaán*)

John:
haádha S-Sanduúq al-
manquúsh jamiil kathiír.
qaddáysh Háqquh?

This carved chest is very beautiful. How much is it?

SaáHib ad-dukkaán:
miit diinaár bass.

100 dinars only.

John:
la, haádha ghaáli kathiír.
shuft Sanaadiíq míthluh wa
sí9rha 'árxaS bi kathiír.

No, that's very expensive. I have seen chests like it and their prices were much lower.

SaáHib ad-dukkaán:
bijuúz, fii Sanaadiíq 'árxaS
bi shwayy laákin haS-
Sanduúq 'ákbar wa 'ájmal
min al-9aáda.

Maybe, there are chests a little cheaper, but this chest is bigger and more beautiful than the usual.

John:
wa 'ídha 'a9Táytak sab9iin
diinaár?

And if I give you 70 dinars?

SaáHib ad-dukkaán:
mush múmkin! laákin
9ashaának baáxudh
mínnak thamaaniín bass.

Not possible! But for you I'll take from you only 80.

John:
'ittafáqna, baáxudhuh bi has-
si9r.

We have agreed, I'll take it at this price.

Vocabulary

laazímnii: *I need* (laázimak = *you need etc.*).

malfuúfa: one *cabbage* (malfuúf = *cabbages in general*).

baTaáTa: *potato* (*singly or in general*).

dukkaán *pl.* dakaakiin: *shop* (*feminine word!*).

laHHaám (-iin): *butcher* (*or welder*). *The fa99aál word structure often indicates someone who works with what is denoted by the root.*

laHm *pl.* luHuúm: *meat.*

muxtálif: *different, various.*

naw9 *pl.* 'anwaá9: *kind, sort.*

Taáza: *fresh* (*invariable adjective*).

laHm xaruúf: *lamb* (laHm ghánam = *mutton*, laHm báqar = *beef*, laHm 9íjil = *veal*, laHm jámal = *camel meat*, laHm xanziír = *pork – usually unobtainable because abominated by Muslims*).

biduún: *without.*

shaHm: *fat* (biduún shaHm = *lean*).

wáraqa: *banknote* (*also "piece of paper"*).

mufaáSala/fiSaál: *bargaining* (*verbal nouns from faáSal (yufaáSil/bifaáSil)*).

musaáwama: *bargaining* (*the verb is* saáwam *someone* 9ála . . .).

e.g. saáwam/faáSal SaáHib ad-dukkaán 9ála S-Sanduúq = *he bargained with the shopkeeper over the chest.*

Sanduúq *pl.* Sanaadiíq: *box, chest, fund.*

manquúsh: *carved* (*a passive participle*).

si9r *pl.* 'as9aár: *price.*

'árxaS: *cheaper* (*from* raxiiS = *cheap*).

9aáda *pl.* 9aadaát: *habit, custom.*

'idha 'a9Táyt . . .: *If I give . . .* (*it is usual to use the perfect after* 'idha *in a conditional clause*).

9ashaának: *for you.*

'ittafáqna: *we have agreed* (*from* 'ittáfaq (yattáfiq/byattáfiq) = *to agree i.e. two parties agreeing between themselves.*

Notes on Grammar and Usage

1. Collectives

In the first dialogue we had the example of the Arabic word for "cabbage" being used first in its "collective" form (*malfuúf*) and then in its "unit" form (*malfuúfa*). The same system operates for many animals, vegetables, fruits, plants and material objects. In Lesson 14 the word *shájara* (a tree) occurred together with some notes on its use:

130

e.g. *shájara* (= a tree)	*shájar* (= trees in general – the word is the "collective")
shajaraát ("trees" – when counted)	*'ashjaár* (= trees – when several varieties are there)
báyDa (= an egg)	*bayD* (= eggs in general)
wáraqa (= a piece of paper)	*wáraq* (= paper in general)

Despite the fact that the English translation of an Arabic collective may be plural (*shájar* = trees), most Arabic collectives are grammatically singular:

e.g. *'al-malfuúf ghaáli l-yawm* = cabbages are dear today.

2. Arab Currencies
In Lesson 15 the *liíra* was used. This is the monetary unit used in the Lebanon and Syria. It is divided into 100 piastres (= *qirsh* pl. *quruúsh*).

The Egyptian pound is called the *junáyh* pl. *junayhaát* (c.f. "guinea") divided into 100 piastres (= *qirsh*). The thousandth part of the pound is called *maliím* pl. *malaaliím*.

The *diinaár* pl. *danaaniír* is used in Iraq, Jordan, Kuwait, Bahrein, and the People's Democratic Republic of Yemen. The *diinaár* is divided into 100 *fils* pl. *fuluús*. The unit's value depends on the country.

The *riyaál* pl. *riyaalaát* is used in Saudi-Arabia, Qatar, Oman and the Yemen Arab Republic.

The U.A.E. currency is the *dírham* pl. *daraáhim*.

Note: the pound sterling is *'al-junáyh al-'isterliíni*. The dollar is *duulaár* pl. *duulaaraát*

3. Weights and Measures

The metric system is understood over most of the Arab World. However, one may occasionally find weights such as:

'uqíyya = 200 grams
raTl pl. *'arTaál* = 1 pound (in Egypt), about 3 kgs (in Syria), 2½ kgs (in Beirut)

The metric units closely resemble their pronunciation in English or (still better) French. Their plurals are formed by adding *-aat*:

e.g. *litr* (= litre) pl. *litraát*   *graam* pl. *graamaát*

131

4. The Days of the Week
Most of these are based on the numerals:

e.g. (*yawm*) al-'áHad	– Sunday ('*áHad* is a variant of *waáHid*)
(*yawm*) al-'ithnáyn	– Monday ("day 2")
(*yawm*) ath-thalaátha	– Tuesday
(*yawm*) al-'árba9a	– Wednesday
(*yawm*) al-xamiis	– Thursday
(*yawm*) al-júm9a	– Friday ("day of assembly")
(*yawm*) as-sabt	– Saturday ("The Sabbath")

5. The Months of the Year
A full list of these is given in Appendix C.

Exercises

1. *Translate the following into Arabic* (the answers are at the end of the lesson) – consult the glossary for words not known.

(*a*) Give me, please, 3 kilos of tomatoes, 2 kilos of apples and ½ kilo of olives.

(*b*) I want 10 litres of petrol, please (petrol = *banziin*).

(*c*) My village is 3 kilometres from the city. (*btáb9ud 9an . . .*)

(*d*) He haggled with the shop owner about a chair.

(*e*) Are the prices of vegetables high or low? (*ghaáli – raxiiS*)

2. Translate the key question into Arabic. Insert the suggested vocabulary items into the question frame-work. You will have to use the glossary.

How much are eggs today?	*qaddáysh Haqq al-bayD al-yawm?*
+ tomatoes/cabbages/olives/ dates/fish/meat	
How much was cheese yesterday?	*qaddáysh Haqq al-júbna 'umbaariH?*
+ bread/butter/coffee/oil/salt/ sugar	

3.

We need a lot of potatoes every week.	*laazímna baTaáTa kathiir kull 'usbuú9.*
+ I/you (m.s., f.s., pl.)/she/ they	
+ rice/fish/beef/lamb/eggs/ sausages	

4.

I may see him tomorrow	*bijuúz 'ashuúfuh búkra.*
+ you/he/they/we/she	*bijuúz tashuúfuh búkra.*
+ her/them/us/you	
+ next week (= *fil-'usbuú9 al-jaay*)	
– Use *múmkin, yúmkin* & *rúbbama* as variants for *bijuúz*.	
– Past – yesterday/last week	*bijuúz shúftuh 'ams (fil-'usbuú9 al-maáDí)*

5.

I'll speak to him on Sunday.	*'nakállimuh yawm al-'áHad.*
+ other days of the week	

6.

We're going to the cinema with them on – (days of the week)	*minruúH má9hum lis-siínama yawm ...*

7.

Has he asked you for money?	*Tálab mínnak fuluús?*
Never give him any money!	*la ta9Tíih fuluús 'ábadan!*
+ books/a drink/food/fruit	
– substitute she and they in the sentences.	

Answers

1. (*a*) 'a9Tiínii min fáDlak thalaátha kiílu tamaáTim, kiiluwáyn tuffaáH wa nuSS kiílu zaytuún (*tomatoes* = banadáwra *in Greater Syria*).

(*b*) bíddii 9áshar litraát banziín min fáDlak.

(*c*) qáryatii btab9ud thalaáth kilumetraát 9an al-madiína.

(*d*) saáwam/faáSal Saáhib ad-dukkaán 9ála kúrsi.

(*e*) 'as9aár al-xaDrawaát ghaáliya willa raxiiSa?

EIGHTEENTH LESSON – *'ad-dars raqm thamaantá9sh*
ON THE TELEPHONE

(John rings a high official in the Ministry of Planning = *wizaárat at-taSmiím*)

Voice:

'aló	*Hallo.*

John:

'akállim wizaárat at-taSmiim?	*Am I speaking to the Ministry of Planning?*

133

Voice:
la, haádha raqm ghálaT.   *No, this is a wrong number.*
(J. biHaáwil márra thaánya = *John tries again*)

Voice:
'aló   *Hallo:*

John:
wizaárat at-taSmiím?   *The Ministry of Planning?*

Voice:
ná9am, ya 'ustaádh. miin   *Yes, sir, whom would you like?*
bítriid?

John:
bíddii 'atkállam ma9 as-   *I want to speak to (Mr) Khalil*
sáyyid xaliíl 9abd as-   *Abdusalaam, director of the*
salaám, mudiír al-qism al-   *section dealing with roads.*
muhtámm bi T-Túruq.

Voice:
miin byatkállam?   *Who's speaking?*

John:
'ísmii John Smith wa 'ána   *My name is John Smith and I'm*
mumáththil shárikat binaá'   *the representative of a British*
briiTaaníyya.   *building company.*

Voice:
xalliik 9ala l-xaTT, min   *Hold the line, please, I'll connect*
faDlak. raH 'a9Tiik   *you with the secretary of (Mr)*
sekritayr al-'ustaádh 9abd   *Abdusalaam.*
as-salaám.

('as-sekritáyr byitkállam = *the secretary speaks*)

Secretary:
ya místir Smith. ma9 al-'ásaf,   *Mr Smith . . . I'm sorry but the*
al-mudiír mashghuúl   *director is very busy this morn-*
kathiír haS-SabaáH. bítriid   *ing. Do you want an appoint-*
máw9id ma9uh?   *ment with him?*

John:
'áywa, ba9d aD-Dúhur, 'ídha   *Yes, this afternoon, if possible.*
múmkin.

134

Secretary:

muta'ássif, ba9d aD-Dúhur mush múmkin li'ánnuh mush mawjuúd fil-máktab ba9d aD-Dúhur

I'm sorry. The afternoon is not possible because he's not in the office this afternoon.

John:

yúmkin búkra?

Is it possible tomorrow?

Secretary:

'idha jiit lil-wizaára s-saá9a tis9a wa nuSS aS-SubH btíqdar tashuúf al-mudiír.

If you come to the Ministry at half past nine in the morning, you can see the director.

(John Smith wants to arrange a meeting with a local contractor = *J. S. biriíd yá9mal máw9id ma9 muqaáwil maHálli* He rings the contractor = *bitalfin lil-muqaawil*)

John:

'aló. 'ísmii John Smith. múmkin 'áHki ma9 al-'ustaádh záki?

Hallo. My name is John Smith. Can I speak with (Mr) Zaki?

Voice:

mush mawjuúd al-yawm. tálfin márra thaánya búkra 'aw ba9d búkra.

He's not here today. Ring again tomorrow or the day after tomorrow.

John:

'ana musaáfir búkra ba9d aD-Dúhur. múmkin 'átruk luh risaála? ...

I'm travelling tomorrow afternoon. Can I leave him a message? ...

quul luh, 'ídha qadárt 'ashuúfuh búkra aS-SubH, mnáqdir námDi l-kuntraátu. laákin 'ídha ma qadárna nataqaábal búkra, laázim nátruk al-'ámr li múddat shahr wa nuSS Hátta 'ají márra thaánya lil-bilaád. mafhuúm?

Tell him, if I can see him tomorrow morning, we can sign the contract. But if we can't meet tomorrow, we'll have to leave the matter for a month and a half until I come to the country again. Understood?

Voice:

mafhuúm. quul lii min fáDlak raqm talfáwnak. raH 'aquúl lil-'ustaádh záki yattáSil biik, bi 'ásra9 ma yúmkin.

Understood. Tell me please your telephone number. I'll tell (Mr) Zaki to get in touch with you as quickly as possible.

135

John:
    númrat talfáwnii . . .   *My telephone number is . . .*

Vocabulary

raqm *pl.* 'arqaám: *number, numeral (also* númra).
ghálaT *pl.* 'aghlaáT: *mistake.*
biHaáwil: *he tries (from* Haáwal (yuHaáwil/biHaáwil) = *to try.*)
'ustaádh *pl.* 'asaátidha: *professor, teacher, polite form of address.*
'áqdar: *I can (from* qádar (yáqdar/byáqdar) = *to be able.*)
qism *pl.* 'aqsaám: *section, part.*
muhtámm (bi): *concerned (with).*
Tariíq *pl.* Túruq *or* Turuqaát: *road.*
mumáththil (-iín): *representative (also "actor").*
binaá': *building (the process – verbal noun from* bána (yábni/ byábni) = *to build).*
xaTT *pl.* xuTuúT: *line (also airline).*
máw9id *pl.* mawaá9id: *appointment.*
mawjuúd: *present, in existence, to be found (from* wájad = *to find).*
muqaáwil (-iín): *contractor.*
bitálfin (li): *ring/phone someone (from* tálfan (yutálfin/bitálfin). = *to telephone. Note there are 4 root consonants in* tálfan. *"Quadriliteral" verbs of this kind behave like 2nd form verbs – see Lesson 20).*
musaáfir (-iín): *travelling (from* saáfar (yusaáfir/bisaáfir) = *to travel.*)
kuntraátu *pl.* kuntraataát: *contract.*
nataqaábal: *we meet (one another) (from* taqaábal (yataqaábal/ byatqaábal) = *to meet (one another).*)
'amr *pl.* 'umuúr: *matter (with the plural* 'awaámir, 'amr = *order, command).*
raqm/númrat talfáwnak: *your telephone number (note how the possessive goes on the last element –* ghúrfat náwmii = *my bedroom).*
yattáSil (bi): *he gets in touch (with) (from* 'ittáSal (yattáSil/bittáSil) = *to get in touch (bi = with)).*
'ásra9: *faster (comparative from* sarií9 = *fast).*
bi-'ásra9 ma yúmkin: *as fast as possible (also* bi-'á9la ma yúmkin = *as high as possible etc.*).

Questions on the Dialogues

1. J. bitálfin li 'ayy wizaára?   bitálfin li wizaárat at-taSmiím.
2. bídduh yukállim miin?   bídduh yukállim as-sáyyid xaliíl
                                                        9abd as-salaam.

3. 'as-sáyyid xaliíl 9abd as-salaám mudiír 'ayy qism. húwa mudiír al-qism al-muhtámm biT-Túruq.
4. shárikat J. min 'ayy naw9? hiya shárikat binaá'.
5. 'al-mudiír faáDi (= free) l-yawm wílla mashghuúl? húwa mashghuúl.
6. múmkin yaáxudh/yá9mal máw9id ba9d aD-Dúhur? la, mush múmkin.
7. laysh la? (= *why not?*) húwa mush mawjuúd fil-máktab.
8. múmkin búkra? ná9am, máw9id múmkin búkra.
9. fi 'ayy saá9a? 'as-saá9a tís9a wa nuSS aS-SubH.
10. la miin bitálfin J.? bitálfin li muqaáwil.
11. shuu 'ism al-muqaáwil? 'ísmuh l-'ustaàdh záki.
12. 'al-'ustaádh záki mawjuúd? la, húwa mush mawjuúd.
13. 'idha qádar J. yashuúf al-muqaáwil búkra aS-SubH, shuu yúmkin yá9malu? 'idha qádaru yataqaábalu, yúmkin yámDu l-kuntraátu.
14. wa 'idha ma qádaru yataqaábalu? 'idha ma qádaru yataqaábalu, laázim yátruku l-'amr li múddat shahr wa nuSS.

Notes on Grammar and Usage

1. Conditional Sentences

(a) There are three words in Arabic to translate "if". They are *'idha, 'in* and *law*, but *'in* is rather rare except in the expression *'in shaa' 'allaáh* = if God wills, which must be used when speaking of future plans. *'in* follows the rules for *'idha*. Some examples:

(i) *'idha qadárna nataqaábal al-yawm, raH námDi l-kuntraátu* = if we are able to meet today, we shall sign the contract.

Notes: It is usual for a verb following *'idha* to be in the perfect. It is possible to have no verb after *'idha* – e.g. *'idha múmkin* = if possible, *'idha fii 9índak* = if you have any, etc.

(ii) *'idha 'ájat 'umbaáriH, 'ána ma shúftha* = if she came yesterday, I didn't see her.

Notes: Here, some doubt is being thrown on a past event. The pastness of the condition is made clear by the adverb *'umbaáriH* and the perfect tense occurring in the second clause. The tense of the verb in the "result" clause (*jawaáb* (= answer) in Arabic) is that required by the sense (compare example (i)).

137

(iii) *law qadárna nataqaábal al-yawm, kúnna námDi l-kuntraátu* = if we were able to meet today, we would sign the contract.

Notes: This condition is less likely to be fulfilled than (i). The difference is carried in English by the use of a past tense in the conditional clause, in Arabic by the use of *law*. Note too that the appropriate part of *kaan* is usual in the result clause e.g. *kúnna* in (iii).

(iv) *law qadárna nataqaábal, kúnna 'amDáyna l-kuntraátu* = if we had been able to meet, we would have signed the contract.

Notes: This is a condition that was not fulfilled. The difference between (iii) (unlikely) and (iv) (impossible) is conveyed in Arabic by the substitution of the perfect *'amDáyna* for the imperfect *námDi*. It is essential to use the appropriate part of *kaan* with the main verb in the result clause – e.g. *kúnna* + *'amDáyna*.

Conclusions: 'idha is used where the condition is of possible fulfilment, *law* where this is unlikely or impossible.

(*b*) The negative of conditions is formed with *ma*:

e.g. *'idha ma kaan mawjuúd, HuTT 9alaáma* (= mark) *quddaám 'ismuh* = if he's not present, put a mark before his name.

(*c*) *even if* = *Hátta 'idha*:

e.g. *ma biruúH má9ak Hátta 'idha dafá9t luh miit diinaár* = he won't go with you even if you pay him 100 dinars.

even if = *Hátta wa law* (in unlikely or impossible conditions):

e.g. *ma kaan birúuH má9ak Hátta wa law kunt dafá9t luh miit diinaár*. he wouldn't have gone with you even if you had paid him 100 dinars.

unless = *'illa 'idha*:

e.g. *raH 'akállim al-mudiir 'illa 'idha btashtághil 'áHsan* = I'll speak to the director unless you work better.

2. Other Types of Conditions

(*a*) *láwla* (*law* + *la*) = but for, were it not for, had it not been for:

e.g. *láwla 'áHmad kunt saafárt 'ila nyuu yurk* = if it had not been for Ahmed, I would have gone to New York.

138

lawlaáhum kúnna saakniin hállaq fi baariis = were it not for them we would be living now in Paris.

(b) *ya rayt* = would that, I (etc.) wish, if only . . . It is followed by the perfect when referring to the past and the imperfect when referring to the present. Like *láwla, ya rayt* is followed by a noun or a pronoun:

e.g. *ya ráytak tashuúf báytna fi bayruút* = I wish you could see our house in Beirut!
ya rayt 'áHmad kaan húna 'umbaáriH = if only Ahmed had been here yesterday!

(c) Expressions like *kúllma* (= whenever), *máhma* (= whatever), *miin ma* (= whoever), *wayn (fayn) ma* (= wherever), *kayf ma* (= however) may be followed by a perfect tense referring to present or future time, just as in more orthodox conditionals:

e.g. *laazímnii bayt wayn ma kaan yakuún* = I need a house wherever it may be.
máhma qult 'ínta, raH naruúH = whatever you say, we shall go.

Note: kúllma is used (+ imperfect) for "the more . . . the more"

e.g. *kúllma byádrus al-lúgha, kúllma byáfham 'ákthar* = the more he studies the language, the more he understands.

3. Compound Tenses
Occasional examples have already occurred of compound tenses formed with *kaan* + other verb forms. Here is a complete list:

Perfect + Perfect = Pluperfect
kaan   'ája   = he had come
Perfect + Imperfect = Past Continuous
kaan (9am)yashtághil = he was working/he used to work

N.B. *9am* emphasises the continuous nature of the imperfect.

Imperfect + Imperfect   = Future Continuous
bikuún   yáskun húna = he will be living here
Imperfect + Perfect   = Future Perfect
bikuún   kátab maktuúb = he will have written a letter

139

Exercises

1. Translate into Arabic (answers at the end of the lesson)

(*a*) I want to speak to the director. Is he in his office today?

(*b*) No, he has gone on a journey, but hold the line please, I'll connect you with his secretary.

(*c*) I've had interviews with the representatives of all the companies.

(*d*) If I can see you this afternoon (today afternoon) we can talk about the contract.

(*e*) If I could have seen you yesterday, we could have talked about the contract.

(*f*) What's his telephone number? Thank you very much. Don't mention it.

(*g*) Is his bedroom on the 5th or 6th floor of this hotel?

(*h*) If we'd signed the contract, we would now be rich.

(*i*) Had it not been for him, we would have stayed at the Grand Hotel.

(*j*) We wish you had been here yesterday.

(*k*) Wherever you ask, the answer will be the same as ours.

2. Translate the key sentence into Arabic – then use *kaan* to make it past. Make the suggested variations.

I'm working in the middle of the city.	*'ána 9am 'ashtághil fi wasT al-madiina.*
past (+ you/he/she/we/they)	*'ana kunt 9am 'ashtághil fi wasT al-madiina.*
He's bargaining with the shop-keeper	*húwa 9am yatasaáwam ma9 SaáHib ad-dukkaán.*
past (+ she/I/we/they/you)	*húwa kaan yatasaáwam ma9 SaáHib ad-dukkaán.*

3. Translate the key sentence into Arabic – then use the correct form of *kaan* to make the pluperfect (had . . .). Change the persons of the verb. Only one *kaan* is required per sentence to make all perfects pluperfect.

He came to the house and spoke with me	*'ája 9al-bayt wa Háka má9ii.*
pluperfect (+ she/you/they)	*kaan 'ája 9al-bayt wa Háka má9ii*
We went to Baghdaad in the summer (= *Sayf*)	*rúHna li baghdaád fiS-Sayf.*
pluperfect (+ they/you/he etc.)	*kúnna rúHna li baghdaád fiS-Sayf.*

140

4. Translate the key sentences into Arabic, then make the suggested modifications.

(a) If I read all these books, I'll learn a great deal.
'idha qaráyt kull hal-kútub, raH 'ata9állam kathiír.

\+ he/she/we/they

→If I read all these books, I would learn a great deal.
law qaráyt kull hal-kútub, kunt bat9állam kathiír.

\+ he/she/we/they

→If I had read all these books, I would have learnt a great deal.
law (kunt) qaráyt kull hal-kútub, kunt ta9allámt kathiír.

(b) If you enter the house, you'll see my father.
'idha daxált al-bayt, raH tashuúf 'abuúy.

\+ he/we/they

→If you entered the house, you would see my father.
law daxált al-bayt, kunt bitshuúf 'abuuy.

\+ he/we/they

– ›If you had entered the house, you would have seen my father.
law (kunt) daxált al-bayt, kunt shuft 'abuúy.

(c) If they do not eat too much, they will not be ill.
'idha ma 'ákalu 'ákthar min al-laázim, ma biSiiru mariiDiín.

\+ he/she/you

→If they did not eat too much, they would not be ill.
law ma 'ákalu 'ákthar min al-laázim, ma kaánu biSiiru mariiDiín.

\+ he/she/you

– ›If they had not eaten too much, they would not have been ill.
law ma (kaánu) 'ákalu 'ákthar min al-laázim, ma kaánu Saáru mariidiín.

\+ he/she/you

Answers

1. (a) bíddii 'akállim al-mudiír. húwa mawjuúd fi máktabuh al-yawm?

(b) la, húwa musaáfir, laákin xalliík 9ála l-xaTT min fáDlak, raH 'a9Tiík sekritáyruh.

(c) kaan 9índii muqaabalaát ma9 al-mumaththiliín min kull ash-sharikaát.

(d) 'idha qadárt 'ashuúfak al-yawm ba9d aD-Dúhur, mnáqdar náHki 9an al-kuntraátu.

(e) law qadárt 'ashuúfak 'ams, kúnna qadárna náHki 9an al-kuntraátu.

141

(*f*) shuu raqm talfáwnuh? shúkran kathiír. 'al-9áfu.
(*g*) ghúrfat náwmuh fiT-Taábiq al-xaámis 'aw fiT-Taábiq as-saádis min hal-fúnduq?
(*h*) law 'amDáyna l-kuntraátu, kúnna hállaq 'aghniyaá'.
(*i*) lawlaáh, kúnna nazálna fil-fúnduq al-kabiír.
(*j*) ya ráytak kunt húna 'umbaáriH!
(*k*) wayn ma sa'ált, bikuún al-jawaáb mithl jawaábna.

NINETEENTH LESSON – *'ad-dars at-tis9atá9sh*
CONVERSATION AT A PARTY

(Conversation at a party. John has been introduced to Zaki)
(*Hadiíth xilaál Háfla. ta9árraf John 9ála záki*)

John:

tasharráfna.	*Pleased to meet you.*

záki:

'ash-sháraf lána. 'in shaa' 'allaáh HáDratak mabsuúT fi bilaádna.	*The honour is mine. I hope you are happy in our country.*

John:

kathiír mabsuúT.	*Very happy.*

záki:

kam Saar lak húna?	*How long have you been here?*

John:

Saar lii shahráyn wa nuSS fil-bilaád.	*I've been two and a half months in the country.*

záki:

HáDratak mutazáwwij?	*Are you married?*

John:

ná9am, záwjatii má9ii, híya waáqfa hunaák 9ind zaawiyat al-ghúrfa.	*Yes, my wife is with me, she's standing there in the corner of the room.*

záki:

záwjatak, kam Saar láha huna?	*How long has your wife been here?*

John:

búkra raH yakuún láha shahr.	*Tomorrow she will have been here a month.*

142

záki:
btíHki 9árabi miliíH. darást al-lúgha qabl ma jiit?

You speak Arabic well. Did you study the language before you came?

John:
maDDáyt sitt asaabií9 wa 'ána 'ádrus 9árabi qabl ma jiit. wa záwjatii kamaán btíqdar tíHki 9árabi.

I spent six months studying Arabic before I came. And my wife too can speak Arabic.

záki:
mumtaáz? kayf bitlaáqi báytak? munaásib?

Splendid! How do you find your house? O.K.?

John:
ná9am, bass ba9d ma waSált bi shwayy, Saar lii shii ghariib.

Yes, but a little after I arrived, something strange happened to me.

záki:
wálla. xayr 'in shaa' 'allaáh!

Heavens! I hope everything was all right.

John:
'a9Táyt al-9unwaán lis-sawwaáq, laákin lámma waSálna, ma kaan fii 'ayy bayt bi hal-9unwaán.

I gave the address to the driver, but when we arrived, there wasn't any house at this address.

záki:
ya salaám! 9ajiíb!

Good gracious! How strange!

John:
Sirt 'aftákir 'innii kunt 9am báHlum, laákin al-Hall basiíT. 'as-sawwaáq ma kaan yá9raf hal-Hayy wa kaan yastá9mil xariíTa bass kaan maasíkha bil-maqluúb. fa Saar al-junuúb badl ash-shimaál wa Dáyya9 Tariíquh.

I began to think that I was dreaming but the solution was easy. The driver did not know this quarter and was using a map but he was holding it upside down, the South changed places with the North and he lost his way.

záki:
'in shaa' 'allaáh laqáyt al-bayt fin-nihaáya.

I hope you found the house in the end.

143

John:
ma9 'innuh Dáyya9 waqt kathíir, ná9am, laqaynaáh. wa kúllma sakánna fiih akthar, kúllma Habbaynaáh 'ákthar.

Although he wasted a lot of time, yes, we found it. And the more we live in it, the more we like it.

záki:
mabruúk

Congratulations.

John:
'allaah yubaárik fiik.

Thank you.

Vocabulary

Hadiíth *pl.* 'aHaadiíth: *conversation.*

xilaál: *during, through.*

Háfla *pl.* Hafalaát: *party.*

ta9árraf: *has been introduced* (*from* ta9árraf (yata9árraf/ bit9árraf) = *to be introduced* (9ála = *to*).)

Saar: *see Notes on Grammar and Usage* (*from* Saar (yaSíir/ biSíir) – *become, happen, begin.*)

mutazáwwij (-iín): *married.*

záwja (-aát): *wife* (zawj *pl.* 'azwaáj = *husband*).

waáqif(a): *standing* (*the short* i *vowel is often dropped in both the feminine and the plural e.g.* waaqfíin).

zaáwiya *pl.* zawaáya: *corner.*

maDDáyt: *I spent* (*time*) (*from* máDDa (yumáDDi/bimáDDi) = *to spend* (*time*).)

mumtaáz: *excellent.*

bitlaáqi: *you find* (*from* láqa (yulaáqi/bilaáqi) = *to find.*)

munaásib: *suitable.*

wálla!: *by God* (wa + 'allaah).

'a9Táyt: *I gave* (*from* 'á9Ta (yá9Ti/byá9Ti) = *to give.*)

9unwaán *pl.* 9anaawíin: *address, title.*

sawwaáq (-iín): *driver.*

9ajiíb: *amazing.*

'aftákir: *I think* (*from* 'iftákar (yaftákir/biftákir) = *to think.*)

báHlum: *I dream* (*from* Hálam (yáHlum/byáHlum) = *to dream.*)

Hall *pl.* Huluúl: *solution.*

xariíTa *pl.* xaraá'iT: *map.*

maásik: *holding, grasping* (*from* másak (yámsik/byámsik) = *to hold.*)

bil-maqluúb: *upside down.*

144

junuúb: *South.*
badl: *instead of.*
Dáyya9: *he lost* (*from* Dáyya9 (yuDáyyi9/biDáyyi9) = *to lose.*)
laqáyt: *you found* (*from* láqa (yulaáqi/bilaáqi) = *to find.*)
ma9 'ínnuh: *although he.*
laqaynaáh: *we found it* (*note the stress shift to the last syllable because of the object pronoun*).
kúllma ... kúllma ...: *the more ... the more* (+ *perfect tense* – *to be hyper correct* – *or imperfect*).
mabruúk!: *congratulations!* – 'állaah yubaárik fiik (*answer*).

Questions on Dialogue.

1. kam Saar li J. fil-bilaád?

Saar luh shahráyn wa nuSS.

2. huwa mutzáwwij?

na9am, húwa mutzáwwij.

3. kam Saar li záwjatuh fil-bilaád?

búkra, raH yakuún li záwjatuh shahr fil-bilaád.

4. li 'ayy múdda J. dáras 9árabi qabl ma 'ája.

máDDa sitt asaabií9 wa húwa 9am byádrus 9árabi.

5. shuu Saar lámma raáHu ya-shuúfu bayt J.?

ma kaan fii 'ayy bayt bil-9unwaán.

6. laysh?

'as-sawwaáq másak al-xariíTa bil-maqluúb wa Dáyya9 Tariíquh.

7. 'al-bayt munaásib?

ná9am, wa kúllma sákanu fiih 'ákthar kúllma Habbuúh 'ákthar.

Notes on Grammar and Usage

1. The Auxiliary Verb *Saar*
   Saar is a verb with a number of important meanings:
   (*a*) "to happen" –
   e.g. *shuu Saar* (*lak*) = what happened (to you)?
   shuu 9am biSiir? = what is happening?
   (*b*) "to become" –
   e.g. *baSiir mariiD* = I am getting ill.
   Saárat mu9állima = she became a teacher.
   (*c*) "to begin" (+ verb in the imperfect – similar construction with '*áxadh* and '*áSbaH*) –
   e.g. *Sírna náktub* = we began to write.
   Saáru/'áxadhu/'áSbaHu yaákulu = they began to eat.

145

(d) "have been" –

e.g. *Saar lii yawmáyn húna* = I've been here two days.

kaan Saar lis-safíir sána fi bayruút = the ambassador had been a year in Beirut.

kaan Saar li muHámmad thalaáth siniín 9am yádrus 9árabi fi baghdaád Muhammad had been studying Arabic in Baghdad for a year.

Saar lii waáqif húna saa9táyn = I've been standing here for two hours.

2. "To owe" – this may be rendered by the prepositions *'il* or *li/la* + noun or pronoun indicating the creditor and *9ind, ma9* or *9ála* + noun or pronoun to indicate the debtor:

e.g. *'ilii 9indhum thalaáth danaaniír* = They owe me 3 dinars.

qaddáysh 'ilak má9ii? = How much do I owe you?

li muHámmad 9aláyya liíra = I owe Muhammad a pound.

3. "as/so long as" – this can be expressed by *Taálama* or *ma daam* (*ma* is not a negative here). Both may be followed by noun, pronoun or verb:

e.g. *Taálama 'áHmad byashtághil húna, laázim yashtághil kuwáyyis* = as long as Ahmed works here, he must work well.

Taálama 9am yáqra kitaáb, húwa mabsuúT = as long as he is reading a book, he is happy.

ma daam may be followed by object pronouns as attached to verbs:

e.g. *ma daámnii mashghuúl, la tutálfin lii fil-máktab* = so long as I am busy, do not ring me at the office.

4. "Still . . . not yet" – we have already used the word *lissa* in the expression *lissa bakkiír* (= it is still early). The word *ba9d* may also be used. Both words may bear object pronouns as attached to verbs:

e.g. *bá9dhum 9aa'ishiin fi baghdaád* = they are still living in Baghdad.

lissaánii fil-máktab = I am still in the office.

In negative sentences they have the meaning "not yet":

e.g. *lissaáhum ma 'áju* = they haven't come yet

or *ma 'áju lissa*

Note particularly:

'ája l-bariíd? (= has the post come?) – *lissa* (= not yet)

5. "in order to" – may be translated by *li*, *minshaán*, or *Hátta* + clause:

e.g. *jiit li 'ashuúfak* = I've come in order to see you.
ruHt 9al-bayt minshaán 'aákul = I went home to eat.
9amált ba9D ash-shughl Hátta 'asaá9dak = I did some of the work to help you.

6. "for, for the sake of, for the use of" – may be translated by *li* (*'il* before attached pronouns) and *minshaán*:

e.g. *hal-maktuúb lil-mudiir* = this letter is for the director.
ma 9índii waqt 'ílha = I don't have time for it.
fii barqíyya minshaán 'áhmad = there's a telegram for Ahmed.

Note: In Egypt, and sometimes elsewhere, *9ashaán/9alashaán* may be used instead of *minshaán*.

Exercises

1. Translate into Arabic. Answers are at the end of the lesson.
(*a*) How long have they been with the company?
(*b*) They have been with the company for six years.
(*c*) What's happening in the ministry? I don't know.
(*d*) I weighed the potatoes three hours ago.
(*e*) They've been staying at the hotel for a week.
(*f*) He owes me five dinars, but he does not want to pay.
(*g*) So long as he holds the map the wrong way up, he will never find the house.
(*h*) They started travelling this morning but have still not arrived.
(*i*) They phoned me to make an appointment with you.

2. Translate the key sentence, then make the suggested substitutions.

He became a teacher two years ago.	*Saar mu9állim qabl sanatáyn.*
+ she/you/they	*Saárat mu9állima . . .*
+ 6 months ago/4 weeks ago/3 etc. years ago.	*Saáru mu9allimiín . . .*

3.

What happened on Sunday?	*shuu Saar yawm al-'áHad?*
– Nothing happened on Sunday	*– ma Saar shii yawm al-'áHad.*
+ Monday/Tuesday/Wednesday etc.	

4. Translate the key sentence. Make the suggested substitutions. Use all the verbs you know that mean "begin".

They began to eat

+ I/you/she/we
+ drink/talk/wash/pay/dress/ read etc.

Saáru/ 'áxadhu/qaámu/ 'ibtádu/ 'áSbaHu yaákulu.

5.
I have been in Beirut for 4 days.

+ in Damascus/in Baghdad/in Cairo/ in Amman etc.
+ for 6 weeks/3 months/2 days etc.
+ you have been/he has been/ they etc.

Saar lii 'árba9t ayyaám fi bayruút.

6.
You owe me 3 dinars
+ 15 pounds/4 dinars/105 pounds . . .
+ he owes me/she . . ./they . . .
+ he owes them/. . . her/ . . .you etc.

'ilii 9aláyk thalaáth danaaniir
'ilii 9aláyk xamastá9shar junáyh.

7.
As long as he wants to go, let him go!
+ she/they
+ he wants to talk/bargain/ telephone
Substitute *ma daam* for Taalama

Taálama biriíd yaruúH, xalliih yaruúH!

ma daámuh biriíd yaruúH, xalliih yaruúH!

8.
As long as they are in Egypt, they can study Arabic.
+ we/he/she/you (all forms)
+ in Syria/Jordan/Saudi-Arabia/Kuwait/Bahrein/Iraq

ma daamhum fi maSr, byáqdaru yádrusu 9árabi.

N.B. Kuwait = *'al-kuwáyt*
Bahrein = *'al-baHráyn*

(Substitute *Taála ma* for *ma daam*) *Taala ma hum fi maSr . . .*

9.

They are still waiting for you	*bá9dum/lissaáhum bintaZiruúk.*
+ we are/he is/she is/I am	
+ for him/her/them/us etc.	

10.

| Have they arrived? Not yet. | *hum wáSalu? lissa.* |
| + has he/she/we/I | |

11.

| This house is for you | *hal-bayt minshaának/'ilak.* |
| + him/her/us/them/you (all forms) | |

12.

I went to the market to buy vegetables.	*ruHt 'ila s-suuq minshaán/ Hátta/li 'ashtári xaDrawaát.*
+ you/he/she/we/they	
+ fruit/meat/cigarettes etc.	

Answers

1. (*a*) kam Saar láhum fish-shárika?
   (*b*) Saar láhum sitt siniín fish-shárika.
   (*c*) shuu 9am biSiír fil-wizaára? – ma bá9rif.
   (*d*) wazánt al-baTaáTa qabl (or min) thalaáth saa9aát.
   (*e*) Saar láhum 'usbuú9 naazliín fil-fúnduq.
   (*f*) 'ilii 9aláyh/9índuh/má9uh xams danaaniír, bass/laákin ma bídduh yádfa9.
   (*g*) Taálama/ma daámuh byámsik al-xaáriTa/al-xariíTa bil-maqluúb, ma raaH yulaáqi l-bayt 'ábadan.
   (*h*) Saáru/'áxadhu/báda‘u yusaáfiru SabaáH al-yawm, bass/ laákin ma wáSalu lissa/ba9d.
   (*i*) tálfanu lii li/minshaán/Hátta yaáxudhu/yá9malu máw9id má9ak.

TWENTIETH LESSON – 'ad-dars al-9ishriín

GOING ON LEAVE

Narrative – *riwaáya*

| kull sána John bisaáfir li bilaáduh fi 'ijaáza. | *Every year, John travels to his country on leave.* |

149

'áwwal shii biráttib al-bayt wa biHáDDir 9áfshuh, ba9dáyn bisákkir al-bayt wa byárkab táksi lil-maTaár.

9ála marr as-siniín, 'al-maTaár Saar 'ákbar wa 'ákbar, wa hállaq fii Tayyaaraát kathiíra biTTiír li 'uruúpa wa 'ameérka wa 'aásiya.

laákin J. byitadhákkar kayf kaan al-maTaár Saghiír bi 'ayyaámuh wa ma kaan fii 'illa kam Tayyaára.

hállaq kull waáHid ta9áwwad 9ála r-rafaahíyya l-jadiída 'illi 'ájat ma9 al-baTráwl.

lámma btánzil aT-Tayyaára, J. biruúH lil-'amn al-9aamm wa biqáddim jawaáz sáfaruh.

wa ba9dáyn byárkab baaS ma9 baqíyyat ar-rukkaáb wa byaaxúdh-hum al-baaS liT-Tayyaára.

'as-sawwaáq biwáqqif al-baaS janb aT-Tayyaára wa byánzal ar-rukkaáb wa byáTla9u 9aT-Tayyaára.

ba9d as-sáfra, kull ar-rukkaáb biwaáfiqu 'inha kaánat muriíHa kathiír.

J. bídduh yazuúr 'awlaáduh al-'ithnáyn 'illi byádrusu fi mádrasa daaxilíyya li'án tarbiyáthum bit-hímmuh jíddan.

li Husn al-HaZZ 'áhluh byahtámmu bil-'awlaád fi ghiyaábuh wa bizuuruúhum bi 'intiZaám fil-mádrasa.

First of all, he arranges the house and prepares his luggage, then he closes the house and takes a taxi to the airport.

In the course of the years, the airport has become bigger and bigger and now there are many aeroplanes flying to Europe, America and Asia.

But J. remembers how small the airport was in the past and how there were only a few aircraft.

Now everyone has become accustomed to the new prosperity (luxury) which has come with the oil.

When the plane lands, J. goes to "Public Security" and presents his passport.

Then he gets on a bus with the rest of the passengers and the bus takes them to the plane.

The driver stops the bus near the plane, the passengers get off and board the aircraft.

After the journey, all the passengers agree that it was very comfortable.

J. wants to visit his two children who are studying in a boarding school because their upbringing concerns him greatly.

Fortunately, his family concern themselves with the children in his absence and visit them regularly in the school.

Vocabulary

bisaáfir: *he travels* (*from* saáfar (yusaáfir/bisaáfir) = *to travel*.)

'ijaáza (-aát): *leave, holiday*.

biráttib: *arrange, set in order* (*from* ráttab (yuráttib/biráttib) = *arrange*).

biHáDDir: *he prepares* (*from* HáDDar (yuHáDDir/ biHáDDir) = *to prepare*).

9afsh: *luggage, household effects, furniture*.

bisákkir: *he closes* (*from* sákkar (yusákkir/bisákkir) = *to close*).

maTaár (-aát): *airport*.

Tayyaára (-aát): *aircraft*.

biTTiír: (*she, it, they*) *fly* (*from* Taar (yaTiír/biTiír) = *to fly*).

byit(a)dhákkar: *he remembers* (*from* tadhákkar (yatadhákkar/ byit(a)dhákkar) = *to remember*.)

ma kaan fii 'illa: *there were only* . . .

kam: *a few* (*followed by singular – as with* kam? = *how much/many*).

ta9áwwad (9ála): *has got used* (*to*) (*from* ta9áwwad (yata9áwwad/ byit9áwwad) = *to become used* (9ála = *to*)).

rafaahíyya: *luxury, comfort, prosperity*.

baTráwl: *oil* (*other words are* nafT *and* zayt).

'amn: *security*.

9aamm: *public, general*.

jawaáz sáfar *pl.* jawaazaát sáfar: *passport* (*also* basbuur(-aat)).

baaS (-aát): *bus* (*also* baSS (-aát)).

baqíyya *pl.* baqaáya: *rest, remainder*.

raákib *pl.* rukkaáb: *passenger, rider*.

waqqaf: *he stopped* (*something*) (*from* wáqqaf (yuwáqqif/ biwáqqif) = *to stop* (*tr.*)).

byánzal ar-rukkaáb wa byáTla9u . . .: *when the verb precedes a plural subject, it may be in the singular, as is* byánzal *in this example*.

byáTla9u: *they board* (*from* Tála9 (yáTla9(byáTla9) = *board, climb, go away*).

sáfra (-aát): *journey*.

biwaáfiqu: *they agree* (*from* waáfaq (yuwaáfiq/biwaáfiq) = *to agree* – *agree to* = waáfaq 9ála, *but* 9ála *not necessary before* 'inn).

yazuúr: *he visits* (*from* zaar (yazuúr/bizuúr) = *to visit*).

'awlaáduh al-'ithnáyn: (*better than* waladáynuh).

tárbiya: *upbringing, education* (*verbal noun from* rábba).

bit-hímmuh: *it* (*f.*) *concerns him* (*from* 'ahámm (yuhímm/ bihímm) = *to concern*).

li Husn al-HaZZ: *fortunately* (*i.e. by the goodness of fortune*).

151

'áhluh: *his family* (*i.e. the nuclear family + relatives*). *The word is* 'ahl *pl.* 'aháali. (*the plural means "inhabitants" of an area*).

byahtámmu (bi): *they concern themselves* (*with*) (*from* 'ihtámm (yahtámm/byahtámm) = *to concern oneself* (bi = *with.*)

ghiyaáb: *absence.*

bi 'intiZaám: *regularly* (*i.e. with regularity*).

Questions

1. laysh J. bisaáfir kull sána li bilaáduh?
   bisaáfir fi 'ijaáza.

2. shuu byá9mal 'áwwal shii?
   biráttib al-bayt.

3. wa ba9dáyn?
   ba9dáyn, biHáDDir 9áfshuh, wa bisákkir al-bayt.

4. kayf biruúH lil-maTaár?
   biruúH bi táksi lil-maTaár.

5. shuu Saar bil-maTaár 9ála marr as-siniín? (*happened to*)
   'al-maTaár Saar 'ákbar wa 'ákbar.

6. shuu sábbab (= *caused*) rafaahíyyat al-bilaád?
   'al-baTráwl sábbab rafaahíyyat al-bilaád al-jadiída.

7. kaan fii Tayyaaraát kathiíra fil-maáDi?
   la, ma kaan fii 'ílla kam Tayyaára.

8. 'áymta J. biruúH lil-'amn al-9aamm?
   biruúH lil-'amn al-9aam lámma T-Tayyaára btánzal.

9. shuu biqáddim lil-'amn al-9aamm?
   biqáddim jawaáz sáfaruh.

10. kayf J. biruúH liT-Tayyaára?
    byárkab baaS.

11. wayn as-sawwaáq biwáqqif al-baaS?
    biwáqqifuh janb aT-Tayyaára.

12. shuu byá9malu r-rukkaáb?
    byánzalu min al-baaS wa byáTla9u 9aT-Tayyaára.

13. biwaáfiq ar-rukkaáb 'inn as-sáfra kaánat muriíHa?
    ná9am, biwaáfiqu 'ínha kaánat muriíHa.

14. J. bizuúr miin?
    bizuúr 'awlaáduh al-'ithnáyn.

15. wáynhum?
    hum byádrusu fi mádrasa daaxilíyya.

16. miin byahtámm bil-'awlaád fi ghiyaábuh?
    'áhluh byahtámmu bil-'awlaád fi ghiyaábuh.

17. 'áhluh bizuúru l-'awlaád?
    na9am, bizuuruúhum bi 'intiZaám fil-mádrasa.

1. Derived Forms of Verbs

In Lesson 7, a quick sketch was given of the derived forms of the verb. In the present lesson, further details are given of Forms 2 to 6, showing not only the forms of the perfect and imperfect tenses but also how to construct the important participles and verbal nouns.

The various parts of the verbs are given first in the $f - 9 - 1$ formula, then examples are given of actual words used in the course. The forms shown are those of the literary language and ultra correct speech. Those vowels which either fall out completely or become indistinct when used in speech are bracketed.

2nd Form

Perfect	Imperfect	Act. Part	Pass. Part.	Verbal Noun
fá99al	*y(u)fá99il*	*m(u)fá99il*	*m(u)fá99al*	*taf9iil*
wáqqaf	*y(u)sákkir*	*m(u)9állim*	*m(u)9állam*	*taSliiH*
(stop)	(close)	(teacher)	(educated)	(repair)

Notes

1. A 2nd form verb is often causative in meaning, hence *wáqqaf* = "make to stop", *9állam* = "make to learn" i.e. teach.
2. The Active Participle is formed from the Imperfect by replacing *yu* with *mu-*. Its plural is with *-iin* or *-aat* e.g. *mu9allimíin* (male teachers) – *mu9allimaát* (female teachers).
3. The Passive Participle has an *a* instead of an *i* before its final consonant.
4. The Verbal Noun is a form that must be learned. Once learned, important constructions such as the following become possible:

e.g. *laázim taSliiH has-sayyaára* = the repairing of this car is necessary i.e. this car must be repaired.

5. The only irregularities occur in the defective verbs. Note particularly the verbal noun.

Perfect	Imperfect	Act. Part.	Pass Part.	Verbal Noun
rábba	*y(u)rábbi*	*m(u)rábbi*	*m(u)rábba*	*tárbiya*
(bring up)		(educator)	(well-bred)	(bringing up)
		or		
		(breeder)		

3rd Form

Perfect	Imperfect	Act. Part.	Pass. Part	Verbal Noun
faá9al	*y(u)faá9il*	*m(u)faá9il*	*m(u)faá9al*	*m(u)faá9ala/*
				fi9aál
Haáwal	*y(u)waáfiq*	*m(u)saá9id*	*m(u)saá9ad*	*m(u)Haáwala*
				– difaá9
(try)	(agree)	(assistant)	(helped)	(attempt –
				defence)

Notes

1. A 3rd form verb often, though not always, relates the meaning of the 1st form verb to another person, hence *kaátab* = correspond with, as opposed to *kátab* = write (letter etc.).
2. The 3rd form's fundamental characteristic is the long *aa* vowel after the first root consonant, otherwise its vowelling is very similar to the 2nd form.
3. The Verbal Noun for most 3rd form verbs is *mufaá9ala* but some verbs take *fi9aál*, and some take both. Examples of verbal noun use:

e.g. *'ad-difaá9 9an hal-bilaád Sa9b* = the defence of this country is difficult.

muqaáranat al-kaatibáyn muhímm = the comparison of the two writers is important.

4. Again any irregularities exist in the defective verbs:

Perfect	Imperfect	Act. Part.	Pass. Part.	Verbal Noun
laáqa	*y(u)laáqi*	*m(u)laáqi*	*m(u)laáqa*	*m(u)laaqaát/*
(meet,				*liqaá'*
find)				(meeting)

Note particularly the verbal nouns (remember *'ila l-liqáa'* = Au revoir)

4th Form

Perfect	Imperfect	Act. Part.	Pass. Part.	Verbal Noun
'áf9al	*yúf9il*	*múf9il*	*múf9al*	*'if9aál*
(*'a)raád*	*y(u)riíd*	*m(u)riíd*	*m(u)raád*	*'iraáda*
(wanted)	(want)	(aspirant)	(desired)	(will,
				desire)
'ámla	*yúmli*	*múmli*	*múmla*	*imlaá', imla*
(dictated)	(dictate)			(dictation)

154

1. *'arsal* is a regular 4th form verb. The hollow verb *'araád* and the defective berb *'ámla* have irregularities because of the missing consonants. In the dialects 4th form verbs are often difficult to distinguish from 1st form verbs and because of this the causative meaning typical of the 4th form has tended to be taken over by the 2nd form. The participles and verbal nouns remain distinctive however:

e.g. *mudiír* (= director) – active participle from *'adaár* = to make revolve i.e. to administer.

'idaára (= administration) – verbal noun from *'adaár*.

'imDaá' (= signature) – from *'ámDa* (= to sign)

Example of verbal noun usage:

e.g. *takállam 9an 'idaárat ash-shárika* = he spoke of the running of the company.

5th Form

Perfect	Imperfect	Act. Part.	Pass. Part.	Verbal Noun
t(a)fá99al	*yat(a)fá99al*	*mut(a)fá99il*	*mut(a)fá99al*	*t(a)fá99ul*
t(a)'áxxar	*yat(a)dhákkɑɪ*	*mut(a)kállim*		*t(a)9állum*
(was late)	(remembers)	(speaker)		(learning)

Notes

1. The 5th form is often the reflexive of the 2nd:

e.g. *wáqqaf* = stop (something/someone), *t(a)wáqqaf* = stop (oneself).

2. The only irregularities occur, as usual, with the defective verbs.

Perfect	Imperfect	Act. Part.	Pass. Part.	Verbal Noun
ta)ghádda	*yat(a)ghádda*	*mut(a)gháddi*	*mut(a)ghádda*	*t(a)gháddi/ gháda*
(lunched)	(lunches)			(lunching/ lunch)

6th Form

Perfect	Imperfect	Act. Part.	Pass. Part.	Verbal Noun
t(a)faá9al	*yat(a)faá9al*	*mut(a)faá9il*	*mut(a)faá9al*	*t(a)faá9ul*
t(a)saáwam	*yat(a)saáwam*	*mut(a)saáwim*	—	*t(a)saáwum*
(haggled)	(haggles)	(haggler)		(haggling)

Notes

1. The 6th form is often the reciprocal of the 3rd form.
   saá9ad = help (someone), *t(a)saá9ad* = help one another.
2. The only irregularities occur in the defective verbs.

Perfect	Imperfect	Act. Part.	Pass. Part.	Verbal Noun
t(a)naása	*yat(a)naása*	*mut(a)naási*	*mut(a)naása*	*t(a)naási*
(pretend to forget)				

Exercises

1. Translate into Arabic. Answers at the end of the lesson.

(*a*) She agreed to clean the bedrooms on Wednesdays.

(*b*) Tell me if you need any help.

(*c*) He told me that the running of the company was not at all good.

(*d*) Cooperation between the two countries (*baladáyn*) was not good (definite article with abstractions like "cooperation").

(*e*) I was late for my appointment with the director (*ta'áxxar 9an*).

(*f*) Before signing the cheque, he asked how much money he had in his account (signing = *'imDaá'* or *'imDa*).

(*g*) He asked me to close the door (ask = *Tálab* NOT *sá'al*).

2. Word formation exercise. The verbs given below are all important. Some you will have met, some not. You are asked to supply various words derived from these verbs. Answers at the end of the lesson.

(*a*) *fákkar* (= think) active participle = thinker . . . ?

(*b*) *sájjal* (= record) verbal noun = recording . . . ?

(*c*) *náDDaf* (= clean) imperative = clean . . . ?

(*d*) *Haáma* (= defend) active participle = lawyer . . . ?

(*e*) *9aáraD* (= oppose) verbal noun = opposition . . . ?

(*f*) *saá9ad* (= help) imperative = help! . . . ?

(*g*) *Haárab* (= fight someone) active participle = combatant . . . ?

(*h*) *'ashaár* (= indicate, advise) verbal noun = hint, allusion advice . . . ?

(*i*) *ta'áxxar* (= be late) active participle = latecomers . . . ?

(*j*) *taqáddam* (= advance) verbal noun = progress . . . ?

(*k*) *taxáSSaS* (= specialise) active participle = specialist . . . ?

(*l*) *taghádda* (= have lunch) past = we lunched . . . ?

(*m*) *taqaá9ad* (= retire on pension) act. part. = pensioners . . .?

(*n*) *tafaáham* (= understand one another) vb. noun = mutual comprehension . . .?

(*o*) *ta9aáwan* (= cooperate) imperative = cooperate! . . .?

3. I lunched at 12 and dined at 7   *taghaddáyt as-saá9a 'ithná9sh wa ta9ashsháyt as-saá9a sáb9a.*
+ you/he/we/she/they etc.
+ at 1/1.20/1.25/7.15/7.30/ 7.35/7.45 etc.

(*b*) Put the above into the present. (*yataghádda* conjugates like *yánsa*)

4. Take each verb in the narrative and conjugate fully in both tenses. What are the active participles and verbal nouns of each verb?

Answers

1. (*a*) waáfaqat 9ala tanDiíf ghúraf an-nawm 'ayyaám al-'árba9a.

(*b*) quul lii 'ídha laázimak 'ayy musaá9ada.

(*c*) qaal lii 'inn 'idaárat ash-shárika mush kuwáyyisa 'ábadan.

(*d*) 'at-ta9aáwun bayn al-baladáyn ma kaan kuwáyyis.

(*e*) ta'axxárt 9an máw9idii ma9 al-mudiír.

(*f*) qabl 'ímDa sh-shayk, sá'al qaddáysh 9índuh fuluús fi Hisaábuh.

(*g*) Tálab mínnii taskiír al-baab.

2. (*a*) mufákkir (*b*) tasjiíl (*c*) náDDif! (*d*) muHaámi (*e*) mu9aáraDa (*f*) saá9id! (*g*) muHaárib (*h*) 'ishaára (*i*) muta'axxiriín (*j*) taqáddum (*k*) mutaxáSSiS (*l*) taghaddáyna (*m*) mutaqaa9idiín (*n*) tafaáhum (*o*) ta9aáwan!

TWENTY-FIRST LESSON – *'ad-dars al-waáHid wa 9ishriín*

TRAVEL

Narrative – *riwaáya*

9ind wuSuúluh li lundun, 'ittáSal J. bi waáliduh 'illi saákin fil-mínTaqa l-gharbíyya min al-bilaád.   *On arriving in London, J. contacted his father who lives in the western region of the country.*

'al-'ab 'inbásaT 'inn 'íbnuh rája9 wa qaal luh raH yantáZiruh fi maHáTTat síkkat al-Hadiíd fil-madiína 'illi saákin fiíha.

The father was happy that his son had returned and told him he would wait for him at the railway station in the town where he lived.

J. názal min al-maTaár li lúndun wa rákib at-trayn 'illi kaan raáyiH li bálad 'abuúh. ba9d kam daqiíqa 'at-trayn másha wa wáqaf ba9d saa9táyn.

J. went from the airport to London and took the train which was going to his father's town. After a few minutes the train started and stopped two hours later.

J. názal mínnuh wa shaaf 'abuúh naáTiruh fil-maHáTTa.

J. alighted and saw his father waiting for him at the station.

'al-'ab 'ishtára sayyaára jadiída 'ajnabíyya, láwnha 'áHmar. li'án al-qadiíma ta9áTTalat.

The father had bought a new foreign car, red in colour, because the old one had broken down.

'as-sayyaára ma kaánat briiTaaniyya laákin mustawrada min al-yaabaán.

The car was not British but was imported from Japan.

'ábu John muftáxir bíha wa 'ixtaárha li'ánha mawjuúda bi káthra.

John's father is proud of it and he chose it because it was readily available.

záwjat J. kaánat wáSalat fi briiTaánya qabl 'usbuu9áyn wa bá9dma zaárat al-'awlaád fil-mádrasa, saáfarat li 'ameérka minshaán tazuúr 'áhlha wa raH tárja9 ba9d kam yawm.

J.'s wife had arrived in Britain two weeks before and after she had visited the children in school, she travelled to America to visit her family. She will return in a few days.

J. bya9táqid hállaq 'ínnuh laázim yáTlub min ash-shárika náqluh 'ila briiTaánya bi sábab ar-riHlaát al-kathiíra 'illi kaan laázim ya9mílha húwa wa záwjatuh.

J. believes now that he must ask the company for his transfer to Britain because of the many journeys which he and his wife have had to make.

Vocabulary

'ittáSal (bi): *got in touch* (*with*) (*from* 'ittáSal (yattáSil/ bittáSil) = *to get in touch* (*with* = bi)).
mínTaqa *pl.* manaáTiq: *region.*

158

ghárbi: *western* (gharbíyya (*f.*) gharbiyyiín (*pl.*)).

'inbásaT: *was happy* (*from* 'inbásaT (yanbásiT/byanbásiT) = *to be/become happy/have a good time*).

yantáZir: *he waits for* (*from* 'intáZar (yantáZir/byantáZir) = *to wait for.*)

maHáTTa (-aat): *station* (*railway, taxi, broadcasting* . . .).

síkkat al-Hadiíd: *the railway* (síkka = *path*, Hadiíd = *iron*).

trayn (-aát): *train.*

wáqaf: *it stopped* (*from* wáqaf (yáwqaf/byáwqaf) = *to stop*).

naáTir: *waiting.*

'ájnabi: *foreign.*

ta9áTTalat: *it stopped working* (*from* ta9áTTal (yata9áTTal/ byat9áTTal) = *be idle, stop working, break down*).

mustáwrad: *imported* (*passive participle from* 'istáwrad (yastáwrid/byastáwrid) = *to import*).

muftáxir (bi = *of*): *proud* (*of*) (*active participle from* 'iftáxar (yaftáxir/byaftáxir) = *to be proud* (bi = *of*)).

'ixtaár: *he chose* (*from* 'ixtaár (yaxtaár/byaxtaár) = *to choose*).

káthra: *abundance* (bi káthra = *in abundance*).

naql: *transfer.*

bi sábab: *because of.*

ríHla (-aat): *journey.*

Questions on the Narrative

1. shuu 9ámal J. 9ind wuSuúluh li lúndun?

   'ittáSal bi waáliduh.

2. wayn saákin 'ábu J.?

   saákin fil-mínTaqa l-gharbíyya min al-bilaád.

3. 'al-'ab, wayn raH yantáZir 'íbnuh?

   raH yantáZiruh fi maHáTTat síkkat al-Hadiíd.

4. 'ayy maHátta?

   'al-maHáTTa fil-bálad 'illi saákin fiih.

5. lámma J. tárak al-maTaár, la wayn raaH?

   názal li maHáTTa fi lúndun.

6. John, miin shaaf lámma názal min at-trayn?

   shaaf 'abuúh.

7. shuu 'ishtára 'ábu J?

   'ishtára sayyaára jadiída.

8. laysh 'ishtára sayyaára jadiída?

   li'an al-qadiíma ta9áTTalat.

9. 'as-sayyaára 'ajnabíyya?

   ná9am, híya yaabaaníyya.

10. laysh 'ixtaár sayyaára mustáwrada min al-yaabaán?

    'ixtaárha li'ánha mawjuúda bi káthra.

159

11. záwjat J., 'áymta kaánat wáSalat fi briiTaánya?	kaánat wáSalat qabl 'usbuu9áyn.
12. la wayn saáfarat?	saáfarat li 'ameérka.
13. bi 'ayy sábab?	minshaán tazuúr 'áhlha.
14. J. shuu raH yáTlub min ash-shárika?	raH yáTlub náqluh 'íla briiTaánya.
15. bi 'ayy sábab?	bi sábab ar-riHlaát al-kathiíra 'ílli laázim ya9mílha húwa wa záwjatuh.

Notes on Grammar and Usage

1. Derived forms 7, 8, 9 and 10.

(*a*) *7th form*

Perfect	Imperfect	Act. Part.	Pass. Part.	Verbal Noun
'infá9al	*y(a)nfá9il*	*m(u)nfá9il*	—	*'infi9aál*
'inkásar	*y(a)nbásiT*	*m(u)nbásiT*		*'inkisaár*
(was broken)	(be glad)	(glad)		(breaking)

Notes
1. The 7th form is usually the passive of the 1st form: e.g. *kásar* = break (something) – *'inkásar* = to be broken, *qásam* (= divide) – *'inqásam* = be divided.
2. It is unusual for the agent to be stated in an Arabic passive sentence. If we wish to say "Ahmed was killed" we may translate it as *'inqátal 'áHmad* (*'inqátal* = be killed – *qátal* = kill). But we cannot translate "Ahmed was killed by Bashir". We would have to make "Bashir" the subject and say *bashiír qátal 'áHmad*.

There is a general tendency to avoid the passive by using the active forms instead: e.g. instead of *'inqaál* = it was said, *qaálu* = they said.

(*b*) *8th form*

Perfect	Imperfect	Act. Part.	Pass. Part.	Verbal Noun
'iftá9al	*y(a)ftá9il*	*m(u)ftá9il*	*m(u)ftá9al*	*'ifti9aál*
'i9táqad	*y(a)shtághil*	*m(u)ntáZir*	*m(u)shtághal*	*'intiqaál*
(believed)	(works)	(waiting)		(transfer)

Notes
1. The 8th form is sometimes the reflexive of the 1st form but there are many verbs where this is difficult to perceive. Very many common verbs are of the 8th form.

2. Various irregularities exist:

(a) When the 1st form begins with *w* or *'*, both these sounds are replaced by *t*. There results a double consonant *tt*:

e.g. *wáSal* = arrive   (8th form) *'ittáSal* = contact
     'áxadh = take   (8th form) *'ittáxadh* = take (measures)

(b) When the 1st form begins with *z*, the inserted *t* of the 8th form is replaced by a *d*:

e.g. *záHam* = press   (8th form) *'izdáHam* = throng

(c) When the 1st form begins with a velarised (or emphatic) consonant, the inserted *t* of the 8th form becomes velarised too:

e.g. *Dárab* = hit   (8th form) *'iDTárab* = be disturbed

(d) An example of a hollow verb is *'ixtaár* (= to choose)

Perfect	Imperfect	Act, Part.	Pass. Part.	Verbal Noun
'ixtaár	*yaxtaár*	*muxtaár*	*muxtaár*	*'ixtiyaár*
(chose)	(chooses)	(chooser)	(chosen)	(choosing)

N.B. "I chose" = *'ixtart*

(e) An example of a defective verb is *'ibtada* (= to begin)

Perfect	Imperfect	Act. Part.	Pass. Part.	Verbal Noun
'ibtáda	*yabtádi*	*mubtádi*	*mubtáda*	*'ibtidaá'*
(began)	(begins)	(beginner)	(begun)	(beginning)

(c) *9th form*

This is rather rare in spoken Arabic and is used for colours and bodily deformities ("blind" etc.). An example is: *'al-bint 'iHmárrat* = the girl blushed (turned red) where the relationship between *'iHmárr* and *'áHmar* (= red) is clear.

Perfect	Imperfect	Act. ·art.	Pass. Part.	Verbal Noun
'iHmárr	*yaHmárr*	*muHmárr*	—	*'iHmiraár*

N.B. "I blushed" = *'iHmarráyt*

(d) *10th form*

Perfect	Imperfect	Act. Part.	Pass. Part.	Verbal Noun
'istáf9al	*yastáf9il*	*mustáf9il*	*mustáf9al*	*'istif9aál*
'istá9mal	*yastá9jil*	*mustáwrid*	*mustáwrad*	*'isti9maál*
(used)	(hurries)	(importer)	(imported)	(use, using)

161

Notes

1. The 10th form often means to wish for oneself the action of the 1st form:

e.g. *'ádhin* = permit   *'istá'dhan* = ask permission (to depart)

It may often have an estimative meaning:

e.g. *Hasan* = be beautiful
'istáHsan = find beautiful

2. Verbs beginning with a *w* replace it with a long *ii* in the verbal noun: *'istáwrad* (verbal noun) *'istiiraád*

3. Hollow verbs are as follows –

Perfect	Imperfect	Act. Part.	Pass. Part.	Verbal Noun
'istaraáH	*yastariiH*	*mustariiH*	*mustaraáH*	*'istiraáHa*
(rested)	(rests)	(resting)	(rested)	(resting)

N.B. "I rested" = *'istaráHt*

'istájwab (= to interrogate) is quite regular.

4. Defective verbs are as follows –

Perfect	Imperfect	Act. Part.	Pass. Part.	Verbal Noun
'istághna	*yastághni*	*mustághni*	*mustághna*	*'istighnaá'*
(did with-out)	(does with-out)	(doing . . .)	(done . . .)	(doing with-out)

Exercises

1. Translate into Arabic. Answers at the end of the lesson.
(*a*) I wanted to sweep the kitchen but the broom broke.
(*b*) They enjoyed themselves very much on their holiday in France.
(*c*) The use of this telephone is forbidden (*mamnuu9*).
(*d*) Waiting for Ahmed was long and tiring (*mut9ib*).
(*e*) I had worked for the oil company in Abu Dhabi but had requested a transfer.
(*f*) If I had the choice, I would have gone by plane.
(*g*) His belief that he was going to become director was not correct.
(*h*) How long have you been importing foreign cars?
(*i*) They are still living in the same house and still waiting for you.
(*j*) Don't hurry! Only a few cars have arrived.

2. Word Formation Exercise. As in the previous lesson supply the parts of the verbs required. Answers at the end of the lesson.

(a) *'inqásam(li)* (= be divided (into)) Vb. Noun = division . . . ?
(b) *'inqaál* (= be said) Present = it is said . . . ?
(c) *'inqaád* (= be led) Pass. Part. = been led . . . ?
(d) *'ishtárak(fi)* (= share (in)) Vb. Noun = participation . . . ?
(e) *'ixtaár* (= choose) Past = I chose . . . ?
(f) *'ishtáka(min)* (= complain (of)) Past = we complained . . . ?   '
(g) *'ibtáda* (= begin) Vb. Noun = beginning . . . ?
(h) *'istá9mal* (= use) Vb. Noun = use . . . ?
(i) *'istáxdam* (= employ) Act. Part. = employer . . . ?
(j) *'istaqaál* (= resign) Act. Part. = someone resigning . . . ?
(k) *'istághna* (9an) (= do without) Imperative = do without! . . . ?

3.

They enjoyed themselves very much on holiday.	*'inbásaTu kathiír fil-'ijaáza*
+ I/he/she/we/you (m., f. & pl.)	*'inbasáTT* (= I enjoyed . . .)

4.

They always wait for me here in the market	*daá'iman byantaZiruúnii húna fis-suuq.*
+ you/he/she + here in front of the ministry/hotel/Saalim's house.	*btantaZírnii* (= you wait for me) N.B. adding pronoun endings may bring stress shifts.

5.

Please sit down! + fem./pl.	*tafáDDal 'istariíH!*

6.

There were many agreements between the two countries. + Britain and the U.S.A. (*'al-wilaayaát al-muttáHida*)/ Russia and the U.S.A./Egypt and Syria etc.	*kaan fii 'ittifaaqaát kathiíra bayn al-baladáyn.*

7.

The users of this bus are all Americans. + English/Egyptians/Syrians/ Lebanese/French etc.	*'illi byastá9milu hal-baaS, kúllhum 'ameerkaán.* *'inkliíz/maSriyyiín*

Answers

1. (*a*) kaan bíddii 'akánnis al-máTbax, laákin al-míknasa 'inkásarat.

(*b*) 'inbásaTu kathiír bi 'ijaazáthum fi fránsa.

(*c*) 'isti9maál hat-talfáwn mamnuú9.

(*d*) 'intiZaár 'áHmad kaan Tawiíl wa mút9ib.

(*e*) kunt 'ashtághil fi shárikat an-nafT fi 'ábu Dábi laákin Talábt 'intiqaál.

(*f*) law kaan lii l-'ixtiyaár, kunt ruHt biT-Tayyaára.

(*g*) 'i9tiqaáduh 'ínnuh kaan raH yaSiír al-mudiír ma kaan SaHííH.

(*h*) qaddáysh Saar lak 9am tastáwrid sayyaaraát 'ajnabíyya?

(*i*) bá9dhum saakniín fi nafs al-bayt wa lissaáhum 9am yantaZiruúk.

(*j*) la tastá9jil! ma wáSalat 'illa kam sayyaára.

2. (*a*) 'inqisaám (*b*) yanqaál (*c*) munqaád (*d*) 'ishtiraák (*e*) 'ixtárt (*f*) 'ishtakáyna (*g*) 'ibtidaá' (*h*) 'isti9maál (*i*) mustáxdim (*j*) mustaqiíl (*k*) 'istághni!

SOME DIFFERENCES BETWEEN THE MAIN DIALECTS

1. The Arabic presented in this book has been a rather elevated variety of colloquial Arabic, the regional flavour being that of the Greater Syrian area (Syria, Lebanon, Jordan and Palestine). The "elevation" of the language (i.e. its movement towards the standards of the literary language) is well shown by the following deviations from typical "Syrian" usage:

    (a) *dh* for *d* and *z* – e.g. *haádha* (for *haáda*) *tilmiidh* (for *tilmiiz*)

    (b) *th* for *t* and *s* – e.g. *thiyaáb* (for *tiyaáb*) *'athnaá'* (for *'asnaá'*)

    (c) the giving of clear literary language type vowellings (especially to verbs) where in the "Syrian" area vowellings might be various or just indeterminate.

2. For the purposes of this section, the intention is to give some elementary details of how the language of three great dialect areas contrast with the Greater Syrian. The dialects chosen are those of Egypt, Iraq (+ Kuwait) and the Gulf/Arabia. North West Africa has been excluded as the dialects in use there are too different to cover in any coherent way.

3. The student should remember that in the Gulf there has been such an influx of "foreign" Arabs that in many areas the natives are outnumbered. Because of the great prestige of other dialects such as Egyptian and Palestinian, it is becoming rare to find pure Gulf Arabic spoken and the inhabitants both readily understand expressions peculiar to other dialects and attempt to imitate them.

4. Egypt

I Sounds:

    (a) In Cairo and Lower Egypt generally, the *q* is pronounced as the glottal stop ' (*'áhwa* for *qáhwa*, *Ha'ii'a* for *Haqiiqa*, *shar'* for *sharq*). In Upper Egypt and the Sudan, the *q* is pronounced as *g* (*gáhwa* for *qáhwa*, *Hagiiga* for *Haqiiqa*, *sharg* for *sharq*). *q* remains in words like *'al-qur'aán* (the Koran) and *'al-qaáhira* (= Cairo).

    (b) In Cairo and Lower Egypt the *j* is pronounced as *g* (*gayb* for *jayb*, *xaliig* for *xaliij*). This hard *g* is regarded as the most characteristic element of Egyptian pronunciation.

    (c) The stressed syllable in words may come later than in the Syrian dialect (*madrása* for *mádrasa*, *mu9allíma* for *mu9állima*).

II Formal Phrases:

    (a) Egyptians and Sudanese use the word *'izzáy?* (= how?) for *kayf?* Hence *'izzáyak?* (= how are you?) and *'izzáy l-Haal?*

III Grammar:

(a) The usual words used instead of *bidd* (= want) are *9aáwiz* (m.s.), *9áwza* (f.s.) and *9awziín* (pl.). They are in fact active participles and are used as follows:

'ána 9aáwiz kitaáb = I want a book.
hiya 9áwza tímshi lis-siínama = she wants to go to the cinema.
hum 9awziín 'igaáza fi l-'iskandaríyya = they want a holiday in Alexandria.

Because of the great prestige of the Egyptian dialect, this construction is understood everywhere.

(b) Instead of *tába9* to indicate possession, *bitaá9* is used in precisely the same way, except that *bitaá9* has to agree with its noun:

'al-bayt bitaá9 al-mudiír = the director's house
'al-binaáya bitá9t ash-shárika = the company's building (f.)
'al-'awlaád bituú9 al-mudiír = the director's children (pl.)

(c) Instead of *haádha* etc. Egyptians use the following constructions with demonstratives:

'al-bayt da (= this house) for *haádha l-bayt*
'al-bint di (= this girl) for *haádhi l-bint*
'al-máT9am daak (= that restaurant) for *haadhaák al-màT9am*

i.e. the definite article precedes the noun while the final syllable of the demonstrative follows.

(d) The negatives of verbs have two elements *ma . . . sh*:

ma katábsh = he did not write (for *ma kátab*)
'ana ma shuftáksh = I did not see you (for *'ana ma shúftak*)
hiya ma bitsaa9idhúmsh = she does not help them

Forms ending in a short vowel lengthen the vowel when negatived:

byaáklu (= they eat)   *ma byaakluúsh*
ghasáltu (= you washed)   *ma ghasaltuúsh*

Forms ending in a long vowel (which always indicates the presence of the *u(h)* pronoun meaning "him" or "it") add *huu-sh*:

shuftuú(h) (= I saw him)   *ma shuftuhuúsh*
nisií(h) (= he forgot it)   *ma nisihuúsh*

Note also *fii* (= there is)   *ma fiish* (= there is not)

(e) The future is indicated by the particle *Ha* instead of *raH*:

Ha yímshi (= he will go)   *mush Ha yímshi* (= he will not go)

IV Vocabulary

Some common words are characteristic of Egyptian Arabic:

166

e.g. *Tarabáyza* (= table) for *Taáwila*
tallaája (= refrigerator) for *barraáda*
9arabíyya (= car) for *sayyaára*
Haága (= thing) for *shii*
bikám? (= how much?) for *qaddáysh?* (asking about prices)
9ayyaán (= sick) for *mariiD* (though *mariiD* is understood)
'in-nahaár da (= today) for *'al-yawm*
dil-wakti (= now) for *hállaq*
raágil (= man) for *rájul*

There is an Egyptian tendency to use what are in fact diminutive forms of certain nouns and adjectives:

máwya (= water)   *Sugháyyir* (= small)

5. Iraq

I Sounds:

(*a*) The *k* is often pronounced as *ch* (as in "*ch*urch") especially in conjunction with vowels like *i*, *ii* and *ay*:

cháyfak? = how are you? (m.s.) (for *káyfak?*)
cháyfich? = how are you? (f.s.) (for *káyfik*)
muu chída? = isn't it? etc. (for *mush kída/mush hayk?*)

(*b*) The *q* is pronounced as a *g*:

gaálat = she said (for *qaálat*)
fawg = above (for *fawq*)

(*c*) Instead of *D* we may hear *Dh* (emphatic or velarised version of *dh*):

DhíHak = he laughed (for *DáHik*)
mariiDh = ill (for *mariiD*)

(*d*) A genuine *p* may be heard:

puliís = police (for *buliís*)   *pánchar* = breakdown, puncture

(*e*) Diphthongised versions of *ay* and *aw* coexist with the pure vowel versions.

II Formal Phrases:

(*a*) *shláwnak?* or *shlawn káyfak?* = how are you? (for *kayf al-Haal?*)
(*b*) *'allaáh bil-xayr* = Good day
(*c*) *zayn* (= good) is a reply to enquiries about health.

III Grammar:

(*a*) The *b-* prefix to imperfects (used in both Syrian and Egyptian dialects) is not used in Iraqi.
(*b*) "to want" is expressed by (*'a*)*raad – yariid*:

radt fuluús = I wanted money (instead of *kaan bíddii fuluús*)

167

yariiduún yashtaruún sayyaára = they want to buy a car (for *bíddhum yashtáru sayyaára*)

(*c*) Verb conjugations in Iraqi Arabic are slightly different in the imperfect from the Syrian. An *-n* is added to the "you" (f.) form, to the "you" plural form and to the "they" form:

tilbasiín = you are wearing (f.s.) (for *tálbasi*)
taquuluún = you are saying (pl.) (for *taquulu*)
ya9rafuún = they know (for *yá9rafu*)

(*d*) "There is/are" is expressed by *'áku*, "there isn't/aren't by *máku* (instead of *fii* and *ma fii*). These words are regarded as being very typical of Iraqi Arabic.

(*e*) Instead of *tába9* to indicate possession, the word *maal* is used. *maal* has a feminine singular *maálat* and a feminine plural *maalaát* which are used when possessive suffixes are attached. When a noun follows, *maal* usually remains invariable. Like *tába9* and *bitaá9*, *maal* is not often used for family relationships:

'al-fúndug maáluh = his hotel (for *'al-fúnduq tába9uh*)
'al-Hadíiga maáltii = my garden (for *'al-Hadiiqa tába9ii/tabá9tii*)

(*f*) *da* is used as a prefix before the imperfect to indicate the continuous tense instead of *9am*:

da yusawwíiha hássa = he is doing it now (for *9am ya9málha hállaq*)

IV Vocabulary

(*a*) *fadd* = one, a (i.e. an indefinite article) (for *waáHid*) *ta9arráft 9ála fadd fransaáwi al-yawm* = I became acquainted with a Frenchman today *9índak fadd diinaár?* = Have you a dinar?

(*b*) *kúllish* = very (for *kathíir*). Used with adjectives:

fiilm kúllish zayn = a very good film

(*c*) *xawsh* = good (invariable adjective always used before the noun)

húwa xawsh wálad = he's a nice boy

(*d*) *shinuú?* = what? (for *shuu?*)
(*e*) *shlawn?* = how? what sort of?

shlawn mayz? = what sort of table?   *shláwnak?* = how are you?

(*f*) *baysh?* = how much, what is the price?
(*g*) *shgadd?* = how much? how far? (how many? = *cham/kam?*)
(*h*) *hwaáya* = a lot of

hwaáya fuluús = a lot of money

6 Arabian Peninsula and Gulf

I Sounds:

(*a*) *q* is pronounced as *g*: *gáhwa* (for *qáhwa*)

168

(*b*) *j* is often pronounced as *y*, especially in the Gulf:

riyyaál = man (for *rijjaál*/*rájul*)

(*c*) *Z* is often pronounced as *D* – hence *'ábu Zábi* (the "correct" form) is pronounced *'ábu Dábi*.

(*d*) *k* is often pronounced as *ch*:

'ismich = your name (f.s.) (for *'ismik*)
cham/*kam wálad?* = how many boys?

II Formal Phrases:
    (*a*) As in Iraqi Arabic "how are you?" is either *cháyfak?* or *shláwnak?* The reply is often with *zayn* (= well, good)
    (*b*) Farewells are often the following:

person taking leave: *fi 'amaán allaáh*
person remaining: *fi 'amaán allaáh, ma9 as-salaáma.*

III Grammar:
    (*a*) The usual way of expressing "want to" is with the verbs *yábi* (= he wants) or *yariíd*:

'ábi kitaáb = I want a book
tábi tádfa9? = do you want to pay?
tabiin tashrabiín? = do you (f.s.) want to drink?
yabuún yaakluún = they want to eat

The negative is formed with *ma*: *ma yábi yaákul.*
Other verbs used in the Peninsula are *yábgha* (conjugated like *yánsa*) and *yáshti*:

'ábgha fúndug zayn = I want a good hotel
yábgha yashuúf al-madiína = he want to see the city
yashtuún yashtaruún bayt = they want to buy a house

    (*b*) Instead of *tába9*, *Hagg* (derived from *Haqq*) and occasionally *maal* are used. *Hagg* is usually invariable:

haádha Hággna = this is ours
'as-sayyaára Hagg as-safiir = the ambassador's car

    (*c*) As in Iraqi Arabic the following forms are found in the imperfect:

taktubiín = you (f.s.) write (for *táktubi*)
taktubuún = you (pl.) write (for *táktubu*)
yaktubuún = they write (for *yáktubu*)

    (*d*) A feminine plural form may be found in both 2nd and 3rd persons of both verbs and pronouns:

'intin tádfa9in = you (f. pl.) pay   ⎫ used for women – mixed company
hin yádfa9in = they (f. pl.) pay   ⎬   is masculine

169

(*e*) The *b-* prefix to imperfects is found but usually indicates a future, progressive or habitual meaning:

húwa byíshrab wíiski = he drinks whisky (habitually)
hum bisaafiruún 'íla suúriya = they will travel to Syria

It is likely that the *b*-prefix is spreading under the influence of high prestige dialects such as the Egyptian.

IV Vocabulary

(*a*) *waájid* = very, a lot of (often pronounced *wadyid*)

9índii waájid sagaáyir = I've a lot of cigarettes
'ana waájid zayn = I'm very well

(*b*) *kúllish* = very (but can only be used with adjectives)

múdda kúllish Tawíila = a very long period

(*c*) *muu(b)* = not (for *mush*)

húwa muub mu9állim = He's not a teacher

(*d*) *'aysh?* = what? (for *shuu?* – though *shuu?* and *shínu?* are both possible)

(*e*) *mayz ('amyaáz)* = table
(*f*) *daríisha (daraáyish)* = window
(*g*) *'al-Hiin* = now (for *hállaq*)

ARABIC–ENGLISH GLOSSARY

The glossary includes nearly all words in the course. The few that are omitted are of lesser importance.

The alphabetical ordering has followed the English pattern except for the following necessary adaptations:

(a) the glottal stop is disregarded, hence 'a is the first letter in the alphabet, while 'u is one of the last.

(b) the emphatic letters represented by capitals follow the ordinary ones, hence *T* follows *t*.

(c) the two letter combinations are treated as separate letters and are arranged as follows –

gh after *f*, sh after *s* and *S*, th after *t* and *T*

(d) 9 is the last letter of the alphabet.

Most nouns and adjectives have their plural given in brackets immediately after the singular. Examples of the use of many words are given in brackets after the translation(s) of the Arabic words.

Verbs are given in the 3rd person masculine singular of the perfect tense. Their imperfects are given in brackets immediately after the initial entry. These imperfects are given in a very literary style, which will be understood all over the Arab World.

The only abbreviations used are –

f. = feminine   pl. = plural

Stressed syllables are indicated throughout.

ARABIC–ENGLISH GLOSSARY

'a

'aáxir ('aaxiríin): *adj. last* ('aáxir wálad = *the last boy*) ('awaáxir) *n. end* ('aáxir annahaár = *the end of the day*)

'ab ('aabaá'): *father* ('ábu bashíir = *Bashir's father,* 'abuúh = *his father,* 'abuúk = *your father*)

'ábadan: *adv. never* (ma shúftuh 'ábadan = *I have never seen him*)

'ábyaD (*pl.* biiD *f.* báyDa): *white*

'ahámm (yuhímm): *to concern, interest*

'áhlan wa sáhlan: *welcome!*

'áHmar (*pl.* Humr *f.* Hámra): *red*

'áHsan: *better*

'aHyaánan: *sometimes*

'ája (yíji): *to come*

'ájnabi: *foreign*

'ákal (yaákul): *to eat*

'ákbar: *bigger*

'állaah: *God*

171

'ámDa (yúmDi): *to sign*
'amn: *security* ('al-'amn al-9aam = *public security*)
'amr ('umuúr): *matter, affair* ('awaámir): *orders*
'ams: *yesterday*
'araád (yuriid): *to want, wish* (shuu bitriíd? = *what would you like?*)
'arD[f.] ('araáDi): *land, earth, floor*
'ársal (yúrsil): *to send*
'ásaf: *regret* (ma9 al-'ásaf = *sorry*)
'áswad (*pl.* suud *f.* sáwda): *black*
'áSfar (*pl.* Sufr f. Sáfra): *yellow*
'athnáa': *during*
'áwwal (-iin): *first*
'áwwalan: *firstly* (+ bil-'áwwal)
'ax ('íxwa): *brother* ('áxu bash-iír = *Bashir's brother*, 'axuúy = *my brother*)
'áxadh (yaáxudh): *take*
'áywa: *yes*
'ayy: *any* – 'ayy?: *which?*
'ázraq (*pl.* zurq f. zárqa): *blue*
'á9Ta (yú9Ti): *to give*

b

bakkiír: *early*
bank (bunuúk): *bank*
báqar: *cattle* (báqara = *cow*, laHm báqar = *beef*)
baqíyya: *remainder*
báraka: *blessing*
bariíd: *mail, post*
basiíT (bisaáT): *easy, simple*
bass: *but, only* (kuwáyyis bass ghaáli = *good but dear*, liiratáyn bass = *only two pounds*)
baSS (-aát): *bus*
baTaáTa: *potatoes*
baTráwl: *crude oil*
bawwaába (-aat): *gate*
bayt (buyuút): *house*
ba9d: *after, still* (ba9d sána = *after a year*, bá9dhum húna = *they are still here*)
ba9dáyn: *afterwards, then*
ba9d búkra: *the day after tomorrow*

ba9d ma: *after* (+ *clause*) (ba9d ma 'ája = *after he came*)
ba9iíd (bi9aád): *far* (*from* = 9an)
bi: *in, with* (húwa bi lúndun = *he is in London*, fiínii 'áftaHuh bi mifákk = *I can open it with a screwdriver*)
bidaáya: *beginning* (fil-bidaáya = *in the beginning*)
bidd (+ *pronoun suffixes*): *want, wish* (bíddii kitaáb = *I want a book*, bíddak tíji = *do you want to come?*)
biduún: *without*
bijuúz/yajuúz: *maybe* (bijuúz yíji búkra = *he may come tomorrow*)
binaá': *building, construction*
binaáya (-aát): *building, edifice*
bin-naádir: *rarely*
bint (banaát): *girl, daughter*
bi-súr9a: *quickly*
búkra: *tomorrow*
buliís (buliisíyya): *policeman*

d

daáfa9 (yudaáfi9) + 9an: *to defend*
daáfa9u 9an al-qárya = *they defended the village*)
daáxil: *inside* (daáxil al-mádrasa = *inside the school*)
daáxili (*f.* daaxilíyya *pl.* daaxiliy-yiín): *internal*
dáfa9 (yádfa9): *to pay, push*
dáftar (dafaátir): *notebook, ledger*
dáftar shakkaát: *cheque book*
daqiíq: *precise, exact*
daqiíqa (daqaáyiq): *minute (of time)*
dáras (yádrus): *to study*
dáxal (yádxul): *to enter*
dáyma: *always* (*expression used after drinking coffee*)
difaá9: *defence* ('ad-difaá9 9an al-qárya = *the defence of the village*)
dúghri: *straight ahead*
dukkaán [*f.*] (dakaakiín): *shop* ('ad-dukkaán kabiíra = *the shop is big*)

D

DaábiT (DubbaáT): *officer*

DáHik (yáDHak): *to laugh*

Daruúri: *necessary*

Dáyya9 (yuDáyyi9): *to lose*

Dúhur: *noon* (ba9d aDDúhur = *afternoon*)

f

faáDi: *free, unoccupied*

faáhim: *have/has understood* ('inta faáhim? = *have you understood?*)

faáSal (yufaáSil): *bargain* (faaSálnii 9ála s-sayyaàra = *he bargained with me over the car*)

faákiha (fawaákih): *fruit*

fáDDal (yufáDDil): *to prefer*

min fáDlak: *please*

fáhim (yáfham): *to understand*

fa'ízan: *so, therefore*

faqáT: *only* (liiratayn faqáT = *two pounds only*)

fárja (yufárji): *to show*

fi: *in, into*

fii (+ nii, – k, ha *etc*): *can* (fiína níji = *we can come*)

fii: *there is/are*

fí'a (-aát): *group*

fiilm ('aflaám): *film*

fíkra ('afkaár): *thought*

finjaán (fanaajíin): *cup*

firaásh (fúrush): *bed*

fiSaál: *bargaining*

fransaáwi (*f*. fransaawíyya *pl*. fransaawiyyíin): *French*

fuluús [*f*.]: *money*

fúnduq (fanaádiq): *hotel*

gh

ghaáli (*f*. ghaálya): *expensive*

gháda ('àghdiya): *lunch* (m.)

ghálaT ('aghlaáT): *mistake*

gharb: *west*

ghárbi (*f*. gharbíyya *pl*. gharbiyyíin) western

ghariib (ghúraba): *strange, stranger*

ghásal (yághsil): *to wash*

ghással (yughássil): *to wash*

ghiyaáb: *absence*

ghúrfa (ghúraf): *room* (ghúrfat 'akl = *dining room*, ghúrfat nawm = *bedroom*)

h

haádha *m*.: *this* (haádhi *f*.)

haadhaák *m*.: *that* (haadhíik *f*.)

haadháwl: *these*

haadhawlaák: *those*

haat!: *bring!*

hállaq: *now*

hayy: *here is* (hayy al-kitaáb = *here is the book*, hayyaáh = *here it is*)

húna: *here* – *also* hína *and* hawn

hunaák: *there*

H

HaáDir (-iín): *present, at your orders*

Haal ('aHwaál): *state, condition* (kayf al-Haal? = *how are you?*

Haarr: *hot*

Haáwal (yuHaáwil): *to try*

Habb (yaHíbb): *to love, like* (biHíbbha kathíir = *he loves her very much*, ma baHíbbuh = *I don't like him*, bitHíbbi tàrquSi? = *would you like to dance?*)

Háda: *anyone* (shuft Háda? = *have you seen anyone?* ma fii Háda = *there isn't anyone*

Hadiíqa (Hadaáyiq): *garden*

HáDDar (yuHáDDir): *to prepare*

HáDratak: *you* – *very polite*

Háfla (-aát): *party* (Háflat siínama = *film show*, Háflat 'istqbaál = *reception*)

Hajm ('aHjaám): *size*

Háka (yáHki): *to talk*

Háki: *talking*

Hálam (yáHlum): *to dream*

Hálaq (yáHliq): *to shave*

Hámal (yáHmil): *to carry*

Hamd: *praise* ('al-Hámdu líllaah = *praise be to God*)

173

Hammaám (-aát): *bath, bathroom*
Haqíiqa (Haqaáyiq): *truth, fact*
bil-Haqíiqa: *in fact*
Haqq (Huquúq): *truth, correctness, one's due, legal claim* ('al-Haqq 9aláyk = *you are wrong*)
Hátta: *even, till, so that* (Hátta r-rájul al-9aádi byáf ham haádha = *even a layman understands that*, Hátta s-saá9a sítta = *till 6 o'clock*, báji Hátta 'ashuúfak = *I've come to see you*)
Hátta 'ídha/law: *even if* (*Chapter 18*)
HaTT (yaHúTT): *to put*
Hawsh ('aHwaásh): *courtyard*
HayT (HiiTaán): *wall*
Hayy ('aHyaá'): *quarter – of city*
HaZZ: *fortune, luck* (li suu' al-HaZZ = *unfortunately*, li Husn al-HaZZ = *fortunately*)
Hilu (Hilwíin): *sweet, pretty, nice* (híya bint Hílwa kathíir = *she is a very pretty girl*)
Hisaáb (-aát): *account, bill*

'i

'ibtáda (yabtádi): *to begin* (bi = *with*)
'ibtá9ad (yabtá9id): *to move away from* (= 9an)
'idha: *if* (*See Lesson 18*)
'iftákar (yaftákir): *to think*
'iHmárr (yaHmárr): *to be or to become red, to blush*
'iid *f.* (*dual* – 'iidáyn, *pl.* 'ayaádi): *hand* ('iidáyk = *your hands*, 'iidáyya = *my hands*)
'ijaaza (-aat): *holiday, leave*
'ijtimaá9 (-aát): *meeting*
'il: *to, for* (+ *pronoun suffixes*) ('ilha 9uyuún Hílwa kathíir = *she has very beautiful eyes*, fii shii 'ílii? = *is there anything for me?*)
'ila: *to* (saáfaru 'ila baghdaád = *they travelled to Baghdad*)
'illa: *except* (ma fii 'illa xamst awlaád = *there are only 5 boys*)

'illi: *who, which, he who, that which* (*See Lesson 14 for usage details*)
'in: (*1*) – *if* ('in shaa' 'allaáh = *if God wills*)
(*2*) – *that* (qaal lii 'ínhu raaH yat'áxxar = *he told me that he would be late*)
'inbásaT (yanbásiT): *have a good time, be happy*
'intáZar (yantáZir): *to wait for*
'intiqaál: *transfer, transport*
'intiZaám: *regularity* (bi-'intiZaám = *regularly*)
'irtáfa9 (yartáfi9): *to rise*
'ism ('asaámi): *name*
'irtaáH (yartaáH): *to rest*
'istaraáH (yastariiH): *to rest*
'istá'dhan (yastá'dhin): *to ask permission* ('astá'dhin 'ámshi = *I ask leave to go*)
'istá9jal (yastá9jil): *to be in a hurry*
'istá9mal (yastá9mil): *to use*
'ishtághal (yashtághil): *to work*
'ishtára (yashtári): *to buy*
'ittáfaq (yattáfiq): *to agree* (on = 9ala)
'ittáSal (yattáSil): *to get into contact* (*with* = bi)
'ixtaár (yaxtaár): *to choose*
'i9táqad (ya9táqid): *to believe*
'íyyaa: (+ *pronoun suffixes*) ('a9Tíiha 'iyyaáhum = *give her them*) – *see Vocabulary of Lesson 15.*
'i9tabar (ya9tabir): *to consider*

j

jaab (yajíib): *to bring*
jaáwab (yujaáwib): *to answer* (9ála + *someone*)
jaay (*f.* jaáya *pl.* jaayyíin): *coming, next* ('ash-shahr al-jaay = *next month*)
jadíid (jidaád): *new*
jamíil: *beautiful*
januúb: *south*
janb: *near to, next to*

174

jawaáz sáfar (jawaazaát safar): *passport*

jáwwi: *air* ('al-bariíd al-jáwwi = *air-mail*)

jaw9aán: *hungry*

jayb (juyuúb): *pocket*

jiddan: *very* (fíkra kuwáyyisa jiddan = *a very good idea*)

júm9a: *assembly* (yawm al-júm9a = *Friday*)

k

kaan (yakuún): *to be – past and future meaning only.*

kaátib (kuttaáb): *clerk, writer*

kabiír (kibaár): *big*

kálima (-aát): *word*

kállam (yukállim): *to speak to*

kam?: *how many?* (kam bayt? = *how many houses?*)

kamaála: *change – on purchases*

kamaán: *also* (kamaán márra = *once again*)

kánnas (yukánnis): *to sweep*

kaslaán: *lazy*

kátab (yáktub): *to write*

kathiír: *much, many, very* (xubz kathiír = *much bread*, buyuút kathiíra = *many houses*, Hílu kathiír = *very pretty*)

kayf: *how – in statements and questions*

kiílu (kiiluwaát): *kilo*

kitaáb (kútub): *book*

kitaába: *writing*

kubbaáya (-aat): *tumbler*

kull: *all, every* (kull al-yawm = *all the day*, kull al-banaát = *all the girls*, kull yawm = *every day*)

kull waáHid: *everyone*

kúllma: *whenever, the more . . .* (*See Lesson 18*)

kuntraátu (kuntraataát): *contract*

kúrsi (karaási): *chair*

kuwáyyis: *good*

l

laákin: *but*

laázim: *necessary, must* ('ash-shughl al-laázim = *the necessary work*, laázim taruúH = *you must go*)

lábis (yálbas): *to wear, to put on* (lábis bádla = *he put on a suit*, shuu kaánat laábisa? = *what was she wearing?*)

laHm (luHuúm): *meat* (láHma = *piece of meat*)

láHZa (-aat): *moment*

lámma: *when – not question* (lámma byíji, quul luh . . . = *when he comes, tell him . . .*)

láqa (yulaáqi): *to find*

lawn ('alwaán): *colour*

li'án: *because* (ma 'ája li'ánhu kaan mariíD = *he didn't come because he was ill*)

li/la: *to* (raáHat lil-máktab = *she went to the office*, la wayn raáyiH? = *where are you going to?* shuu qaálu lil-mudiír? = *what did they say to the director?*

liíra (-aát): *pound* (*Lebanese or Syrian*)

líssa: *still, yet* (lissaáhum fil mádrasa = *they are still in the school*, ma 'áju líssa = *they have not yet come*)

lúgha (-aát): *language*

m

maáDi (*f.* maáDya): *past*

mabruúk: *congratulations*

mabsuúT: *happy, in good health*

ma daam: *as long as* (ma daam 'ínta húna, xalliína nashtághil = *as long as you are here, let's work!* (*See Lesson 19*)

madiína (múdun): *city*

máDDa (yumáDDi): *spend time*

mafhuúm: *understood*

máhma: *whatever* (baHíbbuh máhma 9ámal = *I like him whatever he does*) (*See Lesson 18*)

maHálli (*f.* maHallíyya *pl.* maHalliyyín): *local*

makaán ('ámkina): *place*
máktab (makaátib): *office*
maktuúb (makaatiib): *letter*
malfuúf: *cabbages* (malfuúfa = *a cabbage*)
mamnuún: *grateful, thanks*
manquúsh: *carved*
maqluúb: *upside down, inside out* . . . (bil-maqluúb = *upside down*)
márHaba (*dual.* marHabtáyn *pl.* maraáHib): *hello*
mariíD (mariiDiín/márDa): *ill*
márra (-aát): *occasion, time*
mashghuúl: *occupied – person or thing*
ma9: *with, has/have* ('áHmad má9ii = *Ahmed is with me*, má9ii fuluús = *I have money on me*)
marraát kathiíra: *often*
masaá' (masawaát): *evening* (masaá' al-xayr = *Good evening*
másak (yámsik): *to hold, grasp*
maTaár (-aát): *airport*
máTbax (maTaábix): *kitchen*
máT9am (maTaá9im): *restaurant*
mawjuúd: *present, in existence*
maẃ9id (mawaa9iíd): *appointment*
mayy: *water*
ma9 'ann: *although*
ma9luúm: *certainly, of course*
má9na (ma9aani): *meaning*
miin?: *who?*
miin ma: *whoever* quúluh la miin ma biddak = *tell it to whoever you like.*
miizaán (mayaaziín): *scales, balance*
miknasa (makaánis): *broom* (míknasat huúver = *vacuum cleaner*)
miliíH (milaáH): *beautiful, nice, pleasant*
min: *from*
minshaán: *for, so that* (haádha l-kitaáb minshaának = *this book is for you*, báji minshaán 'ashuúfak = *I've come to see you.*
mínTaqa (manaáTiq): *area, region*
múdda (múdad): *period*

mudiír (múdara): *director*
mufaáSala: *bargaining*
muftáxir (bi): *proud (of)*
muhtámm (bi): *concerned (with)*
múmkin: *possible*
mumtaáz: *excellent*
munaásib: *suitable*
muqaábala (-aát): *meeting, interview*
muqaábil: *opposite*
muqaáwil (-iín): *contractor*
muriíH: *comfortable*
musaáfir (-iín): *traveller, travelling*
musaá9id (-iín): *assistant*
mustáwrad: *imported*
mustá9jil: *in a hurry*
muta'ássif: *sorry*
muta'áxxir (-iín): *late, latecomer*
mutazáwwij (-iín): *married*
muwaaSalaát: *communications*
muwáZZaf (-iín): *official*
muxtálif: *different, various*

n

naádir: *rare*
naási: *has/have forgotten, forgetting*
naáTir (-iín): *waiting*
náDDaf (yunáDDif): *to clean*
nafs (nufuús): *soul, same* (fi nafs al-bayt = *in the same house*)
nafT: *oil – of mineral origin*
nihaáya: *end* (fin-nihaáya = *in the end*)
nawm: *sleep*
naw9 ('anwaá9): *kind, type*
názal (yánzil): *to descend, land, stay at hotel* ('aT-Tayyaára názalat = *the aircraft landed*, 'inta naázil fil-fúnduq al-kabiír? = *are you staying at the Grand Hotel?*)
nísi (yánsa): *to forget*
númra (númar): *number* (shuu númrat as-sayyaára? = *what's the license number of the car?*)
nuSS ('anSaáS): *half* (fi nuSS al-layl = *at midnight*)
nuur ('anwaár): *light*

q

qaal (yaquúl): *to say, tell* (quul lii shuu 'ismak = *tell me what your name is*)

qaam (yaquúm): *to stand up, get up* (qaam min an-nawm = *he woke up*)

qaáran (yuqaárin): *to compare*

qabiih (qibaáh): *ugly*

qabl: *before, ago* (ta9aál qabl as-saá9a sítta = *come before six o'clock*, kaan húna qabl láH-Za = *he was here a moment ago*)

qabl ma: *before* (+ *clause*) (qabl ma 'ashuúfuh laázim 'áHki má-9ak = *before I see him, I must talk with you*)

qádar (yáqdir): *to be able* (báqdir 'aruúH má9kum = *I can go with you*)

qáddam (yuqaddim): *to present* (*to* = li)

qaddáysh?: *how much?* (qaddaysh Haqq has-sayyaára? = *how much is this car?*, qaddáysh 9úmrak? = *how old are you?*, darást qaddáysh waqt? = *how long did you study?*)

qadiím: *old – of things*

qáDa (yáqDi): *to spend time, to judge*

qáhwa: *coffee, café*

qaliil (qilaál): *few* ('aqáll = *less*)

qára (yáqra): *to read*

qariib (min): *near (to)*

qárya (qúra): *village*

qaSiir (qiSaár): *short*

qiraáya: *reading*

qirsh (quruúsh): *piastre*

quddaám: *in front of*

r

raábi9: *fourth*

raaH (yaruúH): *to go*

raákib (rukkaáb): *passenger, rider*

raákib (-iin): *travelling, riding*

raáwi: *narrator*

rafaahíyya: *luxury, prosperity*

raH: *"will"* (raH 'ashuúfuh búkra = *I'll see him tomorrow*)

ráHma (-aat): *mercy*

rá'san: *directly, immediately*

raqm ('arqaám): *number* (shuu raqm talfáwnak? = *what's your telephone number?*)

ráttab (yuráttib): *to arrange, put in order*

raxiiS: *cheap*

ríHla (-aát): *journey*

risaála (rasaá'il): *letter*

riwaáya (-aát): *story, novel*

rub9 ('arbaá9): *quarter*

s

saáfar (yusaáfir): *to travel*

saákin (sukkaán): *inhabitant*

saákin (-iin): *dwelling*

sa'al (yás'al): *to ask* (9an = *about*)

saaq (yasuúq): *to drive*

saá9a (-aát): *hour, clock, watch* (qaddáysh as-saá9a? = *what's the time?*, 'as-saá9a sítta = *It's six*)

saá9ad (yusaá9id): *to help*

sábab ('asbaáb): *reason* (bi-sábab al-máTar = *because of the rain*)

sáfra (-aat): *journey*

sáHab (yásHab): *to withdraw* (sá-Hab kull fuluúsuh min al-bank = *he took all his money out of the bank*)

sákan (yáskun): *to dwell*

sákkar (yusákkir): *to close*

sállam (yusállim): *to protect, hand over* (*to* = li)

sáwa: *together*

sawwaáq (-iin): *driver*

sayyaára (-aat): *car* (sayyaárat naql = *truck, lorry*)

sáyyid: *Mr* ('assáyyid . . . = *Mr . . .*)

sekritáyr (sekritayríyya): *male secretary*

sekritáyra (-aát): *female secretary*

sifaára (-aát): *embassy*

sigaára (sagaáyir): *cigarette*
siídii: *sir* (ná9am ya siídii = *yes sir*)
siínama (-aát): *cinema*
síkkat Hadiíd: *railway*
sinn ('asnaán): *tooth*
si9r ('as9aár): *price*
su'aál ('ás'ila): *question* (sá'alu 'ás'ila thaánya = *they asked other questions*)
súr9a: *speed* (bi-súr9a = *quickly*)
suuq ('aswaáq): *market*

S

SaáHib ('aSHaáb): *owner, friend*
Saar (yaSiír): *happen, become, begin* (*See Lesson 19*)
SabaáH: *morning* (SabaáH al-xayr = *Good Morning*)
Sadiíq ('aSdiqaá'): *friend*
Saff (Sufuúf): *row* (*line*) *class*
Saghiír (Sighaár): *small, young*
SaHHtáyn!: *two healths!* – *reply to the coffee drinking greeting* dáyma
SaHííH (SiHaáH): *correct*
Sanduúq (Sanaadiíq): *box, chest*
SáTeH (SuTuúH): *roof*
Sayf: *summer*
SíHHa (-aát): *health*
SíHi (yáSHa): *to wake up* (SiHiít 'as-saá9a sáb9a wa nuSS = *I woke up at half past seven*)
SubH: *morning*

sh

shaaf (yashuúf): *to see*
shaári9 (shawaári9): *street*
shaay: *tea*
shahr (shuhuúr/'ásh-hur): *month*
shájar: *trees* (shájara = *a tree*)
shákar (yáshkur): *to thank*
shakk (-aát): *cheque*
shánTa (shúnaT): *bag, suitcase*
sháraf: *honour* ('ash-sháraf lána = *the honour is ours*)
shárib (yáshrab): *to drink*
shárika (-aát): *company* (shárikat nafT = *oil company*)
sharq: *east*

shá9ar (yásh9ur): *to feel* (básh9ur bit-tá9ab = *I feel tired*)
shii ('ashyaá'): *thing*
shimaál: *north, left* (9ala shimaálak = *on your left*)
shughl ('ashghaál): *work*
shúkran: *thank you*
shuu? = *what?*
shwáyya: *a little* (shwayy shwayy = *slowly*)

t

tába9: *belonging to* (*See Lesson 6*)
tadhákkar (yatadhákkar): *to remember*
tafáDDal: *please sit down/take this/precede me/come in etc.* (*See Lesson 2 Note 10*)
taghádda (yataghádda): *to lunch*
takállam (yatakállam): *to speak*
tálfan (yutálfin): *to telephone* (tal-fánt lil-mudiir = *I rang the director*)
talfáwn (-aát): *telephone*
tamaám: *completely*
tárbiya: *education*
tasaáwam (yatasaáwam): *to bargain* (*with* = ma9)
tashárraf (yatashárraf): *to be honoured* (tasharráfna = *we have been honoured – on being introduced*)
taSliiH (-aát): *repair*
ta9aál!: *come!*
ta9aáwan (yata9aáwan): *to cooperate*
ta9állam (yata9állam): *to learn*
ta9áTTal (yata9áTTal): *to break down*
ta9áwwad (yata9áwwad): *to get used* (*to* = 9ala) (ta9awwádt 9ala T-Taqs = *I got used to the weather*)
taqriíban: *approximately*
ta9áshsha (yata9áshsha): *to dine*
ta9baán (-iin): *tired*
tíkram: *certainly – when acceding to a request*

178

tilmiídh (talaamiídh): *pupil*

T

Taábiq (Tawaábiq): *storey*
Taábi9 (Tawaábi9): *stamp*
Taálama: *as long as* (*See Lesson 19*)
Taar (yaTiír): *to fly*
Taáwila (-aát): *table*
Taáza: *fresh – of food etc.*
Tálab (yáTlub): *to request* (Tálab al-'ídhn mínhu = *he asked him for permission*)
Tálab (-aát): *request*
Taqs: *weather*
Tariíq (Túruq): *road*
Tawiíl (Tiwaál): *long, tall*
Tayyaára (-aát): *aircraft*
Tuul: *throughout* (Tuul an-nahaár = *all day long*)

th

thaálith (-iín): *third – in sequence*
thaáni (*f.* thaánya *pl.* thaanyiín): *second, other*
thawb (thiyaáb): *garment, robe*
thiyaáb: *clothes*
thulth ('athlaáth): *third – fraction*

'u

'umbaáriH: *yesterday*
'usbuú9 ('asaabií9): *week*
'ustaádh ('asaátidha): *professor, teacher, polite form of address*

w

waáfaq (yuwaáfiq): *to agree to* (= 9ála)
waálid (-iín): *father*
waHd + *pronoun suffix: alone* (wáHdii = *I alone*, saákin wáHdak? = *do you live alone?*)
wájad (yuújad – *very rare*): *to find*
wajh (wujuúh): *face*
wálad ('awlaád): *child, boy*

wáqaf (yáwqaf): *to stop, come to a halt* ('al-baSS wáqaf = *the bus stopped*)
wáqqaf (yuwáqqif): *to stop, bring to a halt* ('as-sawwaáq wáqqaf al-baSS = *the driver stopped the bus*)
waqt ('awqaát): *time* (kaan aT-Taqs Hílu Tuul al-waqt = *the weather was good all the time*, Saar waqt al-gháda = *it's lunch time*)
wára: *behind*
wáraq: *paper* (wáraqa = *a piece of paper*)
wasT: *middle*
wáSal (yáwSal): *to arrive*
wáSSal (yuwáSSil): *to give a lift to, convey*
wayn?: *where?*
wázan (yáwzan): *to weigh* (wázan aT-Tard = *he weighed the parcel*)
wazn ('awzaán): *weight* (wáznuh kiílu wa nuSS = *it weighs one and a half kilos*)
wizaára (-aat): *ministry*
wuSuúl: *arrival*

x

xaádim (xuddaám): *servant*
xaárij: *outside* (xaárij al-bayt = *outside the house*)
xaáriji (*f.* xaarijíyya *pl.* xaarijiyyiín) *external*
xaárTa (-aát): *map*
xaáTir (xawaáTir): *mind* (bi-xaáTrak = *good-bye*)
xálli!: *let . . !* (xalliíha tíji má9na! = *let her come with us!*, xalliína naruúH 9al-bayt! = *let's go home*)
xaliíj (xuljaán): *gulf, bay*
xáraj (yáxruj): *go out*
xarbaán (-iín): *broken down, out of order*
xaruúf (xurfaán): *lamb, sheep*
xasaára (xasaáyir): *loss* (ya xasaá-ra! – *exclamation of dismay*)

179

xaTT (xuTuúT): *line*

xayr: *good* (SabaáH al-xayr = *Good Morning*)

xilaál: *during*

xubz: *bread* (xúbza = *a piece of bread*)

xudh!: *take!* – *imperative from* 'áxadh

y

yajuúz/bijuúz: *maybe*

yamiín: *right* (9ála yamiínak = *on your right*)

ya rayt: *if only, would that* (*See Lesson 19*)

yawm ('ayyaám): *day*

yá9ni: *I mean/that is etc.*

yúmkin: *it is possible*

z

zaá'ir/zaáyir (zuwwaár): *visitor*

zaar (yazuúr): *to visit*

zaáwiya (zawaáya): *corner*

záhra (zuhuúr): *flower*

zamiíl (zúmala): *comrade, colleague*

zawj ('azwaáj): *husband, pair* ('ams 'ishtaráyt zawj (*or* jawz) kal-saát = *yesterday, I bought a pair of stockings.*

záwja (-aát): *wife*

Z

Zann (yaZúnn): *to think, consider* ('aZúnn 'in as-si9r ghaáli = *I think the price is high*)

9

9aádatan: *usually*

9aádi (*f.* 9aádya *pl.* 9aadyiín): *usual, normal*

9aáfa (yu9aáfi): *to give good health* ('állaah yu9aafiík = *God give you health*)

9aáfya: *good health* ('állaah ya9Tiík al-9aáfya = *God give you good health*)

9aálam: *world*

9aáli (*f.* 9aálya *pl.* 9aalyiín): *high*

9aa'ish (-iín): *living*

9aamm: *public, general* ('al-'amn al-9aamm = *public security*, 'al-mudiír al-9aamm = *the general manager*)

9ádad ('a9daád): *number* (9ádad min an-naas 'áju = *a number of people have come*)

9add (ya9udd): *to count*

9afsh: *luggage, furniture, household effects*

'al-9áfu: *don't mention it*

9ajiíb: *strange, wonderful*

9alaáma {-aát): *mark*

9ála: *on* – 9aláy *with pronoun suffixes* (hal-mashruúb 9aláyya = *this drink's on me*)

9ámal (yá9mal): *to do*

9an: *from, off, about* (báytii ba9iíd 9an al-madiína = *my house is far from the city*, thalaáth 'amyaál 9an ash-shaTT = *3 miles off the coast*, kaan 9am yáHki 9an al-Harb = *he was talking about the war*)

9árab: *Arabs*

9árabi (*f.* 9arabíyya *pl.* 9árab): *Arab, Arabic*

9áraf (yá9raf): *to know*

9árraf (yu9árrif): *to introduce* (*to* = 9ála)

9ashaán: *for, so that* (hal-kitaáb 9ashaán al-mu9állim = *this book is for the teacher*, ruHt li báytuh 9ashaán 'ashuúfuh = *I went to his house to see him*)

9aTshaán (-iín): *thirsty*

9ijil: *calf* (laHm 9íjil = *veal*)

9ind: *"chez", has/have* (9ind 'áHmad = *at Ahmed's house*, 9indii kitaáb = *I have a book*)

9unwaán (9anaawiín): *address, title*

180

THE CHRISTIAN AND MUSLIM MONTHS

(a) *THE CHRISTIAN MONTHS*

There are two sets of names for the Christian months. Those in column 1 are those which resemble the English names and which are used exclusively in Egypt, though understood everywhere. The ones in column 2 are used in Lebanon, Syria, Iraq and Jordan.

	1	*2*
January	*yanaáyir*	*kaanuún ath-thaáni*
February	*febraáyir*	*shubaáT*
March	*maars*	*'aadhaár*
April	*'abriíl*	*niisaán*
May	*maáyu*	*'ayyaár*
June	*yuúnyu*	*Huzayraán*
July	*yuúlyu*	*tammuúz*
August	*'aghúsTus*	*'aab*
September	*sebtémber*	*'ayluúl*
October	*'uktuúber*	*tishriín al-'áwwal*
November	*nuufémber*	*tishriín ath-thaáni*
December	*disímber*	*kaanuún al-'áwwal*

(b) *THE MUSLIM MONTHS*

The Muslim months are lunar and are therefore of 28 days duration. They are as follows:

1. *muHárram*
2. *Sáfar*
3. *rabii9 al-'áwwal*
4. *rabii9 ath-thaáni*
5. *jamaáda al-'áwwal*
6. *jamaáda l-'aaxíra*

7. *rájab*
8. *sha9baán*
9. *ramaDaán* (month of fasting)
10. *shawwaál* (*'al-9iid as-Saghiír** in this month)
11. *dhu al-qá9da*
12. *dhu al-Híjja* (month of pilgrimage) (*'al-9iid al-kabiir*†)

* *'al-9iid aS-Saghiír* (= the small festival) is at the beginning of *shawwaál* immediately after the end of the fast of *ramaDaán*.

† *'al-9iid al-kbaiír* (also *9iid al-'áDHa* = the feast of the sacrifice) is when the pilgrims offer sacrifice in Mecca.

GAZETTEER

Only a few place names which may present difficulties are offered here. Normally the English versions are sufficient.

AFRICA	'ifriiqiya	Algiers	'al-jazaá'ir
Algeria	'al-jazaá'ir (= the islands)	Khartoum	'al-xarTuúm (= the elephant's trunk)
Cyrenaica	bárqa		
Egypt	maSr	Tripoli	Traáblus
Morocco	'al-mághrib		

SEAS AND RIVERS

ASIA	'aasiya	Atlantic	'al-muHiíT 'al-'aTlasi
China	'aS-Siin		
India	'al-hind	Euphrates	'al-furaát
Japan	'al-yaabaán	Indian Ocean	'al-muHiíT al-híndi
Jordan	'al-'úrdun		
Lebanon	lubnaán	Mediterranean	'al-baHr al-'ábyaD al-mitwássiT
Saudi-Arabia	'as-sa9uudíyya		
AMERICA	'ameérka		
U.S.A.	'al-wilaayaát al-muttáHida	Persian Gulf	'al-xaliij (al-9árabi)
		Suez Canal	qanaát as-suwáys
EUROPE	'uruúba	Tigris	díjla
Austria	'an-námsa	The Red Sea	'al-baHr al-'áHmar
Belgium	baljiika		
Germany	'almaánya		
Greece	'al-yuunaán		

MISCELLANEOUS

Italy	'iiTaálya	Neutral Zone	mínTaqa muHaáyada
U.S.S.R.	'al-'ittiHaád as-suufiyéti	Middle East	'ash-sharq al-'áwsaT
TOWNS		Far East	'ash-sharq al-'áqSa
Alexandria	'al-'iskandaríyya		

ENGLISH-ARABIC GLOSSARY

This glossary is not a dictionary – it lacks the detail and range. But it is fairly full, ranges much wider than the actual lessons as regards vocabulary, and will, it is hoped, prove a springboard for dealing with situations falling outside the scope of the lesson material. There are in fact few fuller glossaries available at the present moment. To go much further the student will need an English–Arabic dictionary – and will require a knowledge of the Arabic script.

Now for some details on the lay-out of the glossary:

1. *Nouns:* The plurals of most nouns are given, sound plurals (see Lesson 9 Note 3) being indicated by merely giving the endings *-iin* or *-aat*:

· e.g. *Hisaáb (-aát)* – the plural is *Hisaabaát*
  mu9állim (-iin) – the plural is *mu9allimiín*

Broken plurals (see Lesson 9 Note 3) are given in full. Where a plural is omitted, this is because the noun in question does not have a commonly used plural.

Collectives (See Lesson 17 Note 1) are dealt with as follows:

e.g. *tuffaáHa* (coll.) *tuffaáH* (pl.) *-aát* (= apple)

This means: *tuffaáHa* (= one apple), *tuffaáH* (= apples in general), *tuffaaHaát* (= apples when a specific number are counted)

2. *Adjectives:* If an adjective has a broken plural, this is given in full. When an adjective takes a sound plural, this has been given in the same way as for nouns, if the adjective is one commonly used with human beings (See Lesson 13 Note 2 Agreement of Adjectives).

3. *Verbs:* First form verbs are presented in the following way: masculine singular of the perfect (or past) tense (the "he" form), then a vowel indicating the vowel of the imperfect, then the verbal noun:

e.g. Enter: *dáxal(u) duxuúl* . . .

(From this information we know that the imperfect is *yádxul*.

Derived form verbs (see Lessons 21 and 22 for details) are given as follows: the masculine singular of the perfect, then the masculine singular of the imperfect given in full, then the verbal noun:

e.g. Teach: *9állam. yu9állim. ta9liím*

The vowellings actually used in the various areas of the Arab World may differ from the ones given here but those presented in the glossary are essentially of the written language and therefore of a rather elevated Arabic appropriate to Arabic speakers on their best behaviour. These vowellings are "correct" and will always be understood.

Abbreviations

adj. – adjective	n. – noun
adv. – adverb	pl. – plural
coll. – collective	prep. – preposition
conj. – conjunction	s. – singular
f. – feminine	tr. – transitive (describes a verb which may take an object e.g. "to raise")
intr. – intransitive (describes a verb which does not take an object e.g. "to rise")	v. – verb
m. – masculine	

Abbreviations have also been used for the following nationalities: E. (= Egyptian), S. (= Syrian), S.A. (= Saudi-Arabian)

ENGLISH–ARABIC GLOSSARY

A

Able (to be): qádar (i) qúdra *adj.* muqtádir (= *able to* . . .), shaáTir (= *clever*)

Aboard (ship): 9ála Dahr . . .

Abolish: qáDa (i) qaDaá' (+ 9ála) 'álgha. yúlghi, 'ilghaá', *e.g.* qáDa 9ála l-wáZíifa = *he abolished the post*

About (concerning): 9an–bi xuSuúS (*approximately*): taqriiban, *e.g. fii xamsiín taqriiban = there are about 50*

above: fawq

Above-mentioned: madhkuúr

Absence: ghiyaáb

Absent: ghaáyib

Absurd: ghayr ma9quúl *lit: other than reasonable*

Abundant: waáfir

Abuse: v. shátam (i) shátim (*insult*) *n.* shatíima (shataáyim)

Accept: qábal (a) qubuúl

Acceptable: maqbuúl

Accident: Haádith (Hawaádith), *e.g.* Haadith fi sh-shaari9 = *an accident in the street*

Accidentally: bi taSaáduf, biS-Súdfa

Accompany: raáfaq. yuraáfiq, muraáfaqa

According to: Hásab

Account: (*financial*) Hisaáb (-aat), (*story*) riwaáya (-aat), (*description*) waSf ('awSaaf)

Accountant: muHaásib (-iin)

Accuracy: tadqiíq/díqqa

Accurate: daqiíq (diqaáq)

Accurately: bi tadqiíq

Get accustomed to: ta9áwwad (+ 9ála), yata9áwwad (+ 9ála), *adj.* (*accustomed to*) muta9áwwad (+ 9ála)

Ache: n. wája9 ('awjaá9)

Acid: n. HaámiD. (HawaámiD)

Get acquainted with: ta9árraf (+ 9ála), yata9árraf (+ 9ála)

Across: 9abr *e.g.* 9abr al-biHaár = *overseas*

Act: v. máththal. yumáththil. tamthiíl (*i.e. in play*)

Action: n. 9ámal ('a9maál)

Active: (*energetic*) nashiíT

Activity: nashaáT (-aát) *e.g.* nashaaTaát 'ijtimaa9íyya = *social activities*

Actor: mumáththil (-iin)

Actual: Haqiíqi, fí9li

184

Actually: (*really*) bil-Haqiiqa
Add: jáma9 (a) jum9 *e.g.* 'ijma9
waáHid wa waáHid! = *add one
and one!*
In addition to: bil 'iDaáfa li . . .
Address: 9unwaán (9anaawiin)
Adequate: kaáfi
Adjacent: mujaáwir
Adjective: Sifa (-aát)
Adjourn: 'ájjal. yu'ájjil. ta'jiil
Adjust: 9áddal. yu9áddil. ta9diíl
Administer: 'adaár. yudiír. 'idaára
Administration: 'idaára
Administrator: mudiír (múdara)
Adult: kabiír (kibaár)
Adultery: zína
Advance: *v.* *intr.* taqáddam
yataqáddam, *e.g.* taqáddam al-
jaysh bi súr9a = *the army
advanced with speed*
v. tr. sállaf. yusállif, tasliíf
(*advance money*), *e.g.* al-bank sál-
laf miit jináyh = *the bank
advanced £100*
n. súlfa (súlaf)
Take advantage of opportunity:
'intáhaz (yantáhiz. 'intihaáz) al-
fúrSa
Adventure: mughaámara.
Advertisement: 'i9laán (-aát)
Advertising: di9aaya
Advice: naSiiHa (naSaáyiH)
Advise: náSaH (a) naSiíHa
Aeroplane: Tayyaára (-aát)
Affair: (*matter*) 'amr ('umuúr)
Afraid: xaáyif (min = *of*)
To be afraid (*of*): xaaf (xift) yaxaáf.
xawf (+ min), *e.g.* xaaf min al-
kalb = *he feared the dog*
After: ba9d, *e.g.* ba9d sana = *after
a year;* bá9dma, *e.g.* bá9dma
waSal = *after he arrived,* *i.e.*
bá9dma *is used before verbs*
Afternoon: ba9d aD-Dúhur
Afterwards: ba9dáyn
Again: márra thaánya, kamaán
márra
Against: Didd (= *opposed to*)
Age: 9umr (9umuúr)

Agency: wikaála (-aát)
Agent: wakiíl (wúkala)
Ago: qabl (*lit: before*) – *precedes the
noun,* *e.g.* qabl thalaáth sin-
iín = *three years ago.*
Agree (*to*): waáfaq. yuwaáfiq.
muwaáfaqa (+ 9ala), e.g. waáfaq
9ála Tálabi = *he agreed to my
request*
Agreement (*to something*): muwaá-
faqa (+ 9ála); (*between two par-
ties*) 'ittifaáq
Agreeable: (*pleasant*) laTiíf (lúTafa)
Agriculture: ziraá9a
Ahead: quddaám (*ahead of
you* = quddaámak)
Aim: *v.* (*take aim with gun*) 'axadh
niishaán, (*intend*) qáSad (i) qaSd
Air: háwa
Air-conditioning: takyiíf háwa
Air-conditioner: mukáyyif háwa
Airport: maTaár (-aát)
Alarm clock: munábbih (-aat)
Alcohol: al-kuHuúl
Alcoholic drinks: mashruubaát
ruuHíyya
Alight: *v.* názal (a) nuzuúl (= *get
down from*) *e.g.* nazált min
albaaS = *I got off the bus*
Alike: mithl ba9D (= *like each other*)
Alive: 9aáyish
All: kull (+ *plural*), *e.g.* kull al-
'awlaád = *all the boys*
Allow: sámaH (a) samaáH li +
person bi + *thing,* *e.g.* al-
mu9állim sámaH lii bid-
duxuúl = *the teacher allowed me
to enter*
Allowance (*financial*): 9alaáwa
(-aát)
Ally: Haliíf (Húlafa)
Almond: lawza (*coll.*) lawz (*pl.*) -aat
Almost: taqriíban/naHw/Hawaáli,
e.g. fii 9índna naHw/Hawaáli 'alf
kitaáb = *we have almost 1000
books* (*see "About"*)
Alms: Sádaqa
Alone: wáHdii = *I alone;* wáH-
dak = *you alone etc.*

185

Along (with): ma9, (the length of)
9ála Tuul ... e.g. másha 9ála
Tuul ash-shaári9 = he walked
along the street
Alongside: bi jaánib
Aloud: bi Sawt 9aáli (lit: in a high
voice)
Also: kamaán/'áyDaan
Alter: v. tr. gháyyar. yugháyyir.
taghyiír e.g. al-Hukuúma
gháyyarat al-qaanuún = the
government changed the law
v. intr. tagháyyar. yatagháyyar.,
e.g. al-Hukuúma tagháyyarat
= the government changed
Alternative: n. badiíl (búdala)
Altogether: sáwa
Alternately: bi dawr
Although: wa law, e.g. laázim 'ash-
tághil wa law 'ána Ta9baán–má9a
'ínnu, e.g. má9a 'ínnu 'ána
Ta9baán, laázim 'ashtághil
Always: dáyman
Ambassador: safiir (súfara)
Ambulance: sayyaárat 'is9aáf (say-
yaraát 'is9aáf)
Ammunition: dhaxiíra.
Among: bayn
Amount: máblagh (mabaáligh) (of
money) kammíyya (-aát)
Amount to (reach): bálagh(a)
buluúgh, e.g. al-qirD bálagh miit
junáyh = the loan amounted to
£100
Amuse: sálla. yusálli. tásliya
Amusement: (entertainment) tásliya.
tasaali.
Analysis: taHliíl
Ancient: qadiím
Angle: zaáwiya (zawaáya)
Angry: za9laán/ghaDbaán
Animal: Haywaán (-aát)
Announce: '9lan. yú9lin. 'i9laán.
Announcement: 'i9laán (-aát)
Annoy: 'áz9aj. yúz9ij. 'iz9aáj
Annoying: múz9ij
Annual: sánawi
Another: thaáni, ghayr, e.g. ghayr
kitaáb = another book (not this

one). One another: ba9D (+
pronoun suffix corresponding to
subject) e.g. shaáfu bá9Dhum
= they saw one another)
Ant: námla (coll.) naml (pl.) -aat
Any: 'ayy, e.g. 'ayy shaxS = any
person
Anybody: 'ayy waáHid (no matter
who) Háda, e.g. ma shuft
Háda = I didn't see anyone
Anything: 'ayy shii e.g. ma qaal
shii = he didn't say anything
Anywhere: fii 'ayy makaán (lit: in
any place)
Apologise: Tálab al-9áfu (lit: ask
for pardon)
Apostle: rasuúl (rúsul), e.g.
muHammad rasuul allaah =
Muhammad is the apostle of God
Apparatus: 9údda (9údad) 'aála
(-aát) (machine), jihaáz ('ájhiza)
Appear: Záhar(a) Zuhuúr (seem &
show oneself)
Apple: tuffaáHa (coll.) tuffaáH (pl.)
-aát
Appoint: 9áyyan. yu9áyyin. ta9yiín
Appointment: (arrangement to meet)
máw9id (mawaa9iíd)
Appreciate: qáddar. _ yuqáddir.
taqdiír
Approach: v. taqárrab (+ min).
yataqárrab. taqárrub
Appropriate: munaásib
Approve: 'istáHsan (find good)
yastáHsin. 'istiHsaán
Approval: 'istiHsaán
Apricot: míshmisha (coll.) míshmish
(pl.) -aát
Arab: 9árabi (9árab)
Arabia: jaziírat al-9árab (lit: island
of the Arabs)
Area: mínTaqa (manaáTiq) (region)
Argue (with someone): jaádal.
yujaádil. mujaádala (with each
other) tajaádal yatajaádal
Arise: qaam (u) qiyaám
Arithmetic: Hisaáb (calculation)
Arm: dhiraá9 ('ádhru9)
Arms: (weapons) 'ásliHa (plural of

186

SilaáH = *weapon or arm of service, e.g.* silaaH al-jaw = *airforce*)
Army: jaysh (juyuúsh)
Around: Hawl
Arrange: (*make arrangements*) dábbar. yudábbir. tadbiír (*set in order*) ráttab. yuráttib. tartiíb
Arrest: wáqqaf. yuwáqqif. tawqiíf
Arrival: wuSuúl
Arrive: wáSal. yuúSal. wuSuul
Art: fann (funuún)
Artificial: ʿiSTinaá9i
Artillery: midfaa9íyya
As: (*like*) mithl
As soon as: Haálama, *e.g.* Haálama y i ji = *as soon as he comes*
Ashamed: xaljaán
Aahes: ramaád
Ash-tray: minfáDDa (-aát)
Ask: (*question*) sáʿal(a) suʿaál. (*request*) Tálab(u) Tálab (+ min), *e.g.* Talábt finjaán shay minnuh = *I asked a cup of tea from him*)
Asleep: naáyim
Assassinate: ʿightaál. yaghtaál ʿightiyaál (= *assassination*)
Assist: saá9ad. yusaá9id. musaá9ada
Assistance: musaá9ada
Astonish: dáhash(a) dáhsha
Be astonished at: ʿindáhash (+ min) ʿindiháash
At (*near*): 9ind, *e.g.* 9ind al-qaSr = *at/near the palace*
At first: fil-ʿáwwal
At home: fil-bayt
At last: ʿaxiiran
At least: 9ála l-ʿaqáll
At most: 9ála l-ʿákthar
At once: Haálan
Atmosphere: jaww
Attaché: múlHaq (-iín)
Attack: hájam (+ 9ála) (a)hujuúm
Attack: n. hujuúm. (hajamaát)
Attempt: Haáwal. yuHaáwil. muHaáwala n. muHaáwala (-aát)
Attend: (*be present*) HáDar(u)

Huduúr (*give attention to*) ʿadaár (yudiir) al-baal li (*lit: turn the mind to*)
Attendance: HuDuúr
Attention: ʿintibaáh
Attentive: muntábih
Attract: jádhab(i) jadhb.
Attractive: jadhdhaáb
Aunt: (*paternal*) 9ámma (-aát), (*maternal*) xaála (-aát)
Authority: sulTa (= *power*)
Authorities: sulTaát
Automatic: ʿawtomaatiíki
Autumn: xariíf
Available: mawjuúd
Average: mu9áddal
Awake: SaáHi (SaaHyiín)
Away: (*absent*) ghaáyib, (*distant*) ba9iíd

B

Baby: Tifl (ʿaTfaál)
Bachelor: 9ázab (ʿa9zaáb)
Back (*of person*): Dahr (Duhuúr)
Backward: muta ʿáxxar (*of country etc.*)
Backwards: li-wara
Bacon: laHm xanziír
Bad (*in most senses*): rádi–baTTaál e.g. mush baTTaál = *not bad.*
Bag: (*shopping bag*) kiis (ʿakyaás), (*suitcase*) shánTa (shúnaT), (*handbag*) shánTaT yad
Bake: (*bread*) xábaz (a) xabz
Baker: xabbaáz (-iín)
Balance: (*scales*) miizaán (mawaaziín), (*remainder*) baáqi
Ball: kurra-aat e.g. kúrrat qádam = football
Banana: máwza (coll.) mawz (*pl.*) -aát
Band: (*music*) muuziíqa, (*group*) jamaá9a (-aát)
Bandage: ribaáT (-aát) rábTa (ribaáT)
Banish. Tárad (a) Tard
Bank: (*financial*) bank (bunuúk), (*river*) Diffa. *e.g.* aD-Diffa l-gharbíyya = *The West Bank*

187

Banker: SaáHib bank. 'aSHaáb
bank (*lit: owner of a bank*),
muwáZZaf (-iín) bank (*lit: official
of a bank*)
Bank-note: wáraqat bank
Bankrupt: múflis (-iín)
Banner: 9álam ('a9láám)
raáya (-aát)
Bar (for drinks): baar(-aát)
Barbed wire: silk sháwki (*lit: thorny
wire*)
Barber: Hallaáq (-iín)
Barefoot: Haafi (-yiin)
Barely: bil-kaad
Bargain: tr. (haggle) faáSal. yufaá-
Sil. mufaáSala–saáwam,
yusaáwim. musaáwama, *e.g.* faa
Saltuh 9ála sh-shanTa = *I bar-
gained with him over the bag. n.
(deal)* Sáfqa (-aát)
Barley: sha9iír
Barracks: thúkna (-aát)
Barrel: (oil) barmiíl (baraamiíl) (*of
gun*) maasuura(t) (banduqiyya)
(banduqíyya = *gun*)
Base (military): qaá9ida (qawaá9id)
Basin: (for washing) mághsala
(maghaásil), (*drainage area,
reservoir*) HawD. ('aHwaáD)
Basis: 'asaás, ('úsus), *e.g.* 9ála 'asaás
al'ishtiraakíyya = *on the basis of
socialism*
Basket: sálla (sálal)
zanbiíl (zanaabiíl)
Bath (room): Hammaám (-aát)
Bathe: taHámmam. yataHámmam
(= *bathe oneself*)
Battalion: fawj ('afwaáj)
Battery: (electrical) baTaríyya
(-aát)
Battle: má9raka (ma9aárik)
Bay: xaliíj (xuljaán)
Bazaar: Suuq ('aSwaáq)
Be: kaan. yakuún. kawn.
Beach: shaTT (shuTuúT)
Beans: faaSuúliya, (*broad beans*)
fuul
Bear: (endure) taHámmal.
yataHámmal, (*give birth to*)

wálad. yáwlad. wilaáda
Beard: liHya (liHa)
Beat: Dárab(i) Darb (= hit
someone or something)
intr. (of heart, engine etc.) daqq (u)
daqq; (*defeat*) ghálab (a) ghálaba
Beautiful: jamiíl/Hilu
Because: li'an/9alashaán
because of: bi sábab
Become: Saar(i) Sayruúra
Bed: firaásh (-aát)/sariír (saraariír)
Bedding: firaásh (-aát)
Bedroom: ghúrfat nawm (ghúraf
nawm)
'áwDat nawm ('úwaD
nawm)
Bee: náHla (*coll.*) naHl (*pl.*) -aát.
Beef: laHm baqr
Beer: biíra
Before: (place) quddaám
prep: (time) qabl *adv:* min qabl,
e.g. 'ája min, qabl = *he came
before. conj.* qáblama, *e.g.*
qáblama yíji = *before he comes*
Beggar: shaHHaád (-iín)
Begin: v. intr. 'ibtáda, yabtádi.
(*begin doing something*) 'áxadh/
Saar('áSbaH) + *present tense,e.g.*
'áxadht/Sirt/'aSbáHt/ibtadáyt
'aktub maktuúb = *I began to
write a letter*
Beginning: bidaáya/'áwwal
Behave: taSárraf. yataSárraf–sálak
(u) Suluúk (*appropriately*)
Behind: wára/xalf
Belief: 'i9tiqaád (-aát).
Believe: (believe that) 'i9táqad
ya9táqid. 'i9tiqaád
Believe: (something or someone)
Sáddaq. yuSáddiq, (*believe in
something*) 'aáman (+ bi)
yú'min. 'iimaán
Bell: járas ('ajraás)
Belly: baTn (buTuún)
Belong to: tába9 (*S.*) maal (*Ir.*)
haqq (*S.A.*) bitaá9 (*E.*), *e.g.* has-
sayyaára tába9 al-mudiír = *this
car belongs to the director*
Beloved: maHbuúb

188

Below: taHt
Belt: Hizaám ('áHzima)
Bench: (*for sitting on*) taxt. (tuxuút)
Bend: (*something*) 9áwwaj.
yu9áwwij ta9wiíj, (*be bent*)
'in9áwaj. yan9áwij. *n.*
(*bend in road*) Hánya (-aát)
Beside: bi jaánib
Best: 'al-'áHsan/'al-'afDal
Better: 'áHsan/'áfDal
Between: bayn
Beyond: wára
Bible: al-kitaáb al-muqáddas (*lit: the holy book*)
Bicycle: bisklaát (-aát)
Big: kabiír (kibaár)
Bill: Hisaáb (-aát)
Bind: rábaT (a) rabT
Biology: 9ilm al-Hayaát (*lit: science of life*)
Bird: Tayr (Tuyuúr) (*little bird*) 9aSfuúr (9aSaafiír)
Birthday: 9iid miilaád
Biscuit: baskuúta
Bite: 9aDD(i) 9aDD
Bitter: murr (*c.f. myrrh in Bible*) (*of struggle*) mariír
Black: 'áswad (*m.*) sáwda (*f.*) suud (*pl.*)
Blacksmith: Haddaád (-iín)
Blame: v. laam (u) lawm
Blanket: n. baTTaaníyya-(aát) Hiraám (-aát)
Blessed: mubaárak
Blind: 'á9ma (*m.*) 9ámya (*f.*) 9amyaán (*pl.*)
Blockade: HiSaár (-aát)
Blood: dam. (díma)
Blotting paper: wáraq nashshaáf
Blow: v. (*of wind*) habb(i) hubuúb *n.* Dárba (-aát)
Blue: 'azraq (*m.*) zarqa (*f.*) zurq (*pl.*)
Board: v. tr. (*ship, aircraft, bus*) rákab (a) rukuúb
n. (*plank*) láwHa ('alwaáH)
n. (*of directors*) májlis. (majaális)
Boast: tafaáxar. yatafaáxar
Boat: márkab (maraákib)

Body: jism ('ajsaám)
Boil: tr. (*cook by boiling*) sálaq(u) salq, *e.g.* bayD masluúq = *boiled eggs*
intr. ghála. yághli, *e.g.* al-mayy yághli = *the water is boiling*
Bold: jasuúr (-iín)
Bolt: v. tr. qáffal. yuqáffil., *e.g.* qáffalu l-baab = *they bolted the door.*
n. (*used in construction*) búrghi (baraághi)
Bomb: n. qánbala (qanaábil)
Bone: 9aZm. ('a9zaám)
Book: kitaáb (kútub)
Book-keeper: maásik dafaátir
Book-keeping: mask dafaátir
Bookseller: bayyaá9 kútub
Bookshop: máktaba (-aát)
Boot: jázma (-aát) (*also shoes*)
Border: n. (*boundary*) Huduud (*plural of* Hadd (= *limit*)
Boring: mumíll
Born: mawluúd
Borrow: 'ista9aár. yasta9iír 'isti9aára.
Boss: ra'iis (rú'asa)
Both: al-'ithnáyn
Bottle: zajaája (-aát) (gazaáza)
Bottom: 'ásfal (= *lowest part*)
Bowl: Taása (-aat)
Box: Sanduúq (Sanaadiíq)
Boy: wálad ('awlaád) Sábi (Sibyaán) (*young boy*)
Brain (*as a thinking instrument*) dimaágh.
Brake: fraam (-aát)/brayk (-aát)
Branch: (*of tree*) ghaSn (ghuSuún), (*of business*) far9 (furuú9)
Brass: naHaás 'áSfar (*yellow copper*)
Brassière: Suutiyaán
Brave: shujaá9 (shuj9aán)
Bread: xubz
Breadth: 9arD
Break: v. tr. kásar(a) kasr *intr.* (*be broken*) 'inkásar yankásir 'inkisaár
Breakfast: v. 'afTar. yúfTir, 'ifTaár

189

n. fuTuúr

Breast: (*chest*) Sadr. Suduúr

Breath: nafs

Breathe: tanaffas. yantanáffas

Bribe: v. bárTal. yubárTil

n. barTiíl (baraaTiíl) ráshwa (-aát) *Take a bribe:* 'irtásha. yartáshi tabárTal. yatabárTal

Brick: 'aajúrra (*coll.*) 'aajurr (*pl.*) (aát)

Bride: 9aruús (9araáyis)

Bridegroom: 9ariís (9ursaán)

Bridge: jisr (jusuúr)

Bring: jaab(i). *Bring!* = *jiib!*

Broad: 9ariíD

Broadcast: n. idhaá9a (-aat)

Broken: maksuúr

Broom: míknasa (makaánis)

Brother: 'ax ('íxwa) ('áxu + *suffixes and nouns, e.g.* 'axuúha = *her brother* 'áxu Hánna = *Hanna's brother*) (*friendly greeting*) ya 'áxii; (*brethren*) 'ixwaán *e.g.* al-'ixwaán al-muslimiín = *The Muslim Brothers*

Brown: 'ásmar (*m.*) sámra (*f.*) súmur (*pl.*), búnni (*coffee-coloured*)

Brush: v. fárrash. yufárrish

n. fúrsha (fúrash)

Brutal: wáHshi

Bucket: n. saTl ('asTaál/suTuúl)

Build: bána. yábni. binaá'

Builder: bannaá' (-iín)

Building: (*edifice*) binaáya (-aát)

Bullet: raSaáSa (coll.) raSaáS (*pl.*) (-aát)

Buried: madfuún

Burn: tr. Háraq(i) Harq

intr. 'iHtáraq. yaHtáriq. 'iHtiraáq

Burst: tr. shaqq(u)

intr. (*be burst*) 'insháqq. yanshíqq. 'inshiqaáq. (*of bomb*) 'infájar. yanfájir 'infijaár.

Bus: baaS (-aát)/baSS (-aát)

Business: 'ashghaál (*plural of* shughl = *work*), *e.g.* al-'ashghaál mush kuwáyyisa = *business is not good;* (*trade*) tijaára, (*business man*) rájul 'a9maál

Busy: mashghuúl

Butcher: laHHaám (-iín). jazzaár (-iin) (*E*) gaSSaáb (-iín) (*S.A. & Gulf*)

Butter: zíbda

Button: (*on garment or machine*) zirr ('azraár)

Buy: 'ishtára. yashtári. (shára)

Buyer: mushtári (mushtariyiín)

By: (*near, at*) janb,/qariíb (min)/bi, *e.g.* 'áju bi sayyaára = *they came by car*

By means of: bi waásiTat . . ., *e.g.* 'áHmad qátal rashiíd bi waásiTat xánjar = *Ahmed killed Rashiid by means of a dagger*

By day: bin-nahaár

By night: bil-layl

C

Cabbage: malfuúfa (*coll.*) malfuúf [*pl.*) -aát

Cake: ka9k

Calculate: Hásab(a) Hisaáb

Calendar: taqwiím

Caliph: xaliífa (*masculine word!*) *pl.*) xúlafa

Call: v. (*call someone*) naáda. yunaádi. nidaá', (*call out to*) SaaH bi, (*call on = visit*) zaar(u) ziyaára, (*give name to*) sámma. yusámmi

Calm: adj. haádi

Camel: jámal (jimaál)

Camp: v. xáyyam. yuxáyyim

n. muxáyyam (= *tented camp* (-aát)

mu9áskar (= *military camp*) (-aát)

Campaign: Hámla (-aát)

Can: v. (*to be able*) qádar(i) qúdra

n. 9ilba. 9ilab

Canal: qanaát *e.g.* qanaát as-suwáys = *Suez Canal*

Cancer: saraTaán

Candle: shám9a (sham9aát)

Cannon: midfa9 (madaáfi9)

Capable: (*able to do something*) muqtádir

Capacity: sí9a (*of container*)
    qúwwa (*of generator*)
Cape: (*headland*) rá'as (ru'uús)
Capital: (*city*) 9aásima. (9awaásim)
    (*money*) rasmaál (rasaamiíl)
Car: sayyaára (-aát). 9arabíyya
    (-aát) (*E.*)
Caravan: (*of camels*) qaáfila.
    (qawaáfil)
Card: (*playing*) wáraqa(t) al-lá9ab
    (wáraq al-lá9ab), (*ticket, label
    etc.*) biTaáqa-aát
Cardboard: kartáwna. kartáwn.
Care for: v. 'ihtámm (+ bi).
    yahtámm 'ihtimaám
Careless: múhmil (-iín)
Cargo: Himl
Car park: máwqif sayyaaraát
    (mawaáqif)
Carpenter: najjaár (-iín)
Carpet: sijjaáda (sajaajiíd)
Carrot: jázara (*coll.*) jázar (*pl.*)
    -aat
Carry: Hámal(i) Haml (*away*)
    shaal(i) shiyaála
Case: (*legal affair*) qaDíyya.
    (qaDaáya)
Cash: n. naqd (nuquúd)
    adv. náqdan = *in cash*
Castle: qaSr (quSuúr)
Cat: qiTT (qíTaT) (*m.*), qíTTa
    (qiTTaát) (*f.*)
Catch: masak(a) mask
Cattle: baqar (= *cows*) (mawaashi)
Cauliflower: qarnabiíTa (*coll.*)
    qarnabiíT (*pl.*) -aát
Cause: n. sábab ('asbaáb)
    v. sábbab. yusábbib
Ceiling: sáqif. (suquúf)
Celebrate: (*an occasion*) 'iHtáfal
    (+ bi) yaHtáfil. 'iHtifaál (*a feast
    day*) 9áyyad. yu9ayyid
Celery: karáfs
Cellar: sirdaáb (saraadiíb)
Cement: 'ismént
Cemetery: máqbara (maqaábir)
Censorship: raqaába
Centre: (*circle, of administration*)
    márkaz (maraákiz), (*middle*)

wasT ('awsaáT)
Century: qarn (quruún)
Ceremony: 'iHtifaál (-aát)
Certain: 'akiid (*inevitable*)
    muta'ákkid (*certain - of person*)
Certainly: (*naturally*) Táb9an, (*of
    course*) ma9luúm, (*yes, do*) bálli
Certificate: shahaáda (-aát)
Chain: sílsila (salaásil) (*also chain of
    mountains*)
Chair: kúrsi (karaási)
Chalk: Tabashiír (*rock and writing
    material*)
Champion: baTl ('abTaál)
Chance: fúrSa (fúraS)
Change: tr. (*alter*) gháyyar (yugháy-
    yir. taghyiír
    intr. tagháyyar. yatagháyyar
    (*change money*) Sárraf. yuSárrif.
    taSriíf
    n. (*small coins*) firaáTa
    n. (*money left over after having
    paid*) kamaála
Chapter: faSl (fuSuúl)
Character: (*personal quality*) Tab9
    ('aTbaá9), (*letter*) Harf (Huruúf)
Chase: Taárad. yuTaárid.
    muTaárada
Cheap: raxiíS
Cheaper than: 'árxaS min . . .
Cheek: xadd (xuduúd)
Cheese: júbna
Chemist: Sáydali (Sayaádila)
Chemist's shop: Saydalíyya (-aát)
Cheque: shakk (-aát)
Chess: saTránj
Chicken: dajaája (*coll.*) dajaáj (*pl.*)
    -aát
Chief: n. ra'iís. rú'asa
    adj. ra'iísi
Child: walad ('awlaád)
Chin: díqin (duquún)
Cholera: kólera
Choose: 'ixtaár. yaxtaár. 'ixtiyaár
Christ: 'al-masiiH
Christian: masiiHi (masiiHiyyiín)
Christmas: 9iid al-miilaád
Church: kaniísa (kanaáyis)
Cigar: siigaár (-aát)

Cigarette: sigaára (sagaáyir)
Circle: daá'ira (dawaá'ir)
Circular: mudáwwar
Circumcise: Tàhhar. yuTáhhir.
  taThiír
City: madiína (múdun)
Cistern: HawD ('aHwaáD)
Civilian: mádani (madaniyiín)
Civilisation: madaníyya
Civilised: mutamáddin
Claim: Taálab, yuTaálib.
  muTaálaba
Clap: Sáffaq. yuSáffiq. taSfiíq
Class: (*in school*) Saff (Sufuúf)
Clean: naDiíf (niDaáf)
  v. náDDaf. yunáDDif. tanDiíf
Clear: adj. (*sky, relations*) Saáfi
  (*facts, attitude*) waáDiH
  v. (*clarity*) wáDDaH. yuwáDDiH.
  tawDiíH
Clearly: waáDiHan. bi-wuDuúH.
Clerk: kaátib (kuttaáb)
Clever: shaáTir (-iín)
Climate: manaáx, háwa (= *air*)
Climb: Sá9ad(a) Su9uúd–, Tála9(a)
  Tuluú9 (*both verbs are transitive
  and intransitive*)
Clinic: 9iyaáda (-aát)
Cloak: 9abaáya (-aát)
Clock: saá9a (-aát)
Close: adj. qariíb
  v. sákkar. yusákkir. taskiír
Cloth: qumaásh
Clothe: lábbas. yulábbis. talbiís
Clothes: thiyaáb. malaábis
Cloud: gháyma (ghuyuúm)
Cloudy: mugháyyim
Club: n. 9ása (9úSi) (*stick*), naádi
  (nawaádi) (*place*)
Clumsy: thaqiíl (thiqaál)
Clutch: n. klutsh (-aát) (*clutch*),
  duubriyaáj (-aát) (*embrayage Fr.*)
Coal: faHm
Coarse: xáshin
Coast: n. saáHil (sawaáHil)
Coat: kabbuút (kabaabiít)
Cockroach: SarSuúr (SaraaSiír)
Cocoa: kakaáw
Coffee: qáhwa (*the drink*), bunn

(*the bean*)
Coin: n. naqd
Cold: rashH. (rushuuHaát) (*disease*)
  adj. baárid (*of things*)
    bardaán (*of people*)
  n. bard (*coldness*)
Colleague: zamiíl. zúmala
Collect: v. tr. jáma9(a) jam9
  v. intr. 'ijtáma9 (*of people*)
Collection: majmuú9a (*thing*)
College: kullíyya (-aát)
Collide: 'iSTáDam. yaSTádim.
  'iStidaám
Colloquial: daárij e.g. al-lúgha
  addaárja = *the colloquial lan-
  guage*
Colonel: za9iím (zú9ama)
Colour: lawn ('alwaán)
Coloured: muláwwan
Comb: mushT ('amshaáT)
Combatant: muHaárib (-iín)
Come: 'ája. yíji
Comfort: n. raáHa
  v. ráyyaH. yuráyyiH. taryiíH
Comfortable: muriíH
Commander: qaá9id (qaáda)
Commando: komándos (*pl.*)
Comment: ta9liíq
Commentator: mu9álliq
Commerce: tijaára
Commercial: tijaári
Commit (*a crime*): 'irtákab
  (jariíma), yartákib. 'irtikaáb
Committee: lájna (lijaán)
Common: 'i9tiyaádi
Communicate (*with*): 'ittáSal.
  yattáSil. 'ittiSaál (+ bi)
Communism: shuyuu9íyya
Communist: shuyuú9i (-iyyiín)
Community: mujtáma9
Companion: rafiíq (rúfaqa)
Company: shárika (-aát) (*commer-
  cial*)
Compass: buúSla
Compel: 'ájbar. yújbir. 'ijbaár
Compensate: 9áwwaD. yu9áwwid
  ta9wiíD.
Compete (*with*) naáfas. yunaáfis
  munaáfasa.

Competence: kafaá‘a

Complain: ‘ishtáka, yashtáki shákwa. (li + *person* min + *thing*)

Complaint: shákwa (shakaáwi)

Complete: adj. kaámil

v. kámmal. yukámmil. takmiíl

Complicated: mu9áqqad

Component: qism (‘aqsaám) juz‘ (‘ajzaá‘)

Comprehensive: shaámil

Compromise: n. Hall wáSaT (*i.e. solution of middle*)

Compulsory: ‘ijbaári

Computer: dimaágh ‘iliktráwni. (‘ádmigha ‘iliktrawníyya) (*i.e. electric brain*)

Conceited: maghruúr

Concentrate: rákkaz. yurákkiz. tarkiíz.(fíkruh9ála = *his thoughts on*)

Concept: fíkra. ‘af kaár

Concern: v. hamm. yahímm. hamm.

Concerning: bi-xuSuúS

Concession: ‘imtiyaáz (*oil concession etc.*)

Concrete: baaTuún (*the material*)

Condition: sharT (shuruúT) (*term of an agreement*): Haal. (‘aHwaal) (kayf al-Haal?)

Conference: mu‘támar (-aát)

Confess: ‘i9táraf. ya9tárif. ‘i9tiraáf

Confidence (in): thíqa (+ bi)

Confident (in): waáthiq (+ bi)

Confiscate: SaáDar. yuSaáDir. muSaáDara

Confuse: sháwwash. yusháwwish. tashwiísh

Congestion: ‘izdiHaám

Congratulate: hánna. yuhánni. táhni‘a

Conquer: fátaH(a) fatH.

Conscription: tajniíd ‘ijbaári (*forced recruitment*)

Conservative: muHaáfiZ (-iín)

Consider: ‘i9tábar. ya9tábir. ‘i9tibaár

Considerable: mush qaliíl

Conspiracy: mu‘aámara (-aát)

Conspirator: muta‘aámir (-liín)

Constipation: ‘imsaák

Constitution (of country): dastuúr. (dasaátir)

Consul: qúnSul (qanaáSil)

Consulate: qunSulíyya (-aát)

Consultant: mustashaár (-iín)

Consume: ‘istáhlak. yastáhlik. ‘istihlaák.

Consumer: mustáhlik (-iín)

Contact (get in contact with): ‘ittáSal (bi) yattaSil. ‘ittiSaál

Contain: Háwa. yáHwi

Contaminate: wássax. yuwássix. tawsiíx.

Contemporary: mu9aásir (-iín)

Continent: n. qaárra (-aát)

Continual: mustamírr

Continue: ‘istamárr. yastamírr, ‘istimraár

Contract: (agreement) ‘ittifaáq kuntraátu (-aát)

Contradict: xaálaf. yuxaálif. muxaálafa

Contrary: n. 9aks (*on the contrary*) bil-9aks

Contribute: tabárra9. yatabárra9. tabárru9 (+ *bi*)

Control: n. SáyTara (*under the control of . . .* = taHt SáyTarat . . .)

v. Dábat(u) DabT (*control machine*)

Conversation: Hadiíth (‘aHaadiíth)

Convince: ‘áqna9. yúqni9. ‘iqnaá9.

Cook: Tabbaáx (-iín)

v. Tábax(u) Tabx

Cooperate: ta9aáwan. yata9aáwan. ta9aáwun (= *cooperation*)

Coordinate: nássaq. yunássiq. tansiíq (= *coordination*)

Copy: n. násxa (núsax)

Coral: mirjaán

Corner: zaáwiya (zawaáya)

Corporal: 9ariíf (9úrafa) (*rank*)

Correct: adj. SaHiíH

Correspondent: muraásil (-iín)

Corridor: mamárr (-aát)

Corrupt: adj. faásid

Corruption: fasaád

Cost: si9r ('as9aár) (price)
Costly: ghaáli
Cotton: n. quTn.
adj. qúTni
Couch: kánaba (-aát)
Cough: n. sá9la
Council: májlis (majaális)
Count: 9add (i). 9add
Country: bilaád (buldaán) (state)
riif ('aryaáf) (as opposed to town)
Coup: 'inqilaáb (-aát)
Couple: jawz ('ajwaáz)
Courage: shajaá9a
Courageous: shujaá9 (shuj9aán)
Court (of law): máHkama
(maHaákim), (tennis etc) mál9ab
(malaá9ib)
Courteous: laTiif (lúTafa)
Courtesy: luTf
Cover: n. gháTa ('ághtiya)
v. gháTTa. yugháTTi. tághTiya
Cow: báqara. báqar (= cattle) (pl.)
-aat
Coward(ly): jabaán (júbana)
Crate: Sanduúq (Sanaadíiq)
Create: xálaq(i) xalq
Creditor: daáyin (-iín)
Crime: jariíma (jaraáyim)
Criminal: mújrim (-iín)
Cripple: 'á9raj (m.) 9árja (f.) 9urj
(pl.)
Crisis: 'ázma (-aát)
Critic: naáqid (nuqqaád)
Criticism: naqd
Criticise: 'intáqad. yantáqid.
'intiqaád
Crooked: 'á9waj
Cross: Saliíb (Sulbaán) – 'aS-Saliíb
al-'áHmar = the Red Cross
Crowd: jumhuúr (jamaahíir) (large
group) záHma (throng, crush)
Crown: taaj (tiijaán)
Cruel: qaási- (yiín)
Cruelty: qasaáwa
Cube/Cubic: muká99ab
Cucumber: xiyaára (coll.) xiyaár (pl.)
-aát)
Cultural: thaqaáfi
Culture: thaqaáfa

Cup: finjaán (fanaájiin)
Cupboard: xazaána (-aát)
Cure: v. tr. sháfa. yáshfi. shífa
Current (electricity, water): tayyaár
Curtain: sitaára (sataáyir)
Cushion: mixádda (maxaádd)
Custom (habit): 9aáda (-aát) (at bor-
ders) júmruk (jamaárik)
Customer: zabuún (zabaáyin)
Cut: v. tr. qáTa9(a) qaT9
Cutlet: kustalaáta (-aát)
Cylinder (mathematics – engine)
'isTwaána (-aát)

D

Dagger: xánjar (xanaájir)
Daily: adj. yáwmi
adv. yawmíyyan
Dam: n. sadd (suduúd)
Damage: n. Dárar ('aDraár)
v. Darr. yaDúrr
Damp: adj. raTb
Dance: n. raqS (raqSaát)
v. ráqaS (u) raqS
Danger: xáTar ('axTaár)
Dangerous: xáTir
Dark: múZlim (colour = ghaámiq)
Darkness: Zalaám
Data: ma9luumaát
Date: taariíx (tawaariíx) (fruit)
thámra (thámar)
Daughter: bint (banaát)
Dawn: n. fajr
Day: yawm ('ayyaám) (opposed to
night) nahaár
Dead: máyyit (máwta)
Deaf: 'áTrash (m.) Társha (f.)
Tursh (pl.)
Dealings: mu9aamalaát
Dean: 9amiíd (9úmada)
Dear: (beloved) Habiíb/9aziíz, (in
price) ghaáli
Death: mawt
Debris: HiTaám
Debt: dayn (duyuún)
Debtor: madyuún (-iín)
Deceive: ghashsh (u) ghashsh
Decide: qárrar yuqarrir (vb. n =)

194

qaraár N.B. taqriir = report.
Decimal: 9úshri
Decision: qaraár (-aát)
Deck: Dahr (i.e. back of a ship)
Declaration: 'i9laán (-aát)
Declare: 'á9lan. yú9lin. 'i9laán
Decorate: záyyin. yuzáyyin. tazyiín
Decrease: n. nuqSaán
Decree: n. marsuúm (maraasiím)
Deduct: TáraH (a) TáraH ('íTraH
   thalaátha = take away three!)
Deep: adj. 9amiíq
Defeat: n. haziíma (hazaáyim)
   v. házam(i)
Defect: 9ayb (9uyuúb)
Defective: naáqiS
Defence: difaá9
Defend: daáfa9 (9an) yudaáfi9.
   difaá9 e.g. daáfa9 9an báy-
   tuh = he defended his house
Definite: 'akiíd
Degree: dáraja (-aát)
Delay: v. tr. 'áxxar. yu'áxxir. ta'xiír
Delegate: n. manduúb (-iín)
   v. tr. 'intádab. yantádib. 'intidaáb
Delegation: wafd (wufuúd)
Delicious: ladhiídh
Deliver: (cause to arrive) wáSSal.
   yuwáSSil. tawSiíl
Demand: n. Tálab (-aát)
   v. Tálab(u)
Democracy: diimuqraaTíyya
Democrat: diimuqraáTi (-yiín)
Demolish: xárrab. yixárrib. taxriíb
Demonstration (political):
   muZaáhara
Dentist: Hakiím 'asnaán. (Húkama
   'asnaán) (lit: = teeth doctor)
Deny: 'ánkar. yúnkir. 'inkaár
Depart (on journey): saáfar.
   yusaáfir. musaáfara
Department: daáyra (dawaáyir)
Depend: (rely on) 'i9támad (9ála)
   ya9támid. 'i9timaád, (depend on a
   factor) tawáqqaf (9ala). yatwáq-
   qaf. tawáqquf.
Deposit: wadií9a (wadaáyi9)
Depot: mustáwda9 (-aát)
Depth: 9umq

Deputy: naáyib (nuwwaáb)
Descend: názal(i) nuzuúl
Describe: wáSaf. yuúSif/yáwSaf
   waSf
Description: waSf ('awSaáf)
Desert: SáHra (SaHaára)
Deserve: 'istaHáqq. yastaHíqq.
   'istiHqaáq
Design: n. taSmiím (taSaamiím) v.
   Sámmam. yuSámmim
Desk: máktab (makaátib)
Despair: n. ya's
   v. yá'as. yií'as
Despise: 'iHtáqar. yaHtáqir.
   'iHtiqaár
Destination: hádaf. 'ahdaáf
Destroy: xárrab. yuxárrib. taxriíb/
   dámmar etc.
Detail: n. tafSiil (tafaaSiil)
Detect: 'iktáshaf. yaktáshif.
   'iktishaáf
Detergent: munáDDif (-aát)
Develop: v. tr. Táwwar. yuTáwwir.
   taTwiír
   v. intr. taTáwwar. yataTáwwar.
   taTáwwur
Device: jahaáz (-aát/'ajhiza)
Devil: shayTaán (shayaaTiín)
Diagram: rasm (rusuúm)
Dialect: láhja (-aát)
Dialogue: Hiwaár (-aát)
Diameter: quTr
Diarrhoea: 'is-haál
Dictate: (letters) 'ámla. yúmli,
   'imlaá' (9ála = to)
Dictator: diktaatuúr
   (diktaatuuriyya)
Dictionary: qaamuús (qawaamiís)
Die v. maat. yamuut. mawt
Difference: farq (furuúq)
Different: muxtálif
Dig: v. Háfar (i) Hafr
Diggings: Hafriyyaát
Dignity: sháraf
Diligence: 'ijtihaád
Diligent: mujtáhid
Dimension: bu9d ('ab9aád)
Dine: ta9áshsha. yat9áshsha.
   ta9áshsha

195

Dinner: 9ásha (9ashayaát)
Diploma: shihaáda (-aát)
Diplomacy: diplawmaasíyya
Diplomat: diplawmaási (-iyyiín)
Direct: adj. mubaáshir
Direction: jíha (-aát) *e.g.* min jíhat ash-shimaál = *from the North*
Director: mudiír (mudara)
Directory: daliíl
Dirt: wásax ('awsaáx)
Dirty: wásix
Disagree: 'ixtálaf ma9. yaxtálif. 'ixtilaáf
Disappear: 'ixtáfa. yaxtáfi. 'ixtifaá'
Disappointment: xáyba
Disaster: muSiíba (maSaáyib)
Discipline: niZaám
Discover: 'iktáshaf. yaktáshif. 'iktishaáf
Discrimination: tamyiíz
Discuss: báHath(a) baHth + fi, *e.g.* báHath fil-múshkila = *he discussed the problem*
Discussion: baHth ('abHaáth)
Disease: máraD ('amraáD)
Disgust: 'ishmi'zaáz
Disgusted (at): mushma'ízz (min)
Dish: SaHn (SuHuún)
Disinfectant: muTáhhir (-aát)
Dismiss: Sáraf(i) Sarf
Disorder: fáwDa
Dispute: n. nizaá9
Distance: masaáfa
Distil: qáTTar, yuqáTTir. taqTiír
Distilled: muqáTTar, *e.g.* mayy muqáTTar = *distilled water*
Distort: sháwwah, yusháwwih. tashwiíh
Distribute: wázza9. yuwázzi9 tawzii9
Ditch: Húfra (Húfar)
Divan: diiwaán (-aát)
Divide: qássam. yuqássim. taqsiím
Divorce: n. Talaáq
v. tr. Tállaq. yuTálliq
Do: 9ámal(a) 9ámal
Doctor: Tabiíb ('aTibbaá')/Hakiím (Húkama)/doktuúr (dakaàtra)

Doctrine: mábda' (mabaádi')/ 9aqiída. (9aqaáyid)
Dollar: duulaár (-aát)
Domestic: báyti
Donkey: Himaár (Hamiír)
Door: baab ('abwaáb)
Doorman: bawwaáb (-iín)
Dot: núqTa (núqaT)
Doubt: n. shakk (shukuúk)
v. shakk(u)
Down: adv. taHt
Downstairs: taHt
Dozen: dazziína
Drag: v. jarr(u) jarr
Drain: n. máSraf (maSaárif)
Drawer: jaaruúr (jawaariír)
Dream: n. Hilm ('aHlaám)
v. Hálam(a)
Dress: n. (*of woman*) fustaán (fasaatiín)
v. lábas(a) libs *e.g.* lábasat fustaán = *she put on a dress*
Dressmaker: xayyaáTa (-aát)
Drill: v. Hafar(i) Hafr
Drink: n. mashruub (-aát)
v. shárib(a) shurb
Drive: v. saaq(u) sawq
Driver: sawwaáq (-iín)
Drug: (*medicine*) dáwa ('ádwiya), (*narcotic*) muxáddir (-aát)
Drunk: sakraán (-iín)
Dry: adj. naáshif (= *not wet*), yaábis (= *hard*)
v. tr. náshshaf. yunáshshif. tanshiíf
Dumb: 'áxras (*m.*) xársa (*f.*) xurs (*pl.*)/'ábkam (*m.*) bákma (*f.*) bukm (*pl.*)
During: xilaál/'athnaá'
Dust: ghubaár
Duty: waájib (-aát) (*customs*) rasm (rusuúm)
Dwelling: máskan (masaákin)

E

Each: kull (+ *singular noun*)
Ear: 'údhn ('aadhaán)
Early: (*too early*) bakkiír (*early hour*) mubákkir

196

Earn: kásab(i) kasb
Earth: 'arD (*f.*)
East: sharq
Easter: 9iid al-qiyaáma
Eastern: shárqi
Easy: sahl, basiíT
Eat: 'ákal. yaákul. 'akl
Economic: 'iqtiSaáDi
Economy: 'iqtiSaáD
Edge: Tarf ('aTraáf)
Editor: muHárrir (-iín)
Editorial: 'iftitaaHíyya
Educate: 9állam. yu9állim. ta9liím
Education: (*knowledge*) 9ilm (*process of*) tarbiya
Effect: natíija (nataáyij)
Efficiency: fa9aalíyya
Efficient: fa99aál (= *effective*)
Effort: juhd (juhuúd)
Egg: báyDa (bayD)
Either . . . or: ya . . . ya . . .
Elect: 'intáxab. yantáxib. 'intixaáb
Election: 'intixaáb (-aát)
Electric: kahrabaá'i
Electricity: káhraba
Elementary: 'ibtidaá'i
Elephant: fiil ('afyaál)
Eloquent: faSiíH
Embassy: sifaára (-aát)
Emergency: Taári' (Tawaári')
Emigrant: muhaájir (-iín)
Emigrate: haájar. yuhaájir. muhaájara
Emigration: muhaájara
Emotion: 9aáTifa (9awaáTif)
Emperor: 'impraatuúr
Empire: 'impraatuuríyya
Employ: (*recruit*) 'istáxdam. yastáxdim. 'istixdaám, (*use*) 'istá9mal. yastá9mil. 'isti9maál
Empty: faárigh
End: v. *tr.* xállaS. yuxálliS. taxliíS
   n. nihaáya
Enemy: 9ádu ('a9daá')
Energetic: nashiíT (nishaáT)
Energy: nashaáT
Engine: maákina, –muHárrik (-aát)
Engineer: muhándis (-iín)
Enjoy: 'inbáSat. yanbáSat.

'inbiSaáT (+ *bi*)
Enlarge: kábbar. yukábbir. takbiír
Enough: n. kifaáya adj. kaáfi
Enter: dáxal(u) duxuúl
Entertain: sálla. yusálli. tásliya
Entertaining: musálli
Entertainment: tásliya
Entrance: mádxal -madaáxil)
Envelope: Zarf (Zuruúf)
Equal: n. adj. mu9aádil
   v. yu9aádil/yusaáwi
Equator: xaTT al-'istiwaá'
Equip: jáhhaz. yujáhhiz. tajhiíz
Equipment: mu9addaát
Erect: v. bána. yábni
Espionage: jaasuusíyya
Et cetera, etc.: wa 'ila 'axírihi
Evaporate: tabáxxar. yatabáxxar. tabáxxur
Eve: láylat . . . e.g. láylat 9iid al-miilaád = *Christmas Eve*
Evening: masaá' ('amsiyaát)
Ever: 'ábadan
Every: kull (+ *singular noun*)
Everybody: kull waáHid
Evidence: daliíl (dalaáyil)
Evil: sharr (shuruúr)
   adj. shariír
Ex-: saábiq, e.g. waziír saábiq = *former* (ex) *minister*
Exact: adj. maZbuúT
Exaggerate: kábbar. yukábbir. takbiír
Examination: 'imtiHaán (-aát)
Example: máthal ('ámthila)
Exceed: zaad. yaziíd. ziyaáda (+ 9an)
Excellency (*as title*) sa9aáda e.g. sa9aádat al-waxiír = *His Excellency the Minister*
Excellent: mumtaáz
Except: prep. 'illa
Exception: shudhuúdh (= *anomaly*)
Exceptional: ghayr 'i9tiyaádi
Exchange: n. mubaádala (*of money*) Sarf
   v. intr. tabaádal. yatabaádal. tabaádul
Excite: háyyaj. yuháyyaj. tahyiíj

Excrete: 'áfraz. yúfriz. 'ifraáz
Excursion: ríHla (-aát)
Excuse: n. 9udhr (9udhuúr)
v. tr. 9ádhar(i) 9udhr
Execute: (*kill*) 'á9dam. yú9dim.
'i9daám (*implement*) náffadh.
yunáffidh. tanfíidh
Exempt: 'á9fa. yú9fi. 'i9faá'
Exercise: n. tamriín (tamaariín)
v. tr. márran. yumárrin. tamriín
v. intr. tamárran. yatamárran.
tamárrun
Exhibition: má9raD (ma9aáriD)
Exile: v. tr. náfa. yánfi. náfi
Existing: mawjuúd (= *found*)
Exit: máxraj (maxaárij)
Expenditure: maSruúf (maSaariíf)
Expensive: ghaáli
Experience: n. xibra
v. tr. & intr. 'ixtábar. yaxtábir.
'ixtibaár
Experiment: tájriba (tajaárib)
Expert: xabiír (xúbara)
Explain: sháraH(a) sharH–fássar.
yufássir. tafsiír
Explode: v. intr. 'infájar. yanfájir.
'infijaár
Export: n. Saádir (-aát)
v. Sáddar. yuSáddir. taSdiír
Expulsion: TarD
Extend: v. tr. madd(u) madd
v. intr. 'imtádd. yamtádd.
'imtidaád
External: xaáriji
Eye: 9ayn (9uyuún) (*f.*)

F

Face: n. wahj (wujuúh)
v. tr. waájah. yuwaájih.
muwaájaha
Fact: haqíiqa (haqaáyiq)
Factor: 9aámil (9awaámil)
Factory: máSna9 (maSaáni9)
Fail: fáshal(a) fashl
Fair: n. má9rad (ma9aáriD) (= *ex-
hibition*)
adj. 9aádil (= *just*)
Fairness: 9adaála (= *justice*)

Faith: 'iimaán (bi = *in*)
Faithful: mú'min (= *believer*)
'amiín (= *honest*) muxliS
(= *sincere*)
Fall: v. wáqa9. yáwqa9. wáq9a
False: adj. kaádhib (= *lying*) mush
SaHíiH (= *not correct*)
Fame: shúhra
Family: 9aá'ila (9awaá'il)
Famine: juu9
Fanatic: muta9ássib (-iín)
Fanaticism: ta9ássub
Far: adj. ba9iíd
Fare: ta9riífa
Farm: mázra9a (mazaári9)
v. tr. & intr. zára9(a) ziraá9a
Farmer: fallaáH (-iín) (= *peas-
ant*) muzaári9 (-iín)
Fashion: máwDa (múwaD)
Fashionable: 9al-máwDa
Fast: adj. sarií9 (= *quick*)
v. Samm (u) Sawm (= *not eating*)
Fat: adj. samiín (simaán)
Father: 'ab ('aabaá') ('abu +
suffixes and nouns e.g. 'abuú-
ha = *her father*)
Fault: n. ghálaT ('aghlaáT)
Fear: n. xawf (min = *of*)
v. xaaf (min). yaxaáf. xawf
(xift = *I feared*)
Feast: 9iid ('a9yaad) (= *feast-day*)
waliíma (walaáyim) (= *banquet*)
Feather: riísha (ríyash)
Features (*of face or situation*):
malaámiH
Federal: 'ittiHaádi
Federation: 'ittiHaád (-aát)
Feel: shá9ar (bi) (a) shu9uúr)
Fence: n. siyaáj ('asyaáj)
Fertile: xáSib
Fertilise: xáSSab. yuxáSSib. taxSiíb
Fertiliser: samaád ('ásmida)
Festival (*artistic etc.*): mahrajaán
Feudalism: 'iqTaa9íyya
Fever: Húmma
Feverish: maHmuúm
Few: qaliíl (qilaál)
Field: Haql (Huquúl)
Fig: tiina (*coll.*) tiin (*pl.*) -aát

Fight: v. tr. Haárab. yuHaárib.
muHaáraba.
File: n. mábrad (mabaárid) (=
tool), miláff (-aát) (for papers)
v. HaTT bil-miláff (i.e. put in the
file)
Fill: mála' (a) mal'
Film: fiilm ('aflaám)
Final: nihaá'i
Finance: tamwiil (= financing)
Financial: maáli
Find: v. tr. láqa yulaáqi. mulaaqaát
Fine: n. gharaáma (-aát) (= pen-
alty)
Finger: n. 'usbú9 ('asaabi9)
Fire: n. naar (niiraán)
Fire-brigade: 'iTfaa'íyya
Firm: adj. thaábit
First: 'áwwal (m.) 'uúla (f.)
Fish: n. sámaka (coll.) sámak (pl.)
-aát
Fisherman: SayyaáD samak
(-iín . . .)
Fishing: SayD sámak
Fix: v. tr. thábbat (e.g. nail).
yuthábbit. tathbiít
Flag: 9álam ('a9laám)
Flat: n. sháqqa (-aát) (= dwelling)
adj. muSáTTaH (= level)
Flea: barghuút (baraaghiít)
Float: v. intr. 9aam (u)
Flood: n. Tawafaán
v. tr. Táwwaf. yuTáwwif. taTwiíf
Flour: TaHiín
Flow: v. intr. jára. yájri. jarayaán
Flower: n. záhra (zuhuúr)
Flu: fluu
Fluctuate: tagháyyar. yatagháyyar.
tagháyyur
Fluency: Talaáqa
Fly: n. dubbaána (coll.) dubbaán
(pl.) -aát
v. intr. Taar(i) Tayaraán
Fog: n. Dabaáb
Follow: tába9(u)
Food: 'akl/Ta9aám
Fool: majnuún (majaaniín (= mad)
'áHmaq (m.) Hámqa (f.) Humq
(pl.) (= stupid)

Foot: qádam ('aqdaám)
For: prep. li/la. minshaán. 9ashaán
Forbid: mána9(a)
Forbidden: mamnuú9
Force: n. qúwwa (-aát) (physical &
military)
Foreign: 'ájnabi
Foreigner: 'ájnabi ('ajaánib)
Foreman: ra'iís 9ummaál (= head
of workers)
Forget: nísi. yánsa. nisyaán
Forgive: saámaH. yusaámiH.
musaámaha
Fork: n. sháwka (-aát) (implement)
Form: n. shakl ('ashkaál)
v. tr. shákkal. yushákkil. tashkiíl
Formalities: rasmiyyaát
Former: adj. saábiq
Fortnight: 'usbuu9áyn
Forward: adv. li quddaám
Found: v. tr. 'ássas. yu'ássis.
ta'siís
Founder: mu'ássis (-iín)
Fraction: n. juz' ('ajzaá')
Frame: n. 'iTaár (-aát)
Franchise: 'imtiyaáz
Frank: adj. SariíH
Fraud: 'iHtiyaál
Free: adj. Hurr ('aHraár)
v. tr. Hárrar. yuHárrir. taHriír
Freedom: Hurríyya
Freeze: thállaj. yuthállij. tathliíj
Freight: shaHn
Fresh: TaáZa (invariable adjective
applied to fruit etc.)
Fresh water: mayy Hílwa
Friend: SaáHib ('aSHaáb)–Sadiiq.
'aSdiqaá'
Friendship: Sadaáqa
Frighten: xáwwaf. yuwáwwif.
taxwiíf
Frogman: ghaTTaás (-iín)
From: prep. min
Front: n. (military) jábha (-aát) (of
building) waájiha (-aát)
adj. quddamaáni
Frontier: Huduúd (plural of Hadd)
Frozen: muthállaj
Fruit: faákiha (fawaákih)

Fry: qála. yáqli (*fried eggs* = bayD máqli)
Fuel: wuquúd
Full: mal'aán (*of* = bi)
Fundamental: 'asaási
Funeral: jinaáza (-aát)
Funny: múDHik
Furnish: fárash(u) farsh
Furnished: mafruúsh
Furniture: farsh/9áfash
Future: n. & adj. mustáqbal

G

Gadget: 'aála Saghiíra (= *small device*) ('aalaát Saghiíra)
Gale: 9aásifa (9awaásif)
Gallon: galáwn
Gallows: máshnaqa (mashaániq)
Gamble: n. mughaámara (-aát) (= *risk*) *v.* qaámar. yuqaámir. muqaámara
Game: n. lú9ba (lú9ab)
Gang: n. zúmra (zúmar)
Gap: fájwa (-aát)
Garage: karaáj (-aát)
Garbage: zibaála (-aát)
Garden: n. junáyna (janaá'in)
Gardener: junáynii
Garlic: tuum
Gas: ghaaz
Gasoline: banziín
Gate: bawwaába (-aát)
Gatekeeper: baawwaáb (-iín)
Gateway: mádxal (madaáxil)
Gather: jáma9(a) jam9
Gay: farHaán (-iín) mabsuúT (-iín)
Gazelle: ghazaál (ghuzlaán)
Gear: 9ídda (= *equipment*)
General: fariíq (furuúq) (*military*) *adj.* 9aamm
Generate: wállad. yuwállid. tawliíd
Generation: tawliíd (*process*), jiil ('ajyaál) (*period*)
Generator: muwállid (-aát)
Generous: kariím (kúrama)
Genuine: 'aSiíl
Geographical: jughraáfi
Geography: jughraáfya

Geological: jiyuláwji
Geologist: jiyuláwji (-yyiin)
Geologist: jiyuláwjya. 9ilm Tabaqaát al-'arD (= *science of the layers of the earth*)
Geometry: hándasa
Get up: qaam(u) qiyaám
Gift: hadíyya (hadaáya)
Girder: jisr (jusuúr)
Girl: bint (banaát)
Give: 'á9Ta. yú9Ti. 'i9Taá'.
Give back: rájja9. yurájji9. tarjií9
Give birth to: wállad. yuwállid. tawliíd
Glass: zujaáj (*substance*) zujaája (*vessel*) kubbaáya (-aát) (*drinking glass*)
Glasses: naZZaaraát
Glimpse: n. lámHa (-aát) *v. tr.* lámaH(a) lámHa
Glorious: 9aZiím/majiíd
Go: raaH(u) rawaáH
Go back: rája9(a) rujuú9
Go down: názal(a) nuzuúl
Go in: dáxal(u) duxuúl
Go out: xáraj(u) xuruúj
Go up: Tála9(a) Tuluú9
Goal: hádaf ('ahdaáf)
Goat: maá9iz (*coll*) má9ze (*pl.*) ma9aázi
Gold: dháhab
Good: kuwáyyis
Goods: biDaá'i9
Gospel: 'injiíl
Govern: Hákam(u) Hukm
Government: Hukuúma (-aát)
Governor: Haákim (Hukkaám)
Graduate: n. xirriíj (-iín) *v. intr.* taxárraj. yataxárraj. taxárruj
Grammar: qawaá9id al-lúgha (= *rules of the language*)
Grandfather: jadd (juduúd)
Grape: 9ínaba (*coll.*) 9ínab (*pl.*) -aát
Graph: rasm (rusuúm)
Grasp: v. tr. másak(i) mask (= *grip*), fáham(a) fahm (= *understand*)

Grateful: mutashákkir/shaákir
Grave: n. qabr (qubuúr)
adj. xaTiír
Graveyard: máqbara (maqaábir)
Gravy: Saálsa
Grease: dihn
Great: 9aZiím/kabiír
Green: 'áxDar (*m.*) xaDraá' (*f.*)
xuDr (*pl.*)
Grey: ramaádi
Grievance: shákwa (shakaáwi)
Grocer: baqqaál (-iín)
Ground: 'arD (= *earth, floor*) (*f.*)
Group: jamaá9a (-aát)
Grow: v. tr. rábba. yurábbi. tárbiya
(= *cultivate*), kábur(u) (= *get
bigger, older*)
Guarantee: n. kafaála. Damaána
v. tr. káfal(a). Dáman(a)
Guard: n. Haáris (Hurraás)
v. tr. Háras(u)
Guest: Dayf. Duyuuf
Guilt: dhanb (dhunuub)

H

Habit: 9aáda (-aát)
Habitual: 9aádi
Haggle: v. tr. saáwam. yusaáwim.
musaáwama
Hair: sha9r (*single hair* = shá9ra)
Hairdresser: muzáyyin sha9r
Half: nuSS ('anSaáS)
Hall: qaá9a (-aát)
Halve: qásam(i) bin-nuSS
Ham: laHm xanziír
Hammer: míTraqa (maTaáriq),
shaakuúsh (shawaakiísh)
Hand: yad.('ayaádi)
v. sállam. yusállim. tasliím (*li* =
to)
Handkerchief: máHrama
(maHaárim), mandiíl (manaádiil)
Handle: máska (-aát)
Handsome: maliíH (*of appearance*)
Hang: v. tr. 9állaq. yu9álliq. ta9liíq
(9ála = *on, to*), shánaq(u) shanq
(= *hang on gallows*)
Happen: HáSal(u) HuSuúl

Happening: Haáditha (Hawaádith)
Happiness: sa9aáda
Happy: sa9iíd (-iín)
Harbour: miinaá' (mawaáni)
Hard: qaási (= *firm*), Sa9b (Si9aáb)
(= *difficult*)
Hardship: Diiqa
Harem: Hariím (= *women*)
Harm: Dárar ('aDraár)
v. 'ádha(bi). ya'dhi
v. tr. 'aDárr. yuDírr. 'iDraár
Harmful: muDírr. mú'dhi
Harvest: HiSaád
v. tr. HáSad(u)
Haste: 9ájala
Hasten: 9ájjal. yu9ájjil. ta9jiíl
Hat: burnáyTa (baraaniíT)
Hate: n. bughD
v. tr. kárih(a) karaáha
Hateful: kariíh. –makruúh
Have: 9ind + *pronoun endings, e.g.*
9índii = *I have*
Have to: laázim
Hawk: Sáqar (Suquúr)
Head: ra's. ru'uús (*physical*), mudiír
(múdara) (*of company*), ra'iís
rú'asa) (*of state*)
v. tr. rá'as(a) (= *lead delegation
etc.*)
Headache: wája9 ra's
Headquarters: márkaz (maraákiz)
Heal: v. tr. sháfa(i) shafaá'
Health: SíHHa
Heap: káwma (-aát)
Hear: sáma9(a) samaá9
Heart: qalb (quluúb)
Heat: n. Haraára. suxuúna
v. tr. sáxxan. yusáxxin. tasxiín
Heavy: thaqiíl (thiqaál)
Hedge: siyaáj
Height: 9ulúww
Help: v. tr. saá9ad. yusaá9id.
musaá9ada
n. musaá9ada
Helper: musaá9id. mu9aáwin
Hen: dajaája (*coll.*) dajaáj (*pl.*) -aát.
Hero: báTal ('abTaál)
Hesitate: taráddad. yataráddad.
taráddud

201

High: 9aáli
Highness (*title*): sumúww. ya SaáHib as-sumúww = *your Highness!*
Hill: jábal (jibaál) (*mountain*), tell ('atlaál) (*hill*)
Hire: v. tr. 'istá'jar. yasta'jir. 'istiijaár
History: taáriix (tawaariíx)
Hit: v. tr. Dárab(u) Dárba
Hold: v. tr. másak(i). mask
Hole: Húfra (Húfar)
Holiday: fúrSa (fúraS), 9úTla (9úTal)
Home: bayt (buyuút)
Homeland: wáTan ('awTaán)
Homesick: mushtaáq lil-bayt/lil-wáTan
Honest: Saádiq/'amiín
Honey: 9ásal
Hook: Sinnaára (Sanaaniir) (*fish-hook etc.*)
Hope: n. 'ámal ('aamaál)
v. 'ámal(a)
Horizon: 'ufq ('aafaáq)
Horizontal: 'úfqi
Horn: n. qarn (quruún) (*animal*), buuq ('abwaáq) (*on car, instrument*)
Horrible: faZii9
Horse: HiSaán. (*pl.*) xayl
Hospital: mustáshfa (-yaát)
Hospitality: Diyaáfa
Host: muDiíf (*one who has guests*)
Hostage: rahiína (rahaá'in)
Hostile: mu9aádi
Hotel: fúnduq (fanaádiq)/lukánda -aát)/'uutáyl (-aát)
Hour: saá9a (-aát)
House: bayt (buyuút)
Hover: Haam(u)
How: kayf
However: laákin/bass.
Human being: 'insaán (naas) (= *people*)
Humble: mutawaáDi9 (-iín) (*not arrogant*)
Humid: raTb
Humidity: ruTuúba

Hunger: juu9
Hungry: juu9aán (-iín)
Hunt: 'iStaád. yaStaád. 'iStiyaád
Hunter: Sayyaád (-iín)
Hurry: n. 9ájala
v. intr. ta9ájjal. yatá9ajjal. ta9ájjul
v. tr. 9ájjal. yu9ájjil. ta9jiíl
Hurt: n. wája9
v. tr. wájja9. yuwájji9. tawjií9
Husband: zawj/jawz ('azwaáj)
Hut: kuux ('akwaáx)
Hygienic: SíHHi

I

Ice: thalj. (thuluúj)
Icebox: thalaája (-aát)/barraáda (-aát)
Icecream: buúZa
Idea: fíkra ('afkaár–fíkar)
Identity: huwíyya (-aát)/dhaatíyya (-aát)
Ideology: 9aqaa'idíyya (-aát)
Idle: adj. 9aáTil (= *out of work*), kaslaán (= *lazy*)
Ignite: wálla9. yuwálli9. tawlií9
Ignition: tawlií9
Ignorance: jahl
Ignorant: jaáhil
Ignore: v. tr. tajaáhal. yatajaáhal. tajaáhul
Ill: mariíD (márDa)
Illegal: ghayr qaanuúni
Illiteracy: 'ummíyya
Illiterate: 'úmmi
Illness: máraD ('amraáD)
Illuminate: Dáwwa'. yuDáwwi'. tawDií'
Imaginary: xayaáli
Imagine: v. tr. taxáyyal. yataxáyyal. taxáyyul/taSáwwar. yataSáwwar. taSáwwur
Imam: 'imaám
Imitate: qállad. yuqállid. taqliíd
Imitation: taqliíd
Immediate: adj. mustá9jil (= *urgent*)
Immediately: Haálan.
Immerse: gháTTas. yugháTTis.

202

taghTiís
Immersion: taghTiís
Immigrant: muhaájir (-iín)
Immigrate: haájar. yuhaájir.
  muhaájara
Impact: Sádma (= *collision*),
  ta'thiír (= *effect*)
Impartial: ghayr mutaHáyyiz
Impartiality: 9ádam at-taHáyyuz
Impatient: ghayr Sabuúr
Imperfect: ghayr kaámil/naáqiS
Imperialism: 'isti9maár (-aát)
Imperialist: n. & adj. 'isti9maárì
  (-yyiín)
Importance: 'ahammíyya
Important: muhímm
Impossible: mustaHiíl
Impractical: ghayr 9ámali
Imprison: sájan(u) sajn/Hábas(i)
  Habs
Improbable: ghayr muhtámal
Improbability: 9ádam al-'ihtimaál
Improve: v. tr. Hássan. yuHássin.
  taHsiín
v. intr. taHássan. yataHássan.
  taHássun
Inability: 9adam al-qúdra
Incentive: daáfi9 (dawaáfi9)
Incident: Haádith (Hawaádith)
Incite (to): HárraD. yuHárriD.
  taHriíD (9ála)
Include: shámal(a) shámal
Income: daxl
Inconvenient: ghayr munaásib
Independence: 'istiqlaál
Independent: mustaqíll
Indicate: dall (9ála) (u) dalaála
Indigestion: suu' haDm
Individual: fard ('afraád) (= *person*)
Industrial: Sinaá9i
Industrious: mujtáhid (-iín)
Industry: Sinaá9a (-aát)
Infancy: Tufuúla
Infant: Tifl ('aTfaál)
Infantry: mushaát (*f.*)
Inferior: waáTi (= *low*), 'áwTa
  (= *lower*)
Inflammable: sarií9 al-'iltihaáb
  (= *quick of flaming up*)

Influence: n. ta'thiír (= *effect*)
  (-aát) nufuúdh (= *power*)
Influential: SaáHib nufuúdh
Influenza: 'influwánza
Inform: xábbar. yuxábbir. taxbiír
Informal: ghayr rásmi
Information: ma9luumaát
Inhabit: sákan(u) sakn
Inhabitant: saákin (sukkaán)
'Inherit: wárith. yárith/yáwrath.
  wirth
Initiative: mubaádara (-aát) (= *new
  line of action*)
Injection: Húqna (Húqan), 'íbra
  ('íbar) (= *needle*)
Injure: járaH(a) jurH
Injury: jurH (juruúH)
Ink: Hibr
Inlet: xaliíj Saghiír (= *small bay*)
Inner: daáxili
Innocence: baraá'a
Innocent: barií' ('ábriya)
Inquire: 'istáfsar. yastáfsir.
  'istifsaár/'istá9lam. yastá9lim.
  'isti9laám
Inquiry: 'istifsaár/'isti9laám
Insect: Háshara (-aát)
Inside: daáxil
Inspect: fáttash. yufáttish. taftiísh
Inspector: mufáttish (-iín)
Install: rákkab. yurákkib. tarkiíb.
Installation: tarkiíb
Instead (of): bádlan (min)
Institute: n. má9had (ma9aáhid)
  mu'ássasa (-aát)
  v. tr. 'ássas. yu'ássis. ta'siís (= *to
  found*)
Instruct: 9állam. yu9állim. ta9liím
Instructor: mu9állim (-iín) mudárris
  (-iín)
Insult: v. tr. 'ahaán. yuhiín. 'ihaána
  n. 'ihaána (-aát)
Insurance: ta'miím
Insure: 'ámmam. yu'ámmim.
  ta'miím
Intelligent: dháki. 'ádhkiya
Intend: qáSad(i) qaSd.
Intense: qáwi (= *strong*), shadiíd
  (= *violent, extreme*)

Intention: níyya (-aát)
Intentional: maqSuúd
Interact: tafaá9al. yatafaá9al. tafaá-9ul
Interaction: tafaá9ul
Intercourse (*sexual*): 9alaáqa jinsíyya = *sexual relationship.*
Interest: n. 'ihtimaám (= *concern*), máSlaHa (maSaáliH) (= *advantage*), faá'ida (fawaá'id) (= *income from loans*)
Interested (*in*): muhtámm (bi)
Interesting: muthiír lil-'ihtimaám (= *stirring of interest, concern*) muhímm (= *of concern to*) N.B. *"interesting" is famous as having no precise translation!*
Interfere (*in:* tadáxxal (fi). yatadáxxal tadáxxul
Interference: tadáxxul
Intermediary: waSiíT (wúSaTa)
Intermediate: mutawáSSiT
Internal: daáxili
International: dúwali
Interpret: fássar. yufássir. tafsiír (= *explain*) tárjam. yutárjim. tárjama (= *oral or written translation*)
Interpretation: tafsiír/tárjama.
Interrogation: 'istijwaáb
Interview: muqaábala (-aát)
Intestinal: muSraáni
Intestine: muSraán (maSaariín)
Intimidation: taxwiíf
Intoxicate: 'askar. yúskir. 'iskaár
Introduction: muqáddama (-aát) (*of book*) ta9riíf (*of person*)
Invasion: gházwa (ghazawaát)
Invent: 'ixtára9. yaxtári9. 'ixtiraá9
Invention: 'ixtiraá9
Inventory: jard
Invest: wáZZaf. yuwáZZif. tawZiíf
Investigate: Háqqaq (fi). yuHáqqiq. TaHqiíq
Invitation: dá9wa, –9aziíma (9azaá'im)
Invite: dá9a(u) dá9wa–9ázam(i) 9aziíma
Invoice: faatuúra (fawaatiír)

Iron: Hadiíd (*the metal*), mákwa (makaáwi) (*the implement*)
v. tr. káwa (i) kayy
Irrigate: sáqa(i) siqaáya
Irrigation: siqaáya/rayy
Island: jaziíra (jazaá'ir)
Isolate: 9ázal(i) 9azl
Ivory: 9aaj

J

Jack: jak (-jakaát) (*where English spoken*) kriik (-aát) (*where French is spoken*)
jacket: jakáyta (-aát)
Jam: murábba (-aát)
Jar: martbaán (maraatabiín)
Jealous: ghayraán (-iín)–Hasuúd (-iín)
Jealousy: ghiíra/Hásad.
Jesus: yasuú9 (almasiíH = *Messiah*) 9iísa (*the Muslim word*)
Jew: yahuúdi (yahuud)
Jewel: jáwhara (jawaáhir)
Job: shughl, –9ámal (= *work*), waZiifa (waZaá'if) (= *post*)
Join: v. tr. Damm (*u*) Damm (*things*) Damn (*thing*) li (= *to*) (*something*)
v. intr. 'inDámm li (*join a club etc.*) yanDámm. 'inDimaám
Joke: núkta (núkat)
Journey: ríHla/sáfar ('asfaár)
Joy: fáraH
Judge: n. qaádi (quDaát)
v. Hákam(u) Hukm 9ála (*person*), bi (*the penalty*) + *pass judgement on something*
Jug: 'ibriíq ('abaariíq)
Juice: 9aSiír
Jump: v. qáfaz(i) qáfaz
n. qáfza (qafazaát)
Just: adj. 9aádil (-iín) (*fair*)
adv. hállaq (*now*) bass (*only*)
Justify: bárrar. yubárrir. tabriír

K

Keep: v. tr. 'ábqa. yúbqi. 'ibqaá'

(= *make stay, retain*), 'iHtáfaZ
(bi) yaHtáfiZ. 'iHtifaáZ (= *retain
possession of*)
Kerosene: gaaz
Kettle: ghallaáya (-aát)
Key: miftaáH (mafaatiíH)
Kick: v. tr. lábaT(u) lábTa
n. lábTa (-aát)
Kidnap: xáTaf(i) xaTf
Kidney: kúlwa (kalaáwi)
Kill: v. tr. qátal(u) qatl
Kind: n. naw9 ('anwaá9)
adj. laTiif (liTaáf)
Kindergarten: ráwDat 'aTfaál
(= *children's meadow*)
King: málik (muluúk)
Kingdom: mámlaka (mamaálik)
Kiss: v. tr. baas(u) baws
n. buúsa-aát
Kit n. 9údda
Kitchen: máTbax (maTaábix)
Knee: rúkba (rúkab)
Kneel: ráka9(a) rukuú9
Knob: máska (masakaát)
Knock: v. tr. daqq(u) dáqqa *e.g.*
daqq al-baab (= *knock on the
door*)
n. Dárba (Darabaát) (= *blow*)
Knot: n. 9úqda (9úqad)
Know: 9áraf(i) má9rifa
Knowledge: má9rifa (ma9aárif)

L

Laboratory: muxtábar (-aát)
Labourer: 9aámil (9ummaál)
Lack: n. naqS
v. tr. náqaS(u) naqS, *e.g.* naqáSni
waqt (= *I lacked time*)
Ladder: súllam (salaaliím)
Lady: sáyyida (-aát)
Lake: buHáyra (-aát)
Lamb: xaruúf (xurfaán)
Lame: 'á9raj (*m.*) 9árja (*f.*) 9urj
(*pl.*)
Lamp: miSbaáH (maSaabíH)
Land: n. 'arD ('araáDi) (*f.*)
v. intr. hábaT(u) hubuúT (*of
plane*)

Language: lúgha (-aát)
Lantern: faanuús (fawaaniís)
Last: adj. 'aáxir (*m.*) 'úxra (*f.*)
Late: muta'áxxir (-iín) (*belated*)
'almarHuúm (*the late lamented*)
Lately: 'axiíran/mu'áxxiran
Latin: laatiíni
Latitude: xaTT al*9arD (*line of
breadth*)
Laugh: DáHik(a) DaHk (*at =
9ála*)
n. DáHka (-aát)
Lavatory: bayt mayy (buyuút
mayy)
Law: qaanuún (qawaaniín)
Lawyer: muHaámi (-yiín)
Lazy: kaslaán (-iín)
Leaf: wáraqa (wáraq)
Lean (meat): laHm 'áHmar/habr
Learn: ta9állam. yata9állam.
ta9állum
Lease: v. tr. 'ájjar. yu'ájjir. ta'jiír
Leather: jild (juluúd)
Leave: v. tr. tárak (u) tark (*a place*)
v. intr. saáfar. yusaáfir. musaáfara
(= *go away, on journey*)
n. 'ijaáza (-aát)
Lecture: n. muHaáDara (-aát)
v. intr. HaáDar. yuHaáDir.
muHaáDara
Ledge: n. raff (rufuúf)
Left: adj. yasaár–shimaál
Leg: rijl ('árjul) (*f.*)
Legal: qaanuúni
Leisure: faraágh (*empty time*)
Lemon: laymuúna HaámiDa (*coll.*)
laymuún HaámiD (*pl.*) -aát
HaamiDa
Lend: 'a9aár(i) 'i9aára. –'áqraD.
yúqriD. 'iqraáD
Length: Tuul
Less: 'aqáll
Lesson: dars (duruús)
Lest: li'álla
Let: v. tr. xálla. yuxálli. táxliya.
sámaH(a) samaáH li + *person*
bi + *thing, e.g.* 'al-mu9állim
sámaH lii bid-duxuúl = *the teacher
allowed me to enter*

205

Letter: n. maktuúb (makaatiíb) *(message)* Harf (Huruúf) *(of alphabet)*

Lettuce: xaSS

Level: mústawa

Liberate: Hárrar. yuHárrir. taIIriir

Liberty: Hurríyya

Library: máktaba (makaátib)

Licence: n. rúxSa (rúxaS)

Lid: n. ghaTaá' ('ághTiya)

Lie: v. intr. tamáddad. yatamáddad. tamáddud (= *recline*) kádhab(i) kadhb (= *tell a lie*)

Lieutenant: mulaázim (-iín)

Life: Hayaát

Lift: n. míS9aD (maSaá9id) *v. tr.* ráfa9(a) raf9

Light: n. nuur ('anwaar) Daw'. 'aDwaá'.

adj. xafiíf (xifaáf) *(not heavy)*

Lighter: n. wallaá9a (-aát) *(for cigarettes)*

Lighthouse: manaára (manaáwir)

Like: v. tr. Habb(i) Hubb *prep.* mithl, ka-, *e.g.* kaSadiíq = *like a friend*

Line: n. xaTT (xuTuúT)

Link: n. Síla (-aát)

Liquid: n. saá'il (sawaá'il)

List: n. qaá'ima (qawaá'im)

Listen: 'istáma9 (li). yastámi9. 'istimaá9

Little: adj. Saghiír (Sighaár) *(small)* qaliíl (qilaál) *(small quantity)*

Live: adj. Hayy ('aHyaá')

v. intr. 9aash(i) 9aysh

Liver: kibd ('akbaád)

Load: n. Himl/sháHna (-aát)

v. tr. Hámmal. yuHámmil. taHmiíl

Loaf: n. raghiíf ('árghifa) *(of bread)*

Loan: n. 'i9aára (-aát)

Local: adj. maHálli

Lock: n. qufl ('aqfaál)

v. tr. 'áqfal. yúqfil. 'iqfaál

Locust: jaraáda (jaraád)

Lone: adj. waHiíd

Long: adj. Tawiíl (Tiwaál)

Longitude: xaTT aT-Tuul (xuTuúT aT-Tuul)

Look: n. náZra (-aát)

v. taTálla9 (9ála) yataTálla9. taTállu9 = *look (at)*

Loose: adj. raxw

Lorry: láwri (lawaári)/kamiyuún (-aát)

Lose: Dáyya9. yuDáyyi9. Day9

Loud: 9aáli

Love: n. Hubb

v. tr. Habb(i) Hubb

Low: waáTi

Lubricate: záyyat. yuzáyyit. tazyíit –sháHHam. yusháHHim. tashHiim

Luggage: 9afsh, shanTaát (= *bags*)

Lunch: n. gháda ('ághdiya) *v. intr.* taghádda. yataghádda

Lung: rí'a (-aát)

Luxury: rafaáha

M

Machine: maákina (-aát)/'aála (-aát)

Mad: majnuún (-iín)

Magazine: majálla (-aát)

Magistrate: qaáDi (quDaát)

Magnet: maghnaaTiís (-aát)

Magnify: v. tr. kábbar. yukábbir. takbiír

Maid: xaádima (-aát) *(servant)*

Mail: bariíd

Maintain: v. tr. Saan(u) Siyaána *(road, machine etc.)*

Maintenance: Siyaána *(machine etc.)*

Majesty: jalaála (SaáHib al-jalaála = *his/your majesty*)

Major: muqáddam (-iín) *(military rank)*

Majority: 'aktharíyya.

Make: n. Tiraáz (Túruz) *(of car etc.)*

v. tr. 9ámal(a) 9ámal

Man: n. rájul (rijaál)–rijjaál (rajaajiíl)

Manage: v. tr. 'adaár. yudiír. 'idaára (= *administer*)

Management: 'idaára

206

Manager: mudiír (múdara)
Manner: Tariíqa (Túruq)
(= *method*)
Manners: suluúk
Manure: simaád ('ásmida)
Many: kathiír/9adiíd
Map: xariíTa (xaraá'iT)
Margin: haámish (hawaámish)
(*edge of paper etc.*)
Marine: báHri
Mark: n. 9alaáma (-aát) (*sign, feature*)
Market: n. suuq ('aswaáq)
v. tr. sáwwaq. yusáwwiq. taswiíq
Marmalade: murábba burtuqaál
Marriage: zawaáj
Marry: v. tr. tazáwwaj. yatazáwwaj. tazáwwuj
Mason: Hajjaár (-iín)
Mat: sijjaáda (sajaajiíd), bisaáT (búsuT)
Match: n. kibriíta (*coll.*) kibriít (*pl.*) kabariít. mubaára (-aát) (*contest*)
Material: maádda, qumaásh ('áqmisha) (= *cloth*)
Mathematics: riyaaDiyyaát
Maybe: yúmkin/múmkin/yajuúz
Mean: v. tr. 9ána. yá9ni. 9ány
Meaning: má9na (ma9aáni)
Measure: v. tr. qaas(i) qiyaás
Measuring tool: miqyaás (maqaayiís)
Meat: laHm (láHma = *piece of meat*)
Mechanic: n. miikaaniíki
Mechanical: 'aáli (*of machines*)
Mediate: tawáSSaT. yatawáSSaT. tawáSSut (bayn = *between*)
Medical: Tíbbi
Medicine: dáwa ('ádwiya) (*remedy*) Tibb (*the science*)
Meet: qaábal. yuqaábil. muqaábala (*interview*), laáqa. yulaáqi. mulaáqa (*by chance*)
Meeting: 'ijtimaá9 (*of council etc.*)
Member: 9úDu ('a9Daá')
Memorial: dhíkra
Memorise: HáfiZ(a) HifZ
Memory: dhaákira (*mental power*),

dhíkra (dhikriyaát) (*something remembered*)
Mention: v. tr. dhákar (u) dhikr
Menu: qaá'imat 'akl
Message: risaála (-aát)
Messenger: rasuúl (rúsul), rasuúl allaáh (= *messenger of God i.e.* Muhámmad)
Metal: má9dan (ma9aádin)
Metallic: má9dani
Metre: mitr ('amtaár)
Method: Tariíqa (Túruq)
Midday: Zuhr
Midnight: nuSS al-layl
Middle: wasT ('awsaáT)
Migrant: muhaájir (-iín)
Migrate: haájar. yuhaájir. muhaájara
Migration: híjra
Military: 9áskari
Milk: n. Haliíb
Minaret: manaára (-aát)
Mind: n. 9aql (9uquúl)
v. 'ihtámm (+ *bí*) yahtamm. 'ihtimaam
Minister: n. waziír (wúzara)
Ministry: wizaára (-aát)
Mint: ná9na9 (*herb*)
Minute: daqiíqa (daqaá'iq)
Mirror: miraáya (-aát)
Miser: baxiil (búxala)
Mist: Dabaáb xafiíf (= *light fog*)
Mistake: n. ghálTa (-aát/'aghlaáT)
Mix: v. tr. xálaT(u) xalT
Mixture: maxluúT (maxaaliíT)
Mobile: adj. mutaHárrik
Moderate: adj. mu9tádil (-iín)
Modern: adj. 9áSri (-yyiín)
Modest: mutawaáDi9 (-iín) (*humble, insignificant*)
Modification: ta9diíl (*amendment*) taghyiir (*change*)
Modify: 9áddal. yu9áddil. ta9diíl gháyyar. yugháyyir. taghyiir
Moist: raTb
Moisten: ráTTab. yuráTTib. tarTiib
Molecular: dhárri
Moment: láHZa (-aát)

Monarch: 9aáhil (9awaáhil), *e.g.*
'al-9aáhil as-sa9uúdi = *the Saudi*
monarch. málik (muluúk) (=
king)
Money: fuluús/maSaári
Monopoly: 'iHtikaár (-aát)
Month: shahr ('ash-hur/shuhuur)
Monthly: sháhri *adv.* shahríyyan
Moon: qámar ('aqmaár)
Moral: adj. 'axlaáqi
Morals: 'axlaáq (*plural of* xulq)
Morale: ma9nawiyyaát
More: 'ákthar
Morning: SabaáH/SubH
Moslem: múslim (-iin)
Mosque: jaámi9 (jawaámi9) (*large*)
  másjid. masaájid (*smaller*)
Mosquito: naamuúsa (*coll.*)
  naamuús (*pl.*) -aát
Mother: 'umm ('ummahaát)
Mountain: jábal (jibaál)
Mouse: faar (fiiraán)
Moustache: shaárib (shawaárib)
Mouth: n. famm ('afmaám) (*of per-*
  son)
Move: v. tr. Hárrak. yuHárrik.
  taHriík
v. intr. taHárrak. yataHárrak.
  taHárruk
Movement: Háraka (-aát)
Much: kathiír
Mud: waHl/Tiin
Mule: baghl ('abghaál)
Multiply: v. tr. Dárab(u) Darb
  (+ fi) *e.g.* Dárab 'ithnáyn fi
  xámsa = *he multiplied two by five*
Municipality: baladíyya (-aát)
Murder: n. qatl
v. tr. qátal(u) qatl
Murderer: qaátil (quttaál)
Murmur: v. tr. támtam. yutámtim.
  támtama
Muscle: n. 9áDala (-aát)
Museum: mátHaf (mataáHif)
Music: n. muusiíqa
Mustard: xárdal
Mutton: laHm xaruúf
Mutual: mutabaádil
Mysterious: ghaámiD

N

Nail: n. mismaár (masaámir)
v. tr. sámmar. yusámmir. tasmiír
Name: n. 'ism ('asaámi)
v. tr. sámma. yusámmi. tásmiya
Napkin: fuúTa (fúwaT)
Narrow: adj. dáyyiq
Nation: 'úmma ('úmam), *e.g.* 'al-
  'umam al-muttáHida = *the Uni-*
  ted Nations. dáwla (dúwal) (=
  state)
National: adj. wáTani (*of separate*
  country), qáwmi (*of Arabs as*
  whole)
Nationalism: waTaníyya (-aát)
Nationality: jinsíyya (-aát)
Nationalisation: ta'miím
Nationalise: 'ámmam. yu'ámmim.
  ta'miím
Natural: adj. Tabii9i
Nature: Tabii9a (Tabaáyi9)
Naval: adj. báHri
Navy: baHríyya (-aát)
Near: adj. qariíb (min) (= *to*)
prep. janb (= *near to, next to*)
Neat: muráttab
Neatness: tartiíb
Necessary: Daruúri
Necessity: Daruúra (-aát)
Neck: ráqba (riqaáb)
Need: n. Haája (li = *for*)
v. 'iHtaáj + li. yaHtaáj. 'iHtiyaáj,
  e.g. 'iHtaáj li fuluús = *he needed*
  money
Needle: n. 'íbra ('íbar)
Negative: adj. sálbi (*reply etc.*)
Neglect: n. 'ihmaál
v. tr. 'áhmal. yúhmil. 'ihmaál
Negligent: múhmil (-iin)
Negotiate: faáwaD. yufaáwiD.
  mufaáwaDa
Negotiation: mufaáwaDa (-aát)
Negro: zánji (zunuúj), 9abd (9abiíd)
  (= *slave!*)
Neighbour: n. jaar (jiiraán)
Neighbouring: mujaáwir
Neither: la *e.g.* la 9árabi wála

'inkliízi = *neither an Arab nor an Englishman*

Nephew: 'ibn 'ax (= *son of brother*), 'ibn 'uxt (= *son of sister*). ('awlaád 'ax–'uxt)

Net: n. shábaka (-aát)

Neutral: Hiyaádi (muHaáyid)

Never: 'ábadan

New: jadiíd (júdud)

News: 'axbaár (*item of news* = xábar)

Newspaper: jariída (jaraáyid)

Nice: kuwáyyis, miniiH

Niece: bint 'ax (= *daughter of brother*), bint 'uxt (= *daughter of sister*), (banaát 'ax/'uxt)

Night: láyla (*coll.*) layl (*pl.*) layaáli

Nobody: la waáHid

Noise: SawT ('aSwaáT), Dáwsha (*loud*)

Nomad: bádawi (bádu)

Nonsense: kalaám faárigh (= *empty talk*)

Normal: 'i9tiyaádi (= *usual*), Tabii9i (= *natural*)

North: shimaál
adj. shimaáli

Nose: 'anf ('unuúf)

Nothing: ma shuft shii (= *I did not see a thing, i.e. I saw nothing*) walá shii, *e.g.* shuft shii? (= *did you see anything?*) – walá shii (= *nothing*)

Notice: n. 'i9laán (-aát)
v. tr. laáHaZ. yulaáHiz. mulaáHaZa

Nought: Sifr (= *zero*)

Noun: 'ism ('asaámi)

Novel: n. riwaáya (-aát) (= *narrative*)

Now: 'al-'aan/hállaq/hássa

Nuclear: dhárri

Nuisance: 'iz9aáj (-aát)

Number: n. 9ádad ('a9daád)

Nurse: mumárriDa (-aát)

Nut: jáwza (*coll.*) jawz (*pl.*) -aát (*eatable*), Samuúla (Sawaámil) (*of a bolt*)

O

Obedient: muTií9 (-iín)

Obey: v. tr. 'aTaá9. yuTií9. 'iTaá9a

Object: n. shii ('ashyaá') (= *thing*) hádaf ('ahdaáf) (= *aim*)
v. intr. 'i9táraD (9ala). ya9táriD. 'i9tiraáD

Objection: 'i9tiraáD (-aát) (9ála = *to*)

Obligation: waájib (-aát)

Obligatory: 'ijbaári

Oblige: v. tr. 'ájbar. yújbir. 'ijbaár (= *force*)

Observe: v. tr. raáqab. yuraáqib. muraáqaba (= *watch and heed*)

Obsolete: qadiím (qúdama)

Obstacle: n. maáni9 (mawaáni9)

Obtain: HáSal (+ 9ála) (u) HuSuúl

Obvious: waáDiH (= *clear*)

Occasion: n. munaásiba (-aát) bi munaásibat ... (= *on the occasion of*)

Occur: Saar(i) Sayruúra. Hásal(u) HuSuúl

Ocean: muHiíT (-aát)

Offer: v. tr. qáddam. yuqáddim. taqdiím

Office: máktab (makaátib)

Officer: Daábit (DubbaáT) (*uniformed*)

Official: n. muwáZZaf (-iín) mas'uúl (-iín)
adj. rásmi

Often: marraát kathiíra

Oil: n. zayt (*vegetable and mineral*) nafT (*mineral only*)

Old: kabiír (kibaár) (*of people*), qadiím (*of things*)

Olive: n. zaytuúna (*coll.*) zaytuún (*pl.*) -aát

Omelette: 9újja (-aát)

On: 9ála/9a

Once: márra

Onion: báSala (*coll.*) báSal (*pl.*) -aát

Open: adj. maftuúH
v. tr. fátah(a) fatH
v. intr. 'infátaH. yanfátiH. 'infitaáH

209

Operate: v. intr. 'ishtághal. yashtághil 'ishtighaál (= *work*),
9ámal 9amalíyya(a) 9aml
(= *carry out*) *operation on* (=
li)

Operation: n. 9amalíyya (-aát)
(*medical or other*)

Opinion: rá'y ('aaraá')

Opponent: xaSm (xuSuúm)

Opportunity: fúrSa (fúraS)

Oppose: 9aáraD. yu9aáriD.
mu9aáraDa

Oppress: Zálam(i) Zulm

Oppression: Zulm

Optimism: tafaá'ul

Optimist: mutafaá'il (-iín)

Optional: 'ixtiyaári

Oral: sháfawi

Orange: n. burtuqaála/burtuqaána
(*coll.*) burtuqaál/burtuqaán (*pl.*)
-aát

adj. burtuqaáli/burtuqaáni

Orchard: bustaán (basaatiín)

Order: n. 'amr ('awaámir)

v. tr. 'ámar(u) 'amr (= *command*)

v. tr. Tálab. (u) Tálab (= *order
goods*)

Ordinary: 9aádi/'i9tiyaádi

Organisation: munáZZama (-aát)
(*body*), niZaám ('ánZima)
(*system*), tanZiím (*process*)

Organise: v. tr. náZZam,
yunáZZim. tanZiím

Origin: 'aSl ('uSuúl)

Out of order: xarbaán (-iín)

Outside: adv. bárra/xaárij adj.
barraáni/xaáriji

Oval: adj. bayDaáwi (*egg-shaped!*)

Oven: furn ('afraán)

Over: adv. & prep. fawq

Overcoat: kabbuút. (kabaabiít)

Overcome: v. tr. taghállab.
yataghállab taghállub (9ala)

Overflow: v. intr. faaD(i) fayaDaán

Overtake: láHiq(a) laHq

Own: v. tr. málak(u) mulk

Owner: SaáHib ('aSHaáb)

Ox: thawr (thiiraán)

Oxygen: 'oksijiín

P

Page: SáfHa (-aát)

Pail: SaTl (SuTuúl)

Pain: n. wája9 ('awjaá9)

v. tr. wájja9. yuwájji9. tawjií9

Paint: n. dihaán (-aát)

v. tr. dáhan(u) dahn (*a house etc.*)

Pair: n. zawj/jawz ('azwaáj/'ajwaáz)

Palace: qaSr (quSuúr)

Palm: náxla (naxl) (*tree*)
kaff (kufuúf) (*of hand*)

Pan: Tánjara (Tanaájir) (*cooking*)

Pants: kalsuún (-aát)

Paper: n. wáraqa (*coll.*) wáraq
(*pl.*) 'awraáq. jariida (jaraáyid)
(*newspaper*)

Parcel: Tard (Turuúd)

Pardon: n. 9áfu

v. tr. gháfar(i) ghufraán

Park: n. junáyna 9aámma (*public
garden*) máwqif (mawaáqif) (*for
cars*)

v. tr. wáqqaf. yuwáqqif. tawqiíf
(*cars*)

Parliament: barlamaán (-aát)

Part: n. qism ('aqsaám (*piece*), dawr
('adwaár) (*role*)

v. tr. qásam(i) qasm

Participate: 'ishtárak. yashtárik.
'ishtiraák (fi = *in*) (ma9 = *with*)

Participle: 'ism faá9il (*active participle*). 'ism maf9uúl (*passive
participle*)

Particularly: xuSuúSan

Partition: taqsiim

Partner: shariík (shúraka)

Party: Háfla (Hafalaát) (*social*),
Hizb ('aHzaáb) (*political*)

Pass: n. taSriíH (taSaariiH)
(*document*) v. tr. máraq (u)
muruúq (min) (= *pass by*)

Passenger: raákib (rukkaáb)

Passport: jawaáz sáfar (jawaazaát
sáfar)

Past: n. & adj. maáDi

Path: Tariíq (Túruq)

Patience: Sabr

210

Patient: adj. Sabuúr
n. mariíD (márDa) (*sick person*)
Patriot: wáTani
Patriotism: waTaníyya
Patrol: n. dawríyya (-aát)
v. intr. tajáwwal. yatajáwwal.
tajáwwul (fi = *in*)
Pause: n. wáqfa (-aát)
Pavement: raSiíf ('árSifa)
Pay: n. 'ajr ('ujuúr) (*wages*), raátib
(rawaátib) (*salary*)
v. tr. dáfa9(a) daf9 (li) (= *pay*
... *to*)
Peas: bisílla
Peace: silm (*absence of war*) salaám
Peanut: fuul suudaáni
Pearl: n. lúlu
Peasant: n. fallaáH (-iín)
Pen: n. qálam Hibr ('aqlaám Hibr)
Pencil: qálam ('aqlaám)
Penetrate: v. tr. 'ixtáraq. yaxtáriq.
'ixtiraáq
Peninsula: shibh jaziíra ('ashbaáh
jaziíra)
Pension: ma9aásh (-aát)
Pensioner: mutaqaá9id (-iín)
People: n. naas (*plural of person*),
sha9b (shu9uúb) (*nation*)
Pepper: fílfil
Peppermint: ná9na9
Perfect: adj. kaámil
v. tr. kámmal. yukámmil. takmiíl
Perfection: n. kamaál
Perfume: 9uTr (9uTuúr)
Perhaps: yijuúz/yúmkin
Period: n. múdda (múdad), waqt
('awqaát)
Permission: 'idhn
Permit: n. rúxSa (rúxaS) *document*)
v. intr. sámaH (li + *person* bi +
thing) (a)samaáH
Perpendicular: 9amuúdi
Person: shaxS ('ashxaáS)
Personally: shaxSíyyan
Persuade: v. tr. 'áqna9. yúqni9.
'iqnaá9
Pessimism: tashaá'um
Pessimist: mutashaá'im (-iín)
Petrol: banziín

Pharmacist: Sáydali (-yyiín)
'ajzaxaáni (-yyiín)
Phase: Tawr ('aTwaár)
Photograph: n. Suúra (Súwar)
Photographer: muSáwwir (-iín)
Physicist: fiiziyaá'i (-yyiín)
Physics: fiiziyaá'
Picture: n. Suúra (Súwar)
Piece: n. juz' ('ajzaá')
Pier: n. raSiíf ('árSifa) (= *jetty*)
Pierce: 'ixtáraq. yaxtáriq. 'ixtiraáq
Pigeon: n. Hamaáma (*coll.*)
Hamaám (*pl.*) -aát
Pile: n. káwma (-aát)
v. tr. káwwam. yukáwwim.
takwiím
Pilgrim: Haajj (Hujjaáj)
Pilgrimage: Hajj
Pill: Hábba (Hubuúb)
Pillow: mixádda (-aát)
Pilot: Tayyaár (-iín)
v. tr. saaq(u) siyaáqa Tayyaára
(= *drive an aeroplane*)
Pin: dabbuús (dabaabiís)
Pipe: 'unbuúb ('anaabiíb)
Pistol: musáddas (*six-shooter!*)
(-aát)
Peace: n. maHáll (-aát) makaán
('ámkina)
v. tr. HaTT(u) HaTT
Plain: n. sahl (suhuúl) (*flat ground*)
Plan: n. xúTTa (xúTaT)
v. tr. 'ixtáTT. yaxtáTT. 'ixtiTaáT
Plant: n. nabaát (-aát) (*growing*)
má9mal. ma9aámil (*factory*)
v. tr. zára9(a) ziraá9a
Plastic: n. blaastiik
Plate: SaHn (SuHuún)
Play: n. masraHíyya (-aát) (*thea-trical*)
v. tr. lá9ib(a) lu9b
Player: laá9ib (-iín)
Pleasant: laTiíf (lúTafa) (*people*)
ladhiídh (lidhaadh) (*food etc.*)
Pleasure: n. suruúr. *With great
pleasure* = bi kull suruúr
Pliers: zaradíyya (-aát)
Plot: n. mu'aámara (-aát) (*conspir-acy*)

v. intr. ta'aámar. yata'aámar. ta'aámur

Plum: *n.* xáwxa (*coll.*) xawx (*pl.*) -aát

Pocket: *n.* jáyb (juyuub)

Point: *n.* núqTa (núqaT) (*spot, point in games etc.*)
v. tr. dall(u) dall (9ála = *to*)

Police: *n.* buliíS (buliiSíyya)

Police-station: máxfar (maxaáfir)

Polish: *n.* buúya
v. tr. lámma9. yulámmi9. talmii9

Polite: *adj.* mu'áddab (-iín)

Politeness: luTf

Political: siyaási

Politician: siyaási (saása)

Politics: siyaása

Pollution: taláwwuth

Pomegranate: rummaána (*coll.*) rummaán (*pl.*) -aát

Pool: *n.* bírka (bírak)

Poor: faqiír (fúqara)

Popular: maHbuúb (*loved*)

Population: sukkaán (*inhabitants*)

Pork: laHm xanziir

Port: miinaá' (mawaani), márfa (maraáfi')

Porter: *n.* Hammaál (-iin) (*carrier*) bawwaáb (-iín) (*doorman*)

Possibility: 'imkaaníyya (-aát)

Possible: múmkin

Post: *n.* márkaz (maraákiz) (*police etc.*) waZiifa (waZaáyif) (*job*), báwSTa/bariid (*mail*), 9amuúd (9awaámid) (*pillar*)
v. tr. bá9ath(a) ba9th bil-bariíd (*send by post*)

Pot: *n.* 'ibriíq ('abaáriiq)

Potatoes: baTaáTa

Poultry: dijaáj

Pound: *n.* liíra (-aát) (*Syrian and Lebanese unit of money*), juneéh (-aát) (*Egyptian currency unit*), juneéh 'isterliíni (*Sterling pound*)

Pour: *v. tr.* Sabb(u) Sabb

Powder: *n.* buúdra

Power: qúwwa (-aát) (*strength*), SúlTa (-aát) (*authority*), Taáqa (*electricity*)

Practical: 9ámali

Practice: *v. tr.* márran. yumárrin. tamriín (*a skill etc.*) maáras. yumaáris. mumaárasa (*profession*)

Praise: *v. tr.* mádaH(a) madH

Pray: *v. tr.* Sálla. yuSálli. Salaát

Prayer: Salaát (Salawaát)

Precaution: 'iHtiyaát (-aát)

Precede: *v. tr.* sábaq (i) sabq

Precedent: saábiqa (sawaábiq)

Precise: daqiíq (diqaáq)

Predict: *v. tr.* tanábba. yatanábba. tanábbi

Prefer: *v. tr.* fáDDal. yufáDDil. tafDiíl

Pregnant: Haámil (Hawaámil) (*despite only applying to females, this adjective remains masculine in appearance*)

Prepare: HáDDar. yuHáddir. taHdiír

Prescribe: *v. tr.* wáSaf. yuúSif. waSf (+ li = *for*)

Prescription: wáSfa

Present: *n.* hadíyya (hadaáya)
v. tr. qáddam. yuqáddim. taqdiím (+ li = *to*)

Preside: *v. tr.* tará"as.yatará"as. tará' 'us

Presidency: ri'aása (-aát)

President: ra'iís (ru'asa)

Press: *n.* SaHaáfa (*"the Press"*) máTba9a (maTaábi9) (*printing . . .*)

Pressure: *n.* DaghT (DughuúT) *v.* DághaT (a) Daght (+ 9ala) (= *exert pressure (on)*)

Prestige: nufuúdh

Pretend: *v. intr.* taZaáhar. yataZaáhar. taZaáhur

Pretty: jamiíl (jimaál) (*lovely*) Hílu (*charming, delightful*)

Prevent: mána9 (a) man9

Previous: saábiq

Price: *n.* si9r ('as9aár)

Prince: 'amiír ('úmara)

Principal: *n.* mudiír (múdara), ra'iís (rú'asa), 9amiíd (9úmada)

Principality: 'imaára (-aát)
Principle: mábda' (mabaádi')
Print: v. tr. Tába9(a) Tab9
Printer: Tabbaá9 (-iín)
Printing-press: máTba9a (maTaábi9)
Prison: sijn (sujuún)
Private: adj. xuSuúSi
n. júndi basiíT (*simple soldier*)
Prize: jaá'iza (jawaá'iz)
Probability: 'iHtimaál
Probable: muHtámal
Problem: múshkila (mashaákil)
Process: n. 9amalíyya (-aàt)
Produce: v. tr. 'ántaj. yúntij. 'intaáj
Product: mantuúj (-aát)
Production: 'intaáj
Profession: míhna (míhan)
Professor: 'ustaádh. ('asaátidha)
Profit: n. ribH ('arbaáH)
Profitable: murábbiH
Programme: n. burnaámij (baraámij)
Progress: v. intr. taqáddam. yataqáddam. taqáddum
n. taqáddum
Progressive: mutaqáddim (*advanced*) taqáddumi (*political*)
Project: n. mashruú9 (-aát)
Prolong: v. tr. madd (u) madd (*time and space*) Táwwal. yuTaẃwil. taTwiíl (*time and space*)
Promise: n. wá9ad (wu9uúd)
v. tr. wá9ad. yuú9id. wa9d
Promote: v. tr. ráqqa. yuráqqi. tárqiya
Promotion: n. tárqiya
Pronounce: láfaZ(u) lafZ
Pronunciation: lafZ ('alfaáZ)
Proof: burhaán (baraahiín)
Propaganda: di9aáya
Propeller: mirwaáHa (maraáwiH)
Property: mulk ('amlaák)
Prophet: nábi ('ánbiya)
Proportion: nísba (nísab)
Proportional: nísbi
Prosecute: v. tr. Haákam. yuHaákim. muHaákama
Prosecutor: muddá9i (-yyiín)

Prosper: v. intr. 'izdáhar. yazdáhir. 'izdihaár
Prosperity: n. 'izdihaár
Protect: Háma. yáHmi. Himaáya
Protection: Himaáya
Protest: v. intr. 'iHtájj. yaHtájj. 'iHtijaáj (9ala = *against*)
n. iHtijaáj (-aát)
Proud: muftákir (-iín) (bi = *of*)
Prove: v. tr. bárhan. yubárhin. burhaán
Proverb: máthal ('amthaál)
Province: n. muHaáfaZa (-aát) (*unit of administration in Syria & Lebanon*) liwaá' ('álwiya) (*in Iraq*)
Psychological: nafsaáni
Public: adj. 9umuúmi
Publish: náshar(u) nashr
Publisher: naáshir (-iín)
Pull: v. tr. jarr(u) jarr
n. jarr
Pump: v. tr. Daxx(u) Daxx
n. miDáxxa (-aát)
Punctual: 9ála l-waqt
Punish: v. tr. 9aáqab. yu9aáqib. mu9aáqaba (bi = *for*)
Punishment: 9iqaáb/qaSaáS
Pupil: tilmiídh (talaamiídh)
Pure: Saáfi (*undiluted, limpid*), Taáhir ('aThaár) (*honest, chaste*)
Purpose: hádaf ('ahdaáf)
Push: v. tr. dáfa9(a) dáf9a
n. daf9a (-aát)
Put: HaTT(u) HaTT
Put together: v. tr. rákkab. yurákkib. tarkiíb
Pyjamas: biijaáma (-aát)
Pyramid: háram ('ahraám)

Q

Qualified: mu'áhhal (-iín)
Quantity: kammíyya (-aát)
Quarrel: v. tr. xaáSam. yuxaáSim. xiSaám
v. intr. taxaáSam. yataxaáSam. taxaáSum (*quarrel one with another*)

213

n. xiSaám (-aát) (*a quarrel*)
Quarter: *n.* rub9 ('arbaá9) (= $\frac{1}{4}$)
Hayy ('aHyaá') (*of town*)
Queen: málika (-aát)
Question: *n.* su'aál ('ás'ila) (*interrogative kind*) más'ala (masaá'il) (*matter*)
Quick: sarii9 (siraá9)
Quickly: bi-súr9a
Quickness: *n.* súr9a
Quiet: *adj.* haádi

R

Rabbit: 'árnab ('araánib)
Race: *n.* sibaáq (-aát) (*contest*) 9únSur. 9anaáSir (*racial*)
v. tr. saábaq. yusaábiq. sibaáq
Racial: 9únSuri
Racial Discrimination: 'at-tamyiíz al-9únSuri
Radar: raadaár
Radio: raádyo
Radish: fíjla (*coll.*) fijl (*pl.*) -aát
Radius: nuSS quTr (= *half diameter*)
Raft: 9awwaáma (-aát)
Railway: síkkat Hadiíd (= *way of iron*)
Rain: *n.* máTar ('amTaár)
v. intr. máTar(u) máTar
Raise: ráfa9(a) raf9
Raisin: zabiíba (zabiíb)
Rank: *n.* rútba (rútab)
Ransom: fídya (fidayaát)
v. tr. fáda (i) fidaá'
Rape: *n.* 'ightiSaáb (-aát) (*woman*)
v. tr. 'ightáSab. yaghtáSib. 'ightiSaáb
Rare: naádir
Rarely: naádiran (bin-naádir)
Rascal: shayTaán (shayaaTiín)
Ratio: nísba (nísab)
Raw: *adj.* niyy (*meat, fruit*), xaam (*materials*)
Raw materials: mawaádd xaam
Razor: 'aálat Hilaáqa ('aalaát Hilaáqa)
React: *v. intr.* tafaá9al. yatafaá9al.

tafaá9ul (*chemical etc.*)
Reaction: radd fi9l (ruduúd fi9l) (*response to . . .*)
Reactionary: *adj.* ráj9i (-yyiín)
Read: qára. yáqra. qiraáya
Reader: *n.* qaári (qúra) (*of book*)
Ready: HaáDir (-iín) (*present*) musta9ídd (-iín) (*prepared*)
Real: Haqiíqi
Realist: waáq9i (-yyiín)
Realise: *v. tr.* 'ádrak. yúdrik. 'idraák (*thought*). Háqqaq. yuHáqqiq. taHqiíq (*property*)
Rear: *n.* mu'áxxar
v. tr. rábba. yurábbi. tárbiya
Reason: sábab ('asbaáb) (*cause*), 9aql. 9uquúl (*intellect*)
Reasonable: ma9quúl
Rebel: *n.* thaá'ir (thuwwaár)
v. intr. thaar(u) tháwra (9ála = *against*)
Rebellion: tháwra (-aát)
Receipt: waSl (wuSuulaát) (*voucher*)
Receive: *v. tr.* 'istálam. yastálim. 'istilaám (*something*), 'istáqbal. yastáqbil. 'istiqbaál (*people*)
Recent: 'axiír
Recently: 'axiíran/mu'áxxiran
Reception: Háflat 'istiqbaál (*party*)
Recipe: wáSfa (-aát)
Reciprocal: mutabaádil
Recognise: *v. tr.* 9áraf (i) má9rifa
Recruit: *v. tr.* jánnad. yujánnid. tajniíd (*for army*)
Rectangle: mustaTiíl (-aát)
Red: *adj.* 'áHmar (*m.*) Hámra (*f.*) Humr (*pl.*)
Reduce: náqqaS. yunáqqiS. tanqiíS
Reed: qáSaba (qáSab)
Refine: Sáffa. yuSáffi. táSfiya. kárrar. yukárrir. takriír
Refined: muSáffa
Refinery: miSfaát. (maSaáf.) má9mal takriír (= *factory of refining*) (ma9aámil takriír)
Reflect: *v. tr.* 9ákas (i) 9aks (*light etc.*)
Reflection: 'in9ikaás (-aát)
Reform: 'áSlaH. yúSliH. 'iSlaáH

n. 'iSlaáH (-aát)
Refreshments: muraTTabaát
Refrigerate: bárrad. yubárrid.
tabriíd thállaj. yuthállij. tathliíj
Refrigerator: barraád (-aát)/
thallaája (-aát)
Refugee: laáji' (-iín)
Refuse: v. tr. ráfaD(u) rafD
Regime: niZaám Hukm ('ánZimat
Hukm)
Region: mínTaqa (manaáTiq)
Registered: musájjal (-iín)
Regular: adj. niZaámi (yyiín)
(*orderly, normal*)
Regular soldier: júndi niZaámi.
(junuúd niZaamiyyiín)
Relation: qariíb ('áqriba) (*family*)
9alaáqa (-aát) (ma9 = *with*,
bayn = *between*)
Release: v. tr. 'áTlaq. yúTliq.
'iTlaáq
Religion: diin ('adyaán)
Reluctance: taráddud (-aát)
Rely: v. intr. 'ittákal. yattákil.
'ittikaál (9ála = *on*)
Remain: báqa. yábqi. baqaá'
Remainder: baáqi (bawaáqi)
Remark: n. mulaáHaZa (-aát)
v. 9ámal mulaáHaZa
Remember: v. tr. tadhákkar.
yatadhákkar tadhákkur
Remit: v. tr. 'ársal fuluús (*send
money*) yúrsil. 'irsaál
Remove: v. tr. shaal (i) shayl
Rendezvous: máw9id (mawaa9iíd)
Renew: jáddad. yujáddid. tajdiíd
Rent: n. 'újra (*money*)
v. tr. 'ájjar. yu'ájjir. ta'jiír (*rent
out*), 'istá'jar. yastá'jir. 'isti'jaár
(*pay rent*)
Repair: v. tr. SállaH. yuSálliH.
taSliíH
n. taSliíH (-aát)
Replace: v. tr. 'istábdal (*something
bi + something else*) yastábdil.
'istibdaál
Reply: v. tr. jaáwab. yujaáwib.
jawaáb–radd 9ála (u) radd
n. jawaáb (-aát)–radd (ruduúd)

Report: n. taqriír (taqaariír)
Represent: máththal. yumáththil.
tamthiíl
Representative: mumáththil (-iín)
Republic: n. jumhuuríyya (-aát)
Request: v. tr. Tálab (u) Tálab (*a
thing* min *the person*)
n. Tálab (-aát)
Rescue: v. tr. xállaS. yuxálliS.
taxliíS
Research: n. baHth (buHuúth)
Resemble: v. tr. shaábah.
yushaábih. mushaábaha
Reserve: v. tr. Hájaz (i) Hajz (*seat*)
Reservoir: xazzaán (-aát)
Resign: v. intr. 'istaqaál. yastaqiíl.
'istaqaála
Resignation: 'istaqaála (-aát)
Resistance: muqaáwama
Resource: máwrid (mawaárid)
Respect: v. tr. 'iHtáram. yaHtárim.
'iHtiraám
n. 'iHtiraám
Responsibility: mas'uulíyya (-aát)
Responsible: mas'uúl (-iín) (9an =
for)
Rest: n. raáHa
v. intr. 'istaraáH. yastariíH.
'istaraáHa
Restaurant: máT9am (maTaá9im)
Result: n. natiíja (nataá'ij)
v. intr. nátaj (u) nitaáj (min =
from)
Retaliate: v. intr. 'intáqam.
yantáqim. 'intiqaám
Retaliation: n. 'intiqaám
Retard: 'áxxar. yu'áxxir. ta'xiír
Retire: taqaá9ad. yataqaá9ad.
taqaá9ud (*on pension*), 'insáHab.
yansáHib. 'insiHaáb (*withdraw*)
Return: v. intr. rája9 (i) rujuú9
v. tr. rájja9. yurájji9. tarjií9
Revenge (*to take*)*:* 'intáqam.
yantáqim. 'intaqaám
Revenue: 'iiraád (-aát)
Reverse: v. tr. 9ákas (i) 9aks
n. 9aks
Revolution: tháwra (-aát) (*political*)
dáwra (-aát) (*of engine*)

215

Reward: n. mukaáfa'a (-aát)
v. tr. kaáfa'. yukaáfi'. mukaáfa'a
Rice: ruzz
Rich: adj. gháni ('ághniya)
Ride: v. tr. rákab (a) rukuúb)
Rider: raákib (rukkaáb)
Rifle: bunduqíyya (banaádiq)
Right: n. Haqq (Huquúq) (inalien-
able) yamiín (hand)
adj. maZbuúT (correct) SaHiíH
(SiHaáH) (correct)
Riot: n. shághab
Rise: v. intr. 'irtáfa9. yartáfi9.
'irtifaá9 (go higher) qaam (u)
qiyaám (stand up) zaad(i) ziyaáda
(increase)
n. 'irtifaá9 (-aát), ziyaáda (-aát)
River: nahr ('ánhur)
Road: Tariiq (Túruq)
Rob: sáraq(i) sáriqa
Robber: saáriq (-iín)
Rock: Sáxra (piece of) (Suxuúr)
Rocket: Saaruúx (Sawaariíx)
Roof: n. saTH (suTuúH)
Room: ghúrfa (ghúraf)–'áwDa
('úwaD)
Rope: Habl
Rose: wárda (ward)
Rough: xáshin
Round: adj. mudáwwar
prep. & adv. Hawl
Routine: n. ruutiín.
adj. ruutiíni
Row: n. Saff (Sufuúf) (line) Dáwsha
(noise)
Royal: málaki
Rubber: n. maTTaáT (substance)
maHaáya (-aát) (eraser)
Rubbish: zubaála
Rug: sijjaáda (sajaajiíd), bisaáT
(búsuT)
Rule: n. niZaám ('ánZima) (regula-
tion)
v. tr. Hákam (u) Hukm (govern)
Ruler: Haákim (Hukkaám),
mísTara (masaáTir) (drawing)
Rumour: n. 'ishaá9a (-aát)
Run: v. intr. rákaD (u) rakD
Run away: hárab (u) harb

Rural: adj. riífi

S

Sabotage: v. tr. xárrab. yuxárrib.
taxriíb
n. taxriíb (-aát)
Saboteur: muxárrib (-iín)
Sack: n. kiis ('akyaás)
Sad: Haziín (Hizaán)
Saddle: n. sharj ('ashraáj)
Safe: adj. saliím (súlama)
n. xizaána (-aát)
Safety: salaáma
Sail: v. intr. 'ábHar. yúbHir.
'ibHaár
Sailor: baHHaár (-iín)
Salad: sálaTa
Salary: raátib (rawaátib)
Salesman: bayyaá9 (-iín)
Salt: míliH
Same: adj. nafs/dhaat, e.g. nafs/
dhaat al-bayt = the same house
Sand: raml (rimaál)
Sandal: Sándal. (Sanaádil)
Sandwich: sandwiísh (-aát)
Satisfactory: múRdi
Sauce: SálSa (-aát)
Sauce-pan: Tánjara (Tanaájir)
Sausage: sújuq
Save: v. tr. xállaS. yuxálliS. taxliíS
(rescue), wáffar. yuwáffir. tawfiír
(money)
Say: qaal (u) qawl
Saying: n. qawl ('áqwaál), máthal
('amthaál) (proverb)
Scale: miqyaás (maqaayiís) (map
etc.)
Scandal: faDiíHa (faDaáyiH)
Scenery: manaáZir (country)
Scent: n. riíHa
Schedule: jádwal (jadaáwil)
Scholar: 9aálim (9úlama)
Scholastic: mádrasi
School: mádrasa (madaáris)
Science: 9ilm (9uluúm)
Scientific: 9ílmi
Scientist: 9aálim (9úlama)
Scissors: miqáSS (pair of . . .)

216

(maqaáSS)
Scorpion: n. 9áqrab (9aqaárib)
Screw: n. búrghi (baraághi)
Screw-driver: n. mifákk baraághi.
(mifakkaát baraághi)
Script: xaTT (xuTuúT)
Sea: baHr (biHaár)
Search: v. tr. fáttash. yufáttish.
taftiísh (9an = for)
Season: faSl (fuSuúl)
Seat: máq9ad (maqaá9id)
Seated: ad. qaá9id (-iín)
Second: n. thaánya (thawaáni) (time unit)
adj. thaáni
Secondary: thaániwi (schools etc.)
Secrecy: sirríyya
Secret: n. sirr ('asraár)
adj. sírri
Secretary: sekritáyr(a) (-iín/-aát)
Sect: Taá'ifa (Tawaá'if)
Section: qism ('aqsaám)
Sector: qiTaá9 (-aát)
Security: 'amn
See: v. tr. shaaf (u) sháwfa
Seed: bizr (buzuúr)
Seek: fáttash. yufáttish taftiísh (9an = for)
Seem: v. intr. Záhar (a) Zuhuúr
Seize: v. intr. 'istáwla. yastáwli. 'istiilaá' (+ 9ala) (land etc.), e.g. 'istáwlu 9ala l-má9mal = they seized the factory
Seldom: naádiran/bin-naádir
Self: n. nafs (nufuús) e.g. 'ája náfsuh = he came himself
Sell: v. tr. baa9 (i) bay9
Seller: bayyaá9 (-iín)
Send: v. tr. bá9ath (a) ba9th, 'ársal. yúrsil. 'irsaál
Sensible: ma9quúl (-iín)
Sentence: n. júmla (júmal) (language) Hukm. 'aHkaám (legal)
Sentry: Haáris (Húrraas)
Separate: v. tr. fáSal (u) faSl
adj. munfáSil (-iín)
Sequence: tasálsul (-aát)
Serious: jíddi (-yyiín) (person), xaTiir (situation)

Seriousness: n. jiddíyya, xuTuúra
Servant: xaádim (xuddaám)
Serve: v. tr. xádam (u) xídma
Service: xídma (-aát)
Set: Taáqim (Tuquúma) (of tools), majmuú9a (-aát) (of things), jamaá9a (-aát) (of people), jahaáz ('ájhiza) (radio)
v. tr. HaTT (u) HaTT (table . . . put down) DábaT (u) DabT (regulate apparatus)
Settee: kánabay (kanabayaát)
Several: adj. 9íddat . . . e.g. 9íddat junuúd = several soldiers
Severe: shadiíd (shidaád) (stern, violent, intense)
Sew: v. tr. xáyyaT. yuxáyyiT. xiyaáTa
Sex: jins ('ajnaás)
Sexual: jínsi
Shade: n. Zill ('aZlaál)
Shallow: DaHl–ghayr 9amiíq (= not deep)
Shame: n. 9ayb (9uyuúb)
Share: n. HiSSa (HíSaS) (portion) sahm ('áshum) (in company)
v. tr. shaárak. yushaárik. mushaáraka
v. intr. 'ishtárak. yashtárik. 'ishtiraák (fi = in)
Shareholder: musaáhim (-iín)
Shark: kalb al-baHr (kilaáb al-baHr)
Sharp: Haadd (of knife)
Sharpen: sann (u) sann (knife)
Shave: v. tr. & intr. Hálaq (i) Hilaáqa
Shed: máxzan (maxaázin) (store)
Sheep: xaruúf (xurfaán), ghánam (collective word)
Sheet: shárshaf (sharaáshif) (on bed)
Sheikh: shayx (shuyuúx)
Shelf: raff (rufuúf)
Shepherd: raá9i (ru9yaán)
Shine: v. intr. láma9 (i) lam9
Ship: safiína (súfun)/márkab (maraákib)
Shipment: sháHna (shaHanaát)

Shirt: qamiiS. (qumSaán)
Shocking: faZii9 (*horrible*)
Shoe: kúndara (kanaádir) (*Western*)
Shoot: v. tr. 'áTlaq an-naar (+ 9ála). yúTliq. 'iTlaáq (= *let loose fire upon*)
Shop: dukkaán (dakaakiín) (*f.*)
v. intr. tasáwwaq. yatasáwwaq. tasáwwuq
Shore: saáHil (sawaáHil) (*of sea*)
Short: qaSiir (qiSaár) (*length*) naáqiS (= *lacking*)
Shortage: naqS
Shorthand: 'ixtizaál
Shorthand writer: n. muxtázil/a
Shorts: banTaluún qaSiir. (banTaluunaát qiSaár/qaSiíra)
Shoulder: katf ('aktaáf)
Shout: n. Sárxa (-aát)
v. intr. Sárax (u) Suraáx (bi = *to*)
Shovel: míjrafa (majaárif)–shibl
Show: v. tr. fárja. yufárji (*Syrian*) ráwwa. yuráwwi (*Gulf*)
Shower: duush (-aát) (*bath*)
Shut: v. tr. 'ághlaq. yúghliq. 'ighlaáq–sákkar. yusákkir. taskiír
Sick: mariiD (márDa)
Side: n. jaánib (jawaánib) jíha (jihaát) (*direction*)
Sign: n. 9alaáma (-aát) (*badge, token*) 'ishaára (-aát) (*gesture*)
v. tr. 'ámDa. yúmDi. 'imDaá'
Signature: 'imDaá' (-aát)
Silence: sukuút
Silent: saákit
Silk: Hariir
Silver: fíDDa
adj. fíDDi
Simple: basiíT (bisaáT)
Sin: n. xaTíyya (xaTaáya)
Since: prep. múndhu/min e.g. múndhu/min haadhaak al-waqt = *since that time*
conj. li'án (= *because*)
Sincere: múxliS (-iín)
Sincerity: 'ixlaáS
Sing: v. tr. ghánna. yughánni. ghinaá'
Sink: v. intr. gháriq (a) gháraq

Sister: 'uxt ('axawaát)
Sit: v. intr. jálas (i) juluús qá9ad (u) qu9uúd (*take seat & remain seated*)
Site: maHáll (-aát)
Situated: adj. waáqi9
Skilful: maáhir (-iín)
Skill: mahaára
Skin: jild (juluúd)
Skirt: tannuúra (tanaaniír)
Sky: samaá' (samawaát)
Slave: 9abd (9abiíd)
Sleep: n. nawm
v. intr. naam. yanaám. nawm (nimt = *I slept*)
Sleeping: adj. naáyim
Sleepy: adj. na9saán
Slim: adj. naHiif (niHaáf)
Slipper: baabuúj (bawaabiíj)
Slow: adj. baTii' (bitaá')
Slowly: adv. shwayy shwayy, bibúT'
Small: Saghiir (Sighaár)
Smash: v. tr. kássar. yukássir. taksiír
v. intr. 'inkásar. yankásir. 'inkisaár
Smell: n. riiHa (*odour*)
v. tr. shamm (u) shamm
Smoke: n. duxxaán
v. tr. dáxxan. yudáxxin. tadxiín (*tobacco*)
Smooth: mústawi (*level*), maális (*not rough*)
Smuggle: v. tr. hárrab. yuhárrib. tahriíb
Smuggler: n. muhárrib (-iín)
Snake: Háyya (-aát)
Snatch: v. tr. xáTaf (u) xaTf
Snow: n. thalj
v. intr. thálajat (u) (*feminine ending because dúnya (f.) (= world) is the supposed subject*)
So and So: fulaán
Soap: Saabuún
Soccer: kúrat al-qádam
Social: 'ijtimaá9i
Socialism: 'ishtiraakíyya
Socialist: n. & adj. 'ishtiraáki (-yyiín)
Society: mujtáma9 (-aát) (*community*) jam9íyya (-aát) (*club*)

Sock: jáwrab qaSiír (jawaárib qaSiíra)

Socket: máqbis. (maqaábis) (*electrical*)

Soft: naá9im, ghayr kuHuúli (*nonalcoholic*)

Soldier: júndi (junuúd)

Some: adj. shwáyya(t) ... (*a little (of)*) ba9D (*a certain number/ amount of*)

Someone: waáHid

Something: shii ('ashyaá')

Sometimes: marraát, 'aHyaánan, fi ba9D al-'awqaát

Son: 'ibn ('abnaá')

Song: 'úghniya ('aghaáni)

Soon: qariíban/ba9d shwayy

Sorrow: Huzn

Sorry: Haziín (*sorrowful*), muta'ássif-iín (*regretful*)

Sort: naw9 ('anwaá9)

Sound: Sawt ('aSwaát)
 adj. saliím

Soup: shuúrba

Sour: HaámiD

Source: 'aSl ('uSuúl) (= *origin*)

South: n. junuúb
 adj. junuúbi

Souvenir: tidhkaár (tadhaákir)

Spacious: waási9

Spade: n. mijrafa (majaárif), shibl

Spare part: qíT9at ghayaár (qíTa9 ghayaár)

Spark: sharaára (-aát)

Speak: v. tr. Háka (i) Hikaáya, takállam. yatakállam. takállum

Speaker: mutakállim (-iín), xaTiíb (xúTaba) (*lecturer, orator*)

Special: xuSuúSi

Specialist: mutaxáSSis (-iín)

Specialise: taxáSSas. yataxáSSas. taxáSSus (bi = *in*)

Specially: xuSuúSan

Specifications: muwaaSafaát (*machine*)

Spectacles: naZZaaraát

Spectator: mutafárrij (-iín)

Speech: xiTaáb (aát) (*formal*)

Speed: súr9a

Spend: v. tr. Sáraf (i) Sarf (*money*), qáDa (i) qaDaá' (*time*)

Spherical: kúrawi (*i.e. ball like*)

Spider: 9ankabuút (9anaákib)

Spill: v. tr. kabb (u) kabb

Spirits: mashruubaát ruuHíyya (*alcoholic drinks*)

Splendid: badii9–9aZiim

Spokesman: n. mutakállim bi ...

Spoon: mál9aqa (malaá9iq)

Sport: riyaáDa (-aát)

Spot: núqTa (núqaT) (*location or mark*)

Spring: rabií9 (*season*)

Spy: n. jaasuús (jawaasiís)
 v. intr. tajássas. yatajássas. tajássus

Square: murábba9 (-aát)

Squeeze: v. tr. 9áSar (i) 9aSr

Stability: 'istiqraár

Stage: márHala (maraáHil) (*in process*), másraH (masaáriH) (*theatre*)

Stair: dáraja (dáraj) (= *stairs*)

Stamp: Taábi9 (Tawaábi9)

Stand: v. intr. wáqaf. yáwqaf. waqf, qaam (u) qiyaám (*stand up*)

Star: najm (nujuúm)

Start: v. tr. báda. yábdi. bidaáya
 n. bidaáya (-aát)

Starve: v. intr. jaa9 (u) juu9

State: dáwla (dúwal) (*country*), wilaáya (-aát) (*federal*), Haal ('aHwaál) (*condition*)

Statement: bayyaán (-aát)

Station: maHáTTa (-aát)

Statistician: 'iHSaá'i (-yyiín)

Statistics: 'iHSaa' (-aát)

Statue: timthaál (tamaathiíl)

Stay: v. intr. báqa. yábqa. baqaá' (*remain*), názal (i) nuzuúl (fi = *in*) (= *at hotel*)

Steal: v. tr. sáraq (i) sáriqa

Steam: buxaár

Steel: fuulaàdh/Sulb

Steep: munHádir kathiír

Steer: v. tr. sáyyar. yusáyyir. tasyiír

Steering wheel: stiírin (*English influenced areas*) váwlan (*from*

French "volant")
Step: xúTwa (-aát) (pace)
Stick: 9áSa (9áSi)
v. tr. lázzaq. yulázziq. talziíq (one thing to another)
Still: adj. haádi (sea . . . air . . .)
adv. lissaba9d e.g. lissa bakkiír (= still early)
Stink: n. riíHa kariíha (= bad smell)
Stocking: kálsa (-aát)
Stomach: mí9da (mí9ad)
Stone: Hájar ('aHjaár)
Stop: v. tr. wáqqaf. yuwáqqif. tawqiíf
Store: máxzan (maxaázin) (depot)
v. tr. xázan (u) xazn
Storey: Taábiq (Tawaábiq)
Storm: 9aáSifa (9awaásif)
Story: qíSSa (qiSaS)
Stove: furn ('afraán)
Straight: adj. mustaqiím
adv. rá'san (directly), dúghri (straight ahead)
Strange: ghariíb (ghúraba)
Stranger: ghariíb (ghúraba)
Stream: májra (majaári), jádwal (jadaáwil)
Street: shaári9 (shawaári9)
Strength: qúwwa (quwwaát)
Strengthen: qáwwa. yuqáwwi. táqwiya
Strike: v. tr. Dárab (u) Darb (hit) 'áDrab. yúDrib. 'iDraáb (stop work)
n. 'iDraáb (-aát)
String: xayT (xuyuúT)
Strong: qáwi (-yyiín)
Student: tilmiídh (talaamiídh) (secondary) Taálib (Tullaáb) (university)
Study: v. tr. daras (u) dars
n. dars (duruús)
Stupid: ghabi (-yyiín)
Subject: n. mawDuú9 (mawaaDií9) (topic)
adj. xaáDi9 (-iín) (li = to)
Subordinate: mar'uús (-iín)
Subsidy: musaá9ada maalíyya

Substitute: v. tr. 'istábdal. yastábdil. 'istibdaál (shii bi shii = one thing for another)
n. badiíl. búdala (min = for)
Subtract: TáraH (a) TarH (shii min. = something from)
Suburb: DaáHiya (DawaáHi)
Subversive: 'inqilaábi (revolutionary)
Succeed: v. intr. nájaH (a) najaáH
Success: najaáH
Successful: naájiH (-iín)
Sudden: mufaáji'
Suddenly: fáj'atan
Suffer: v. tr. 9aána. yu9aáni
Sufficient: kaáfi
Sugar: súkkar
Suggest: v. tr. 'iqtáraH. yaqtáriH. 'iqtiraáH
Suggestion: muqtáraH (-aát)
Suit: bádla (-aát) (of clothes)
Suitable: munaásib (-iín)
Suit-case: shánTa (-aát)
Summarise: v. tr. láxxaS. yuláxxiS. talxiíS
Summary: xulaáSa (-aát) muújaz (-aát)
Summer: Sayf (Suyuúf) adj. Sáyfi
Summon: v. tr. 'istád9a. yastád9i. 'istid9aá'
Sun: shams (shumuús)
Sunrise: shuruúq ash-shams
Sunset: ghuruúb ash-shams
Sunshade: shamsíyya (-aát)
Superintendant: muraáqib (-iín)
Superior: ra'iís (rú'asa) (opposed to mar'uús = subordinate)
Supervise: v. tr. raáqab. yuraáqib. muraáqaba
Supervisor: muraáqib (-iín)
Supper: 9ásha
Supply: v. tr. záwwad. yuzáwwid. tazwiíd (bi = with), (Supplies = mú'na (mú'an))
Suppose: v. tr. 'iftáraD. yaftáriD. 'iftiraáD
Sure: 'akiíd (information), muta'ákkid (person)

220

Surface: SaTeH (SuTuúH)
Surgeon: jarraáH (iín)
Surplus: ziyaáda (-aát) (9an = *over*)
Surprise: *v. tr.* faája'. yufaáji'.
mufaája'a
Surround: *v. tr.* 'aHaáT. yuHiíT.
'iHaáTa (+ bi), *e.g.* suur yuHiíT
bil-madiína = *a wall surrounds
the city*
Surrounding: muHiíT
Survey: *n.* masaáHa (*land*)
v. tr. másaH (a) masaáHa
Surveyor: massaáH (-iín)
Swallow: *v. tr.* bála9 (a) bal9
Sweep: *v. tr.* kánas (u) kans
Sweet: Hílu
Swim: *v. intr.* sábaH (a) sabaáHa
Switch: miftaáH (mafaatiíH)
Sword: sayf (suyuúf)
Symbol: ramz (rumuúz)
Sympathetic: 9aáTif (-iín)
Sympathy: *n.* 9aTf
System: niZaám ('ánZima)
Systematic: niZaámi

T

Table: *n.* Taáwila (-aát) (*Syrian*),
mayz ('amyaáz) (*Gulf*),
Tarabáyza (-aát) (*Egypt*), jádwal
(jadaáwil) (*document*)
Tact: libaáqa
Tactics: taktiík
Tail: dhánab ('adhnaáb)
Tailor: xayyaáT (-iín)
Take: *v. tr.* 'áxadh. yaáxudh. 'axdh
Take off: *v. intr.* 'áqla9. yúqli9.
'iqlaá9 (*aeroplane*)
v. tr. shálaH (a) shalH (*clothes*)
Talk: *v. tr.* Háka (i) Hikaáya/
takállam. yatakállam. takállum
n. Háki/kalaám/Hadiíth
('aHaadiíth) (= *conversation*)
Tall: Tawiíl (Tiwaál)
Tank: dabbaába (-aát) (*military*),
HawD ('aHwaáD) (*cistern*)
Tanker: Haámilat nafT.
(Haamilaát.)
Tap: Hanafiyya (-aát) (*water etc.*)

Tar: zift
Target: hádaf ('ahdaáf)
Task: 9ámal ('a9maál)
Taste: *n.* dhawq ('adhwaáq)
v. tr. dhaaq (u) dhawq
Tax: Dariíba (Daraá'ib)
Taxi: táksi
Tea: shaay
Teach: *v. tr.* 9állam. yu9állim.
ta9liím
Teacher: mu9állim (-iín) (*man*),
mu9állima (-aát) (*woman*)
Team: fariíq (fúraqa)
Tear: *n.* dám9a (dumuú9) (*weeping*)
Tear: *v. tr.* mázzaq. yumázziq.
tamziíq (rip)
Technical: fánni–takniíki
Technician: fánni (yyiín)
Technology: taknawlujíyya
Tedious: mumíll (*boring*)
Telegram: teleghraáf (-aát),
barqíyya (-aát)
Telephone: *n.* talifáwn (-aát)
v. intr. tálfan. yutálfin. tálfana
(+ li), *e.g.* tálfan lil-bank = *he
rang the bank*
Television: taliviiziyáwn
Tell: *v. tr.* 'áxbar. yúxbir. 'ixbaár
(*inform*)
Temperament: mazaáj
Temperature: dárajat Haraára (*de-
gree of heat*)
Tender: *n.* 9arD bi munaáqaSa
(9uruúD . . .) (= *offer at competi-
tion to decide lowest bidder*)
adj. Tari (*fresh, succulent*)
Tennis: ténis
Tension: tawáttur
Tent: xáyma (xíyam)
Terrorism: 'irhaáb
Terrorist: 'irhaábi (-yyiín)
Text: naSS (nuSuúS)
Textbook: kitaáb mádrasi (kútub
madrasíyya)
Thank: *v. tr.* shákar (u) shukr
(9ála = *for*)
Thankful: mutashákkir (-iín)
Theatre: másraH (masaáriH)
Then: *adv.* fi hal-waqt (*at that time*),

ba9adáyn (*after that*), fa'ízan (*therefore*)
Theory: naZaríyya (-aát)
There: hunaák
Therefore: lidhaálik
Thermometer: miizaán Haraára. (mawaaziin Haraára)
Thick: thaxiin
Thickness: thuxn
Thief: saáriq (-iin)
Thin: naHiif (niHaáf)
Thing: shii ('ashyaá')
Thirsty: 9atshaán (-iin)
Thought: fíkra ('afkaár)
Thread: xayT (xuyuúT)
Threat: tahdiid (-aát)
Threaten: v. tr. háddad. yuháddid. tahdiid
Throat: Halq (Huluúq)
Throne: 9arsh (9uruúsh)
Through: prep. min xilaál (*across, out of*), bi waáSita (*by means of*)
Throw: v. tr. ráma. yármi. rimaáya
Thunder: rá9da
Ticket: tádhkara (tadhaákir)
Tidy: muráttab (-iin)
Tie: rábTa (-aát)
v. tr. rábaT (u) rabT
Tile: balaáTa (balaáT)
Till: prep. & conj. Hátta
Time: waqt ('awqaát), zamaán ('ázmina) (*long*), márra (-aát) (*occasion*)
Tired: ta9baán (-iin)
Tiresome: mút9ib
Toast: xubz muHámmas
Tobacco: tabgh, títin (*Iraq*)
Today: 'al-yawm
Together: sáwa
Toilet: n. bayt mayy
Tolerant: mutasaámiH-iin
Tomato: TamaáTim, banaduúra' (-aát)
Tomorrow: búkra
Ton: Tann ('aTnaán)
Tongue: lisaán ('álsina)
Tonight: 'al-láyla
Too: kamaán (*also*), 'ákthar min al-laázim (*more than necessary*)

Tool: 'adaát ('adawaát)
Tooth: sinn ('asnaán)
Toothache: wája9 'asnaán
Torch: baTTaaríyya (-aát)
Total: majmuú9 (-aát)
Touch: v. tr. lámas (i) lams
Tourism: siyaáHa
Tourist: saáyiH (suyyaáH)
Towel: mánshafa (manaáshif)
Town: bálad (bilaád)
Toy: lú9ba (-aát)
Tractor: jarraára (-aát)
Trade: tijaára
Tradition: taqliid (taqaaliid)
Traditional: taqliídi
Traffic: sayr/Hárakat al-muruúr
Train: n. qiTaár (-aát) (*rail*)
v. tr. márran. yumárrin. tamriín
Transfer: v. tr. Háwwal. yuHáwwil. taHwiil (*money*), náqal (u) naql (*personnel*)
Be Transferred: v. intr. 'intáqal. yantáqil. 'intiqaál
Translate: tárjam. yutárjim. tárjama
Translation: tárjama (taraajim)
Translator: mutárjim (-iin)
Transport: v. tr. náqal (u) naql
n. naql
Transport services: naqliyyaát
Trap: maSiida (maSaáyid)
Travel: v. intr. saáfar. yusaáfir. sáfar
n. sáfar ('asfaár)
Traveller: musaáfir (-iin)
Tray: Siiníyya (-aát)
Treasurer: 'amiin Sanduúq
Treaty: mu9aáhada (-aát)
Tree: shájara (*col.*) shájar (*pl.*) shajaraát (*or*) 'ashjaár
Trial: muHaákama-aát
Triangle: muthállath (-aát)
Tribal: 9ashaá'iri
Tribe: 9ashiíra (9ashaá'ir), qabiila (qabaá'il)
Trick: Hiila (Híyal)
Tropical: 'istiwaa'i
Trousers: banTaláwn (-aát)
Truck: láwri (lawaári), sayyaárat shaHn (sayyaaraát . . .)

True: SaHiíH (SiHaáH)
Trust: v. tr. wáthaq. yáwthaq.
thíqa + bi, e.g. wáthaq bi
SaáHibuh = he trusted his friend
n. thíqa (+ bi = in)
Truth: Haqiíqa (Haqaáyiq)
Truthful: Saádiq (-iín)
Try: v. tr. Haáwal. yuHaáwil.
muHaáwala (attempt), Haákam.
yuHaákim. muHaákama (legal)
Turn: n. dawr ('adwaár) (one's turn)
v. intr. daar (u) dawr (revolve)
v. tr. dáwwar. yudáwwir. tadwiír
Type: naw9 ('anwaá9)/Tiraáz
(Túruz)
Typewriter: 'aála kaátiba ('aalaát)
Tyre: duulaáb (dawaaliíb)

U

Ugly: qabiíH (qibaáH)
Uncle: 9amm (9umuúm) (paternal),
xaal ('axwaál) (maternal)
Under: prep. taHt
Underneath: taHt
Understand: v. tr. fáhim (a) fahm
Underwear: thiyaáb taHtaaníyya
Unification: tawHiíd
Unique: waHiíd
Unit: wáHda (-aát)
Unite: v. tr. wáHHad. yuwáHHid.
tawHiíd
University: jaámi9a (jaami9aát)
Unless: 'illa 'idha
Until: prep. & conj. Hátta
Use: v. tr. 'istá9mal. yastá9mil.
'isti9maál
Useful: mufiíd
Useless: biduún faá'ida

V

Vacant: faáDi (unoccupied)
Vaccinate: v. tr. Tá99am. yuTá99im
taT9iím
Vague: mush waáDiH (not clear)
Valley: waádi (widyaán)
Value: qiíma (qíyam)
v. tr. qáddar. yuqáddir. taqdiír

Valve: Simaám (-aát)
Vanish: v. intr. 'ixtáfa. yaxtáfi
Veal: laHm 9ijl
Vegetables: xaDrawaát
Veil: Hijaáb (Hújub)
Ventilate: v. tr. háwwa. yuháwwi.
táhwiya
Veranda: firaánda
Verb: fi9l ('af9aál)
Verdict: Hukm ('aHkaám)
Vibrate: v. intr. 'ihtázz. yahtízz.
'ihtizaáz
Victim: DaHíyya (DaHaáya)
View: mánZar (manaáZir) (scen-
ery), ra'y. ('aaraá') (opinion)
Village: qárya (qúra)
Vinegar: xall
Violent: shadiíd (shidaád)
Virtue: faDiíla (faDaá'il)
Visit: v. tr. zaar (u) ziyaára
n. ziyaára (-aát)
Vocabulary: mufradaát
Voice: Sawt ('aSwaát)
Vote: Sawt ('aSwaát)
v. intr. Sáwwat. yuSáwwit. taSwiít

W

Wage: 'újra ('ujuúr)
Wait: v. tr. 'intáZar. yantáZir.,
'intiZaár, 'istánna. yastánna
Waiter: Sufráji-íyya
Wake: v. tr. SáHHa. y̆uSáHHi
v. intr. SiHi. yáSHa
Walk: v. intr. másha. yámshi. máshi
n. mushwaár (mashaáwir) (stroll)
Wall: HayT (HiiTaán)
Want: v. tr. 'araád. yuriíd. 'iraáda
bíddii, bíddak . . .
War: Harb (Huruúb)
Warehouse: máxzan (maxaázin)
Warm: daáfi
Warn: v. tr. 'ándhar. yúndhir.
'indhaár
Warning: 'indhaár (-aát)
Wash: v. tr. ghásal (i) ghasl
Watch: saá9a (-aát)
v. tr. tafárraj. yatafárraj tafárruj
(+ 9ála), e.g. tafárraj 9ála

l-bayt = *he watched the house*
Water: mayy
Water-melon: n. baTTiíxa (*coll.*)
baTTiíx (*pl.*) -aát
Wave: n. máwja (*coll.*) mawj (*pl.*)
-aát (*or*) 'amwaáj
Way: Tariıqa (Túruq) (*method*)
Weak: Da9iíf (Di9aáf)
Weapon: silaáH ('ásliHa)
Wear: v. tr. lábas (a) libs
Weather: Taqs
Week: 'usbuú9 ('asaabií9)
Weigh: v. tr. wázan. yuúzan. wazn
Weight: wazn ('awzaán)
Welcome: v. tr. ráHHab.
yuráHHib. tarHiíb (+ bi)
N.B. Welcome! = 'áhlan wa sáhlan!
Well: bir ('aabaár)
West: gharb
adj. ghárbi
Wet: adj. raTb (= *damp*). mabluúl (= *soaked*)
Wheel: duulaáb (dawaaliíb)
When: (*question*) 'áymta?
conj. lámma
Where: (*question*) wayn?
conj. wayn
Which: (*question*) 'ayy? (*relative*) 'illi
White: 'ábyaD (*m.*) báyDa (*f.*) biiD (*pl.*)
Who: (*question*) miin? (*relative*) 'illi
Why: laysh?
Wicked: shiriír
Wide: 9ariiD (9iraáD)
Width: 9arD
Wife: záwja (-aát)
Win: v. tr. faaz (u) fawz + bi + *thing*/ + 9ála + *person*

(= *triumph over*)
Wind: riiH ('aryaáH)
Window: shubbaák (shabaabiík)
Wine: nabiídh
Winter: shíta
Wire: silk ('aslaák)
With: prep. ma9
Woman: mára (niswaán)
Wood: xáshab (xáshaba = *piece of wood*)
Wool: n. Suuf
adj. Suúfi
Word: kálima (-aát)
Work: n. shughl ('ashghaál)
(= *works*)
v. intr. 'ishtághal. yastághil. shughl
World: 9aálam
Write: v. tr. kátab (u) kitaába
Writer: kaátib (kuttaáb)
Wrong: adj. ghálaT (*mistake*), *e.g.* haádha ghálaT = *this is a mistake*

Y

Year: sána (siniín)
Yearly: adj. sánawi
adv. sanawíyyan
Yellow: adj. 'áSfar (*m.*) Sáfra (*f.*) Sufr (*pl.*)
Yesterday: 'umbaáriH/'ams
Yet: líssa (*up till now*)
Young: Saghiír (Sighaár)
Youth: shaab. shabaáb (= *"youths"* and *"youth"* in general)

Z

Zero: Sifr ('aSfaár)
Zone: mínTaqa (manaáTiq)